AF378522

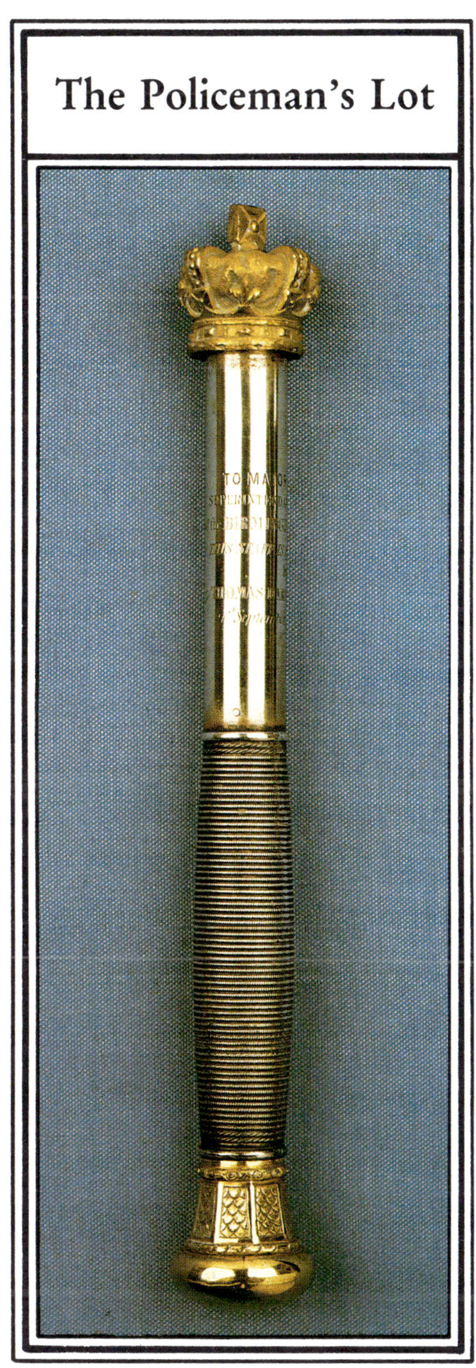

The Policeman's Lot
Antique British Police Equipment

INCLUDING

Truncheons & Tipstaves

Mervyn A. Mitton

FZS, FRGS

Front cover:

Varied collection of tipstaves showing the wide variety of styles and materials.
From left: 1. Geo IV (unknown). 2. Mayor of Bath c.1810. 3. Deputy Chief Constable Worcester 1889. 4. Parish Constable, Jersey. 5. Constable of Boughton. 6. Guernsey, Parish Constable. 7. Magistrate's Baton 8. Bristol GIIIR St. Mary Port Ward. 9. City of London 1755. 10. Silver admiralty oar, 1810. 11. Magistrate's baton for the Viscounts of Leeds 1786. 12. London Dock Company 1804. 13. Manchester GIIIR. 14. Wm IV from Scotland. 15. Tipstaff, probably for Bethnal Green, Geo. III. 16 & 17. 2 unknown tipstaves. Authors collection.

Back cover:
The author with a small part of his police collection. Photographer Homer Sykes.

Half-title page:
Silver, gilt and gold-plated tipstaff presented to Major Shaw – the Superintendent-in-Chief of the Birmingham Police in 1840. Author's collection.

Title page:
Some examples of short truncheons covering the period George III to Queen Victoria. Author's collection.

All photographs by Derek Bird Photography unless otherwise credited.

Design by Tina Dutton; design and production in
association with Book Production Consultants,
Cambridge

Typesetting by Cambridge Photosetting Services

Printed and bound in Yugoslavia by Mladinska Knjiga

First published 1985 by
Quiller Press Ltd
50 Albemarle Street
London W1X 4BD

Copyright text © 1985 Mervyn A. Mitton
      compilation © 1985 Quiller Press Ltd

ISBN 0 907621 50 3

All rights reserved. No part of this book can be reproduced by any means without prior written permission from the publishers.

Contents

To my mother – Mrs. V. M. Mitton

and to

Roy Pickett – whose help in collecting material has been invaluable

Some fine examples of decorated truncheons.
From left: *1. Early Victorian for Dover. 2. Manchester senior officer's truncheon. 3. Whiston, 1813. 4. Plymouth Mace, Governor of the Hospital of Poor's Portion – pre 1800. 5. Victorian truncheon for Merton. 6. George III truncheon-post 1816. 7. Metropolitan Police, senior officer's truncheon about 1870. 8. Bow Street Horse Patrol. 9. Officer of the Corn Exchange – probably Cardiff. 10. Exeter High Constable 1827. 11. George IV tipped truncheon, probably Taunton. 12. Plymouth mace – Hospital Poor's Portion – post 1801. 13. Commemorative truncheon Birmingham 1919. 14. Edinburgh, inspector's short truncheon. 15. Railway truncheon, Manchester & Leeds Railway.* Author's collection.

Introduction

When I first started collecting antique British police equipment, I was still a constable in the Metropolitan Police and, with colleagues, had just finished organising and running the first exhibition of police history to be opened to the public in the Metropolitan Police District. Called 'Police and the East End of London', its various exhibits showed the close links which existed between the police and residents in this unique part of London.

Many members of the public came forward with personal items to loan and only then did I realise the tremendous volume of the police-related historical objects that must be sitting in people's homes. Since 1829, literally hundreds of thousands of men and women have served as police officers, and quite naturally many of them have kept, after their service, mementoes of their careers. The reservoir of material still to be found is therefore vast but, unfortunately, with every year more of the older items become lost, destroyed or irreparably damaged.

Truncheons and tipstaves are two of the objects which are most at risk – leaving aside old uniforms and helmets which, of course, are always likely to have damage from moth and ill-use – and I usually find that young children are to blame. Children are always fascinated by weapons of any description and a 'one-off' truncheon which belonged to 'Great Uncle Charlie' a hundred years ago seems an ideal toy. Even when a truncheon is a valued heirloom, there is always the risk that, when the owner dies, it will be sold off or destroyed with other small items. This is tragic – not for any monetary value, but because of the loss of another piece of British history. While in the field of militaria there may be many examples of a given sword or pistol, when it comes to a decorated police truncheon or, particularly, a tipstaff, it can often be the only one of its kind.

Police development in the British Isles has been a slow one – and always with links to previous years. There can be few countries in the world, where terms still in use, such as 'constable', 'justice of the peace', or 'sheriff', can be traced back some thousand years or where the symbols of those offices have remained virtually unchanged for the same period. Therefore, every time another decorated truncheon or tipstaff of office leaves the country or is damaged or destroyed, it signifies more than the loss of an interesting object – it is the loss of part of our historical heritage.

Perhaps because of the poor reputation of the early peacekeeping forces, and the rather unglamorous equipment of the later police in comparison to the military, the collecting of police equipment – apart from badges and medals – has never been particularly popular. There have been several major collections of truncheons in the past hundred years, but few people have kept the other, more mundane, objects. Even the public and police force museums are not over-burdened with pieces and, as a result, a great deal can still be learned and achieved from the collecting of police-associated items – particularly if the specialised fields of interest can be expanded and the results shared.

My own collection has grown to be one of the largest in the country and I take every opportunity to acquire new pieces and to research their history. I hope that, through the pages of this book, some of the knowledge I have gained will prove helpful to other collectors – and indeed also to the general public and to members of the police.

I will always be most happy to correspond with collectors old or new and to help and advise with any queries they may have. I would also welcome news of any interesting pieces available for sale or coming up at auction.

M. A. Mitton
32 Cleveland Road
Bournemouth BH1 4QG.

CHAPTER ONE

A Short History of Policing in Britain

Amongst the criteria which can be used to judge the degree of civilisation a nation has reached must surely be its own ability to police and control the population for the good of all citizens. The ancient Sumerians, Assyrians, Egyptians, Persians, Greeks and Romans all had their codes of law and, to enforce these, a judiciary backed by either the army or a civil force. The Romans, for example, possessed a well defined hierarchy of magistrates and judges and – for keeping the peace in Rome and other large cities of the Empire – had a militia, or police force, which was separate from the main army and whose chief functions were to guard against civil unrest and to fight fires.

Following the fall of Rome, Europe faced several invasions causing great unrest; whilst influxes of people also took place within the British Isles, they continued on the Continent for a much longer period. The result was that many European countries did not have codified laws and peacekeeping forces until comparatively recent times and very often these were arbitrarily imposed on the populations without regard to a tradition or common usage. This is exactly the opposite to the system which gradually established itself in Britain from the time of the Anglo-Saxons onwards (5th and 6th centuries).

Although over the centuries we have had many changes in the style and administration of the law, these have, however, mostly taken place over considerable periods of time and usually with the understanding and co-operation of the general population. Obviously, there have been many periods when the law has fallen into disrepute and its official guardians held in fear and contempt by ordinary people. Nevertheless, the law has usually reflected the mood of the population at large and it is perhaps for this reason that we are generally regarded as one of the most law-abiding countries – often to the envy of the rest of the world.

Since the main purpose of this book is to outline the history of collectable police equipment, the general background to the history of policing cannot be explored in too much detail. However, an understanding of the origins of the police – mainly in England and Wales – is important and helps towards a general understanding of the way things have developed to the present day.

The Anglo-Saxon period

Even the early ideas on peacekeeping outlined in this section did not just originate overnight, but rather were the distillation of earlier methods and practices. However, many of the ideas and expressions which we use today in connection with the police basically date back to this period.

The Saxon kings had succeeded in gradually spreading their authority until large parts of the country were united under them. Now, for the first time, new peacekeeping methods could be applied to more than just a small area. Probably the most important concept to emerge was that of the 'king's peace'. This meant that for the first time, the king had become responsible for law and order – with twofold implications. Firstly, the 'king's peace' had a general application guaranteeing citizens certain basic rights and freedoms to go about their lawful business without harassment. Secondly it related to the king, his court and his officials and was intended to give them specific protection from attack. The severe penalties for breaking the 'king's peace' – usually death – acted as vital safeguards to administrators such as tax collectors who had to go amongst a people only recently re-introduced to civilisation.

The key to all policing at this time was land tenure, since freemen alone were considered to have rights. The only way that a king could exert strong pressure to have his commands obeyed was to make the thanes, or larger landowners, responsible for all crimes committed in their area – with the threat that if they failed to carry out his instructions, their lands and goods could be confiscated.

However, there were many freemen who did not own land and, since they were also held to be responsible for their own behaviour, they had to either attach themselves to a thane or form a group with other freemen of a similar position, when they could pledge joint property as good behaviour for all of those in the group. The law was quite definite on this point. If freemen were not banded together, then they were not under the protection of law and were not allowed to own cattle. The groups formed by freemen without large estates were called 'tythings' and these consisted of ten homesteads with one man elected as a 'headborough'. Local expressions often changed the word headborough to either 'borsholder' or 'chief frankpledge', depending on the area of the country. From these early beginnings a system evolved which, with many alterations, came right down to the 19th century when headboroughs were still in some areas being elected to represent groups who held police duties. The basic idea behind forcing people to live in these groups was to exert greater control over them and also to make it easier to collect taxes. Anyone entering the country had to join a tything within forty days.

The tything system of ten homesteads led in turn to the institution of the 'hundred', which was a group of ten tythings. A boy was considered to be a freeman and full member of the tything at the age of twelve. Between the ages of fifteen and sixty, all freemen could be called upon to perform three main functions: repelling invasions, crushing rebellions and suppressing riots.

The supervision of the hundred was under either the hundredman or, as he was sometimes called, the reeve, whilst the overall responsibility in the shire for all of the hundreds rested with the sheriff. The sheriff was directly responsible to the king and in times of emergency had the power to muster

An early representation of a Reeve of the 14th century. BBC Hulton Picture Library.

all available men to deal with serious crime or threatened invasion. This muster was known as the 'posse comitatus' and was the origin of the word 'posse' so beloved of the American Wild West.

In theory, all men had police responsibilities. For ease of administration, however, the headboroughs or tythingmen, as they also became known, were in fact held responsible and given the duty of keeping the 'king's peace'.

With many people living settled rural lives, the Anglo-Saxon system worked well. The well-defined responsibilities of a community were easily supervised and strangers closely watched. The Anglo-Saxons also had definite views on the suitable punishment to fit a crime; in fact, offences considered very serious today could often be settled by paying compensation both to the victim and to the king. For example, a scale was laid down whereby, if a cut one inch long was inflicted on the face, there was a fine of two shillings; however, if the cut was under the hairline, the fine was only one shilling. For the loss of an ear the fine was thirty shillings.

This period also saw the origin of another important expression, the 'hue and cry', which again kept its official meaning right down to the end of the 19th century. Backed by the full force of the law, it was the duty of all freemen to raise a hue and cry if they saw a crime being committed. The apprehended person would then be handed over to the headborough or tythingman for appearance at a local court. For less serious crimes the 'folk moot' – a gathering of the tything – was the most likely and in these minor cases the offenders were usually tried by the senior men, or aldermen. However, the more serious cases went to the hundred court, where the reeve or hundredman would pass sentence. Alternatively they could be sent to the shire court for the adjudication of the shire reeve, or sheriff as he eventually became known. The sheriff's responsibility for the law as the king's representative in his shire is embodied in the office of sheriff still to be found in most counties – the accompanying power, however, has long gone and the lord lieutenant is now the royal deputy.

These successful institutions of Anglo-Saxon times were, however, soon put under great strain with the arrival of William I and his conquering Normans.

Norman period

After the initial years of the military conquest when all general laws must have been in a state of suspension, the Normans allowed many of the Anglo-Saxon institutions to be revitalised but ensured that the laws were administered with great rigidity in order to keep the general population under close control.

The sheriff of the shire, now always a Norman, had a new court for the administration of the law – known as the 'court of the tourn' – which, for the first time in English history, went on a circuit of the shire or county every year.

There was much discontent amongst the original Anglo-Saxon population due to the heavy fines and punishments which were meted out by these courts. The fact that there had been only five pence to the old English shilling whereas there were twelve to the new Norman shilling meant that fines were being imposed at nearly two-and-half-times the old level.

The new Norman nobles wielded great power and influence and the more favoured ones could obtain the right to hold their own courts under a steward nominated by the Lord of the Manor – these became known as the 'courts of the leet'. As other nobles also came to demand the right to hold such courts, they soon became a standard feature throughout the country. They had greater civil powers than the old courts and proved so successful that eventually the courts of tourn were abandoned.

The leet court directly involved the residents of its area and each year chose manor officers: a constable, ale-tasters, swine-ringers and bread-weighers. The new office of 'constable' now generally covered the duties of the old headboroughs or tythingmen, including the power of arrest and the calling of the 'hue and cry'. He was generally given a stave of office. The headboroughs or tythingmen did not disappear and would have continued to exert some authority in their tythings, but it was generally the constable who had assumed the real power.

Even today there are many leet courts which still meet on an annual basis and, although they no longer have any function, it is interesting to see such a long unbroken line of tradition. Two which come to mind are the leet court of Wareham in Dorset and that of Hungerford in Berkshire. The latter's two tythingmen still carry early Victorian painted truncheons with the two ale-tasters carrying pewter truncheons.

The evolution of all law at this time was very slow and it was not until the time of Richard I that assize courts for the trial of the more serious cases were set up on a general basis, initially covering six separate circuits under three judges. Again, this system has persisted until the very recent past.

Above and top right: *British coinage covering the late Anglo-Saxon and early Norman period.* BBC Hulton Picture Library.

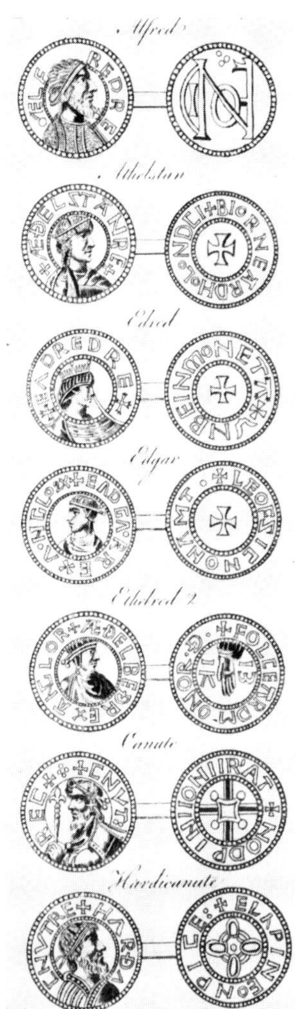

Edward III. BBC Hulton Picture Library.

As the Norman courts continued to be harsh and oppressive, the Magna Carta included certain provisions to curb the excessive fines they imposed. King John undertook to *not make men Justiciaries, Constables, Sheriffs or Bailiffs unless they understood the law of the land and are well disposed to observe it.*

One of the most significant acts of legislation of Norman times was Edward I's Statute of Winchester in 1285. While keeping many of the tried and tested methods of the past, this laid a constitutional duty on the citizens to protect and guard their district. Regulations were also effected for the establishment of town watchmen in the hours of darkness – this was called 'watch and ward'. We should note however that the Statute of Winchester did not apply to London which was covered by its own legislation.

The City of London – perhaps because of its importance as a trading centre and its larger population – has always been fortunate in having reasonable peacekeeping forces. At this time the City was divided into 24 wards, each patrolled by six watchmen who were supervised by an alderman. This alderman acted both as a magistrate and as the leader of the Watch and these dual functions were to be maintained by magistrates for many years to come. Separate to the ward watchmen was a body called the 'marching watch' whose duty was to generally patrol and assist the stationary watchmen when any trouble occurred. The City had a curfew imposed one hour after sunset when the gates were closed and a bell rung to mark this time.

Edward I was also the first king to lay down rules for 'coroners'. Being important law officers of the Crown, there were usually four to a shire or county, and their responsibilities included calling local juries to pass judgement in cases of suspicious death: yet another function carried on to the present day.

The next fundamental development took place in 1361 with Edward III's statute appointing 'justices of the peace' – this office still functions actively today. Below the justices came the 'petty constables' who were appointed annually by the juries of the leet courts. However, it was the magistrates who swore them in and controlled their duties.

The word 'constable' is held to derive from the Latin *comes stabuli*, or Master of the Horse. Because of its Roman origins the word has been used in many countries; however, in England it has generally meant an office of authority under the Crown. The first mention of petty constables was in a writ of Henry III for enforcing 'watch and ward' in 1252; however, the office itself is probably much older.

All these different functionaries can often be confusing but, to make things clear, while a parish could still have many tythingmen who represented their individual tythings, there could only be *one* petty constable – later called 'the parish constable' – who acted with the authority of the king. Again, although the term 'constable' was introduced by the Normans, the ordinary Anglo-Saxon people continued to use their original native words – so that in Middlesex the constable was still called the 'headborough', in Kent the 'borsholder' and, in the west, the 'tything-man'. With the extra functions for the office laid down by the justices, we find that all of the various titles of tythingman, petty constable, parish constable and police constable are names for the same office.

Tudor period

By the 15th century the constable very often no longer worked within a close-knit group such as the old tything system. Nevertheless, as freemen still had the collective responsibility of maintaining the law, the constable could call on any one of them to assist him in his duties.

Other developments were also taking place at this time – although as is common with most progress in public reform in English history, these were slow. However, it was in the 15th century that a scale of punishments was first set down whereby a fine *or* a term of imprisonment could be imposed. For instance, we find that the taking out of a sword within the City of London would incur a fine of ten shillings or a sentence of fifteen days, while wounding with a sword carried a fine of twenty shillings or a term of forty days.

With the growth of trade, the times of Henry VII saw a great increase in the power of the middle classes. Most being town dwellers, they came to demand better protection than the run-down system of the time could provide. Moreover, they resented the compulsory time that all freemen were still obliged to spend as constables with all the numerous and lengthy duties this involved. They therefore began to pay for deputy constables to take their place when their turn came.

A vagrant in Tudor times. BBC Hulton Picture Library.

The livery courts also gained in strength during the Tudor period as they controlled the increased trade and attempted to keep out foreign competition. Many of these livery courts appointed their own beadles and constables to ensure a uniform standard and prevent fraud. Most livery companies today still continue to appoint their own beadles.

Following the dissolution of the monasteries by Henry VIII, England had a great problem with vagrants and beggars, many of whom were young and fit and often became involved in violent crimes. To try to control these men strict laws were enacted and many thousands were hanged. This period really marks the beginning of the harsh penal laws which were allowed to multiply until, by the 18th century, there were over 160 offences for which one could be hanged.

Henry VIII was also responsible for incorporating the whole of Wales into the existing judicial system. He appointed justices of the peace with the same powers as in England – a greatly needed reform, as at that time there were 141 lordships along the borders of England and Wales where the king's law did not apply. The new system was a success and, in 1543, the Welsh justices of the peace were authorised to appoint two men as chief constables of the hundred where they lived with 'special regard to maintaining the king's peace'.

During the time of Edward VI the country was run by a regent or 'Proctector' and there were considerable religious problems. As a result, social unrest was particularly rife and this led to a special statute being passed against unlawful assemblies. Much of its content survived in the Riot Act, which was repealed only recently. To enforce this new Act, an official known as the 'lord lieutenant' was appointed. As the king's representative in each county or shire, he had the power to call men up as an organised body to deal with rioters – a power which had until then belonged to the sheriffs who now ceased to have any military function.

The Tudor period has always been noted for the way ordinary people's lives were controlled. Under Queen Elizabeth many Acts were passed, particularly with regard to food regulations, and special bodies of men were appointed for carrying out these new laws. During Elizabethan times the control and appointment of constables generally lay in the hands of the magistrates and much of their energy was devoted to dealing with the vagrants who still posed a problem. Punishments were very severe and included whipping and branding. Social control extended into such spheres as the times people worked, the length of their meal breaks and even the right of country folk to marry, with two justices of the shire having first to give their permission. This workload placed a very heavy burden on both the justices and the constables and, since they were granted very little official reward, bribery and corruption became widespread.

The Civil War

Normal justice was one of the first casualties during the Civil War. The Assize circuits were stopped, and even marriages, which would normally only have been celebrated in churches, had to be performed by justices of the peace. In effect, the fabric of English life came under great strain.

After Cromwell had finally defeated the Royalists, he was faced with many civil problems – one of the most serious being that essentially justices were Royalists, whilst the constables and tythingmen supported the Commonwealth. However, he did have at his command something which no previous ruler had ever had: a strong standing army. In 1655 England and Wales were divided into twelve police districts, each under a military officer. These men – although usually only of the rank of colonel or major – were known as 'Major Generals' and had control of their district together with the local justices – although in fact this co-operation was usually non-existent. A special force of over 6000 mounted men was assigned to back the Major Generals and, to pay for them, a tax of ten per cent was imposed on the estates of the Royalists. Since this was both a military and a puritanical regime, many new offences additional to those on the statute books were created. However, with the restoration of Charles II in 1660, most of these were quickly repealed and the police districts abandoned.

The Restoration

London at the time of the Restoration was in a sad state of decay and, with the influx of ex-soldiers and the unemployed, the peace officers could do little. Even in daylight there were whole areas of the City in which it was unsafe to venture.

In 1663, by an Act of Common Council, a special force of 1000 'bellmen' was appointed for the City to act as nightwatchmen and guard the streets. These men later became known as 'Charlies' in memory of Charles II. Although equipped with a bell, lantern, rattle and stave, they were not a great success since they were generally elderly men unable to stand up against the baiting they received both from the apprentices and lawbreakers. They represented, however, the only real night police for many years to come.

Jonathan Wild on his way to execution. BBC Hulton Picture Library.

By the end of the 17th century, thieving and robbing was bringing chaos to the country and, with the constant threat and fear of highwaymen, was immobilising travel. Troops were sometimes used to combat this, but not to any great effect, since they did not have the necessary mobility. 1692 saw a new statute offering rewards for the killing or taking of highwaymen and pardons for their accomplices if the latter helped in their downfall. This led to a new breed of amateur thieftakers, anxious only for the rewards and quite uninterested in the guilt – or otherwise – of their victims. Jonathan Wild was the thieftaker who became most famous; his evil organisation actually trafficked in stolen property and then arrested the dealers for the rewards. He ran his own gang of criminals whose lives were always in his hands and it was many years before he was finally caught, convicted and hanged at Tyburn gallows (the site of which is now beneath Marble Arch in central London).

*Contemporary drawing of a
Bow Street Runner –
probably Townsend.*
Metropolitan Police.

Public disorders, one of the marks of this age, continued with very little hindrance from the constables, or the nightwatch, who did not have the power or the organisation to combat them.

Georgian policing

One of the first Acts in the reign of George I was a revision of the Riot Act, indicating how serious the question of law and order had become.

Numerous further Acts were passed but generally without any marked success in the decrease of lawlessness. One crisis tended to merge with another. In 1745, London was under the immediate expectation of being invaded by the forces of the Young Pretender who was marching from Scotland and, for a period of five months, the City militia superceded normal law. These five months, in fact, saw a startling drop in street crimes, since the two City marshalls were not in charge of policing and regular armed sentries were on duty throughout the capital. There was talk eventually of handing policing over to the 'trained bands' or militia – however, as usual, nothing came of it and a chance for reform was lost.

During the first half of the 18th century it was seen as necessary for the public to go out always armed in order to protect themselves. Whilst the City of London, with its paid constables and night watchmen, had a degree of protection for its citizens, the outer areas – particularly Westminster and Middlesex – still kept to the traditional parish constables, supported in some areas by watchmen at night. This combined area had approximately 100 parishes and, without any proper organisation between them, things were to continue to go from bad to worse.

There was some improvement in 1748 when Henry Fielding – a well known author of the time – was appointed Chief Magistrate for Westminster with his office at Bow Street (Bow Street police station now stands nearly opposite the site of the original public or police office). He effected a number of ideas novel for the time, the most important being the formation of a small force of paid constables who did not just serve for the obligatory year. This body, who were really an early detective force, became known as 'Mr. Fielding's People' and had considerable success. They were later to become known as the Bow Street Runners.

Henry Fielding died after only six years in office and was succeeded by his half-brother, John Fielding. He might have seemed an unlikely choice, being blind, but he was so successful that he was later knighted. One of his ideas was a publication, *The Weekly Pursuit,* which was circulated for exhibition in public places and gave details of wanted criminals and their crimes. Probably his most important innovation was the formation of a body of mounted men known as the 'Bow Street Patrol' in 1763.

Under the two brothers, the Bow Street Court and its small force of constables, patrols and detectives became the premier peacekeeping force in the capital – despite the fact that there were at this time nearly 2000 constables, beadles and watchmen employed by the different counties and parishes. Many of their reforms were to receive additional recognition when they were brought into use with the Metropolitan Police in 1829.

June 1780 saw some of the worst riots ever experienced in this country. Known as the Gordon Riots after their chief instigator, Lord George Gordon, they could easily have been contained in the early stages if only

WATCH·HOUSE
ERECTED
1791
DESTROYED   REBUILT
1941   1962

London had possessed a force of 200–300 constables, used to working together under experienced officers. However, such a force did not exist and Gordon was able to fan anti-Catholic feelings to such a large extent – following the repeal of out dated anti-Catholic laws – that, in six days, over 700 people were killed, with untold damage done to property and buildings. Over 60,000 people were involved in the rioting; they even attacked Newgate Prison and released over 300 dangerous prisoners. The Bow Street magistrates' office was also burnt out.

Eventually, there were over 35 fires burning at the same time. Both the King's Bench Prison and Fleet Prison were forced open and their prisoners released. Finally, troops and militia were used with full force and allowed to open fire on the crowds of rioters until, after two days, they had the situation under control.

These riots showed how totally inadequate the peacekeeping forces were and yet nothing was done to strengthen them. However, in 1786 the Dublin Police Act appointed three commissioners and a paid force of constables – so Ireland at least gained from the troubles. This Act is notable for the fact that it officially uses the word 'police' for the first time.

In 1792 seven new police offices were established to administer different parts of London – they were based on the successful Bow Street Office and were at Hatton Garden, Worship Street, Lambeth Street, Whitechapel, Shadwell, Union Hall in Westminster and Great Marlborough Street.

Each police office had three magistrates, six constables and resident clerks, gaolers and housekeepers – all at regular salaries. This meant that London now had eight police offices with a total of 24 magistrates, 48 constables, plus the Bow Street Detective Force and the Bow Street Patrol – this of course was in addition to the City of London forces. The Patrol was particularly active at this time in combating highwaymen and the following extract regarding their duties is taken complete from the *28th Official Government Report on Finance and Police* of 1798. The punctuation is as in the original:

'This useful body of men was established in the lifetime of the late Sir John Fielding, and consists of sixty-eight in number. They are divided into thirteen parties, consisting of a Captain and some have four and other five men to attend them. Eight of these parties are employed in patrolling the different roads leading to the Metropolis, to prevent robberies and detect offenders; and the other five parties are employed in the same way in the different streets of the town. They meet in the evening to go upon duty and continue till twelve o'clock at night, or as much later as their duty may require. It is the business of the men to attend to such directions as they may receive from the Captain; and it is the business of the Captain to see the men attend their duty, to give them directions and to attend with them during the hours of duty; and also to attend at the Office every morning, and report to the Magistrate any neglect of duty in the men, to bring before him any offenders they may have apprehended and to relate any offences they may have heard of, or any other occurrences that may have taken place in the course of the night, necessary to inform the Magistrate of, and to enter such report, in writing, in a book kept at the Office for that purpose, to the truth of which daily report they are sworn by Sir William Addington every Monday morning. They are all appointed by the Chief Magistrate of the Office, who attends to such recommendations as he receives, if the men are fit and able. They are allowed for their trouble, each Captain 5s per night and the men 2/6p each. They are furnished by the Office with arms, each Captain having a carbine, a pair of pistols and a cutlass; and each man having a cutlass. These are all produced before Sir William Addington every Monday morning, for the purpose of his seeing they are kept in proper order. Besides the nightly duty the men perform, they are constantly under the direction of the Magistrates, and are employed upon all occasions when the six Officers are not sufficient for the business of the Office, and a greater number of persons are required, for which they derive an advantage from the persons by whom they are employed, according to the services they perform. They are also employed to preserve the peace upon all public occasions; as processions, meetings, etc., when the whole body are collected, and received directions from the Magistrates for discharging the Duty of the Day. They attend His Majesty to the Houses of Parliament; and other public places, the theatres, ancient music, opera, etc., etc., The original allowance for supporting this establishment was £4,000 per annum, furnished from the Civil List Fund, but it does not quite amount to that sum. It used to be issued to the Magistrates every six weeks, but now forms a part of the quarterly issue of money from the Treasury to Mr. Reeves, the Receiver, for defraying the expenses of the Office. and from the irregularity of this money being issued these men are frequently many months in arrear of their weekly allowance, which, from many of them having large families, and nothing but their allowance to support them, occasions much distress among them, and, it is to be feared, a degree of energy is thereby lost to the public in their services'.

It will be seen from this recently discovered report that the Patrol was well organised and armed and the men well paid – since they earned over twice the weekly official salary of the constables. However, constables also got paid fixed amounts for executing warrants and conveying prisoners – which easily doubled their wages. That the Patrol also formed an escort for the king on public occasions and additionally kept order at all public meetings will be a surprise to many – since it has always been generally believed that its only function was to patrol the main roads.

The new police offices – together with the Bow Street Police Office – were important as being the first regularly organised paid police force in English history.

In 1798 an Act of Parliament established the Thames River Police, a force of some 60 paid constables who patrolled the river in rowing boats in order to prevent piracy and theft from the very many merchant ships which then visited the London docks. Usually ex-sailors, they were armed with swords and proved very successful, so much so that a mob attempted to burn down the Thames Police Office at Shadwell – however, they were repulsed after one police officer was killed. The Thames Marine River Police existed as a separate force until becoming part of the Metropolitan Police in 1839.

Whilst London had seen some improvements in its policing methods, the rural areas of the country were still being administered by justices of the peace and high constables with the aid of parish constables and tythingmen. The system continued to work reasonably well whilst the population was static but, with the social unrest of the time, and the existence of large bodies of unemployed soldiers, it did not have the manpower or flexibility to adequately protect the citizens.

These changes can be well illustrated by quoting an extract from a small book, *The Ringing Grooves of Change,* by the Rev. Paul Lanham, Vicar of Shillington in Hertfordshire. The Rev. Lanham's book, published 1984, traces the recent history of his church and its importance within the parish. Whilst this extract takes us chronologically out of order by extending forward to 1830, it nevertheless details most clearly how the social unrest of the time affected just one small parish. Multiply this by the whole country, and you will have a good idea of the problems which the authorities faced.

'So in 1802 there came to Shillington the first of three major changes that were to alter the entire social structure of the village irrevocably. In order to understand the effect of the Enclosure of the Land, it is necessary to look briefly at the whole nature of Shillington. Up to 1800 it was as though the world was passing it by. Obviously there were changes that it could not avoid, not least in the church itself, but it was essentially a self-contained village. There were no main roads anywhere near it and the new railways would not come closer than three miles away; lacking the links with the outside world it became an introverted community. The main families married and inter-married among themselves for the most part and few people moved into or out of the area. All were wedded to the soil, mostly as ordinary agricultural labourers – though there were a few minor landowners, and group of artisans who created their own trades and practised them in the village. Until 1766 at least, few of the land-owners actually lived in the village, but with the enclosure of the land

All Saints Church at Shillington. Revd. Lanham

all this changed with dramatic suddenness. The enclosure movement aimed to rearrange the land of tenant farmers into smaller units with the aim of using the land more profitably and thus get more income from it. This represented a complete upheaval after a long period of rural stability and it was not helped by the effects of the Napoleonic Wars, notably the huge rise in the cost of food. Within every village there came into existence the evil of the 'roundsmen'. These were the unemployed labourers who were compulsorily taken on by farmers, according to the size of the farm and the rateable value of the property. The registers show how, with dramatic suddenness new people came to Shillington and the whole fabric of the village's society changed. At the same time, there was tremendous social unrest, with new labour drifting into the County and a large body of insecure and potentially riotous workers at large. To add to the trouble there was an air of unrest in the whole of the continent that was to reach its climax in the Revolutions of 1848.

'All this came to a head in Shillington at least between 1827 and 1831. In January 1827 four men from the village were fined ten shillings for damaging the parish wheelbarrows; the alternative sentence was three months in prison. In October that year four were fined a shilling each for 'riot and tumult'. Two months later there came a more serious riot, levelled against William King the parish overseer; five men were gaoled for fifteen months for their involvement in this. In his evidence to the Quarter Sessions, King gave this account of their behaviour "They were assembled in front of my farmhouse in a most riotous and noisy manner and with many oaths and threatening gestures demanded money . . . Their conduct was so violent and disorderly as to cause much fear and alarm to me and my family for the safety of our persons . . . These young men have no just ground for disorderly conduct. I am ready to find them work but they refuse to work and demand money from me, to spend in public houses" (Cirket: The 1830 Riots in Bedfordshire R.H.R.S. lvii 1971. pp 78–79.) Eventually the five were bound over to keep the peace, in the sum of Twenty Pounds each.

'The Vicar of Shillington at that time was John Hull, a local Justice of the Peace and by all accounts a most formidable cleric. In June 1829 there broke out in Kent the "Swing Riots" and these spread to Bedfordshire between late 1830 and the end of 1831. On December 2nd 1830 rioting broke out in Stotford and four days later Hull swore in no less than 212 special constables, forty per cent of the entire male population of the village. One hundred and nine of these were sent to Stotford to help contain the riots, the result of which was the condemning to death of five of those involved. Of these one hundred and nine, there were seventy-four labourers, three shoemakers, thirteen farmers, four gentry, three butchers, two pensioners, two tailors, a coachman, a footman, a blacksmith, a carpenter, a wheelwright, a bricklayer, a glazier and a miller. Most of them were paid a shilling each as wages and they were armed with staves at a cost to the parish of ninepence each. Most of these staves were lost, but a number remain. They bear the crest of King William IV and their size testifies to their effectiveness and the terrible havoc they could wreak. It is said that their red tips were to hide the blood they shed and they were certainly formidable weapons. The riot was put down and peace eventually returned to the area. Today the long-term effect of the trouble is seen in the existence of the many parish allotments of the area often on glebe land own by the church.'

1800 – 1829

While the Act establishing police offices was repealed in 1801 a new one was immediately re-enacted to put the offices on a more permanent basis. There were now ten police offices and these were at Mansion House, Guildhall, Hatton Garden, Worship Street, Whitechapel, Shadwell, Southwark, Queens Street in Westminster, Great Marlborough Street and Wapping. There was, of course, also Bow Street which came under a different Act of Parliament. Mansion House and the Guildhall were for the City, and Wapping was for the River Police. Each police office still had three magistrates, but the number of constables for each was raised to eight.

In 1805 Sir Richard Ford, who was the then Chief Magistrate of Bow Street, extended the Bow Street Horse Patrol to cover an area up to twenty miles from Bow Street, consisting of 52 men plus two inspectors and a clerk. They were to become the first uniformed body of men in the history of English policing and were even more successful than their predecessors, the Horse Patrol. They were later supported by a hundred strong unmounted horse patrol who patrolled at night and, later still in 1822, by a daytime patrol of 27 men. The London which they were set to patrol was far more lawless and disorderly than the one we know today, although

The problem of excessive drink in Georgian London – as seen through the eyes of Hogarth. BBC Hulton Picture Library.

some of the crimes we hear of now have their parallels in those days. The population of the capital and the surrounding areas in the early 1800s was just over one million and to police it there were only the fragmented forces of constables, patrols and watchmen listed previously – perhaps 2500 in all at this time. Crime and vice of every sort was so common that the contemporary reports treat as quite commonplace those incidents which would make headlines today.

There were many thousands of vagrants and abandoned children whose only way of life was to thieve and it is estimated that there were over 8000 receivers of stolen goods in London. Drink was available without restriction and even gin could be bought at under one shilling for a pint. Captain Melville Lee in his *History of Police in England* reports a letter written by the Receiver of Metropolitan Police in 1831 to a distinguished person. Referring to incidents which regularly took place at an annual fair in the West End of London, the Receiver wrote:

> 'It will hardly be credited that within five or seven years . . . people were robbed in open day . . . and women stipped of their clothes, tied to gates by the roadside; the existing police set at defiance.'

Burglary was particularly prevalent in the early 1800s and few of the culprits were ever caught. Similarly, forgery was so common that there was a risk of the currency losing credibility. Between 1805 and 1818 more than 200 people were hanged for forgery – a figure which gives some idea of the problem.

There were many riots and civil disturbances during the first quarter of the 19th century and the responsible authorities were naturally alarmed at this trend, particularly as they had no really effective force with which to combat a rioting mob. The militia – which should have been a final resort – usually represented the only available men in sufficient numbers, and as they were not trained or armed for such peacekeeping duties, they tended to over-react. This happened at Peterloo in 1819 when they killed at random many innocent people.

The time was ripe, therefore, for a complete change in the methods which had worked well in Anglo-Saxon days but which, in the 19th century, had no chance of coping with an expanding population beset with social and economic problems.

1829 – The Metropolitan Police

During the years leading to 1829 a number of parliamentary committees had considered the problems of policing London and had made many recommendations. These were to prove helpful when legislation was being made to establish the Metropolitan Police.

In 1821, however, two important changes were to take place in the existing arrangements. Firstly, the Bow Street Patrol was restricted in its range to give greater protection to the central areas. Actually, sixteen new districts were formed, each with five men on permanent duty, with a reserve of fifteen men stationed at Bow Street for emergencies. Secondly, the Bow Street Horse Patrol was enlarged to 161 men and given wider duties to protect the suburbs. The Dismounted Horse Patrol was now

A contemporary painting of Sir Robert Peel.
Metropolitan Police.

responsible for an area of five miles from Bow Street, whilst the Mounted Horse Patrol covered a radius of approximately twenty miles. Their chief drawback was that they patrolled only the main roads and then still only until midnight – nonetheless they certainly helped to reduce the number of highwaymen around London.

In 1822, Sir Robert Peel, as Home Secretary, established a Bow Street Day Patrol and although it consisted only of three inspectors and twenty-four men, it proved very successful. These semi-experimental and tentative changes were to pave the way for the new force.

A Parliamentary Commission in 1828 made recommendations for policing changes which Sir Robert Peel acted upon immediately and, on 15th April 1829, he put his new Police Bill before parliament. Initially, only Westminster was to be affected, followed by Kensington and Hammersmith, and with the eventual aim of including all the parishes within fifteen miles of Charing Cross. Within two months the Bill was law. The headquarters of the new force were to be at Scotland Yard which would have supervisory duties only and not act as a court. The success of the Metropolitan Police made their take-over much quicker than antici-pated and soon they were policing most of London.

The new police was placed under the authority of two justices of the peace who were known as the 'commissioners'. It is interesting that even today the Commissioner and his deputy in the Metropolitan Police are sworn in as JPs. The Watch were to hand over their duties as the police district expanded and the Bow Street Patrols were also nominally taken over. The first two commissioners were a soldier, Colonel Rowan, and a lawyer, Richard Mayne. They were ideal for their position and for the tasks ahead of them – which must have been colossal, considering that they not only had to train virtually a complete police force, but also to set up relevant administration to run it.

By June 1830 the new police had 17 superintendents, 68 inspectors, 323 sergeants and 2906 constables – whilst the population at that time was approximately 1,200,000. There were 17 divisions each with its own police station and a superintendent in charge.

Details of uniform and equipment are given in the appropriate chapters, but it must be pointed out that much of the new organisation was based on the methods tested with the Bow Street Patrols and, indeed, even the uniform was very similar.

The new commissioners were determined to employ only the best available men as constables and, in the eight years between 1830 and 1838, nearly 5000 were dismissed and a further 6000 resigned – many of these compulsorily.

Great opposition from the public attended the new police and many newspapers made up stories to discredit them. There were also many unprovoked attacks on the constables, who were given nicknames such as 'Blue Devils', 'Peel's Gendarmerie', 'Raw Lobsters', and 'Peelers'. The first death of a constable on duty was that of P.C. Grantham on 29th June 1830 – he was kicked to death while trying to break up a street fight in Somers Town. This was followed on 18th August, 1830 by the death of P.C. Long of the 'G' Division who was stabbed whilst trying to arrest three suspects. They were to be the first of many brave men killed in the execution of their duty.

The original buildings of Scotland Yard.
Metropolitan Police.

Despite these physical and verbal attacks, the success of the new police was assured. In October 1836 the Horse Patrol was finally absorbed into the Metropolitan Police and the constables became the Mounted Branch. The Marine River Police was incorporated into the force during June 1839 and renamed the 'Thames Division'.

Although the City of London was outside the authority of the new Metropolitan Police, it too made reforms in its police force on the pattern of the Metropolitan and as a result, has retained its independence to the present day. Sir Robert Peel had made no secret of his wish to absorb the City into his general new policing arrangements, but the wealth and patronage of the City institutions had proved too strong for him. Eventually, in 1839, a further Act was passed amending the original one of 1829 and extending the authority and boundaries of the Metropolitan Police.

In 1842, the Metropolitan Police formed a branch of men to operate out of uniform. This grew into the CID, which was officially instituted in 1878.

Provincial forces

Whilst London was gradually accustoming itself to an efficient and well run police force, the rest of the country was still in the hands of watchmen, tythingmen and parish constables. But as most of the provincial urban population was also growing rapidly in number and in wealth, this antiquated system was totally unsatisfactory. As an example, Liverpool in

1834 had only 50 watchmen for a population of over 240,000. Another problem that the larger towns faced was that many criminals now left London to look for safer havens. The first attempt to provide a day police outside of London was through the Lighting and Watching Act of 1833 which appointed inspectors to supervise local police; however, it was not a success.

The Municipal Corporations Act of 1835 was more successful and created municipal corporations in the larger towns. Watch committees consisting of the mayor and councillors were set up and they were allowed to appoint a head constable and other constables. These constables were given the authority to act both in the county as well as in the town.

The Rural Police Act of 1839 allowed the justices of a county or shire the right to decide if they wished to appoint a chief constable and permit him to set up a force of organised constables – the expense of which would be charged to the rates. This Act, generally known as the 'Permissive Act', was not a great success due to the choice of its adoption being left to local country people, who were not greatly in favour of change. However, those counties which did adopt it were generally better policed and more efficient. By May 1853, there were 22 counties who had adopted the Act – seven who had partly adopted it and 22 which continued the parochial system. This patchwork was ended in 1856 with the passing of the Rural Police Act, known as the 'Obigatory Act'. Magistrates were immediately ordered to appoint a constabulary force where one did not exist and, if the borough had less than 5000 people, its borough police was to be consolidated with the county police.

In 1842, a further statute had been passed which stated that no petty officer, headborough or tythingman should after that time be appointed to any parish at a court leet, except for the purpose usually connected with the public peace. Thus, from that date, all police powers were effectively removed from the old officers of the law and modern policing as we know it came into full being.

1869 saw the final abolition of the title of 'high constable' which dated back many hundreds of years, but which, with the existence of new police, no longer held any meaning. The last of the old watchmen finally disappeared in the 1870s and, with their passing, the old systems were at an end.

Generally speaking, by the 1860s the whole country was under an efficient police force which, subject to the usual amalgamations and re-organisations, has continued to the present day.

Special police

The appointment of special constables to assist the authorities in times of trouble goes back to the Tudors and, although the first Act of Parliament for the appointment of specials was passed in 1673, in the early days they were not called upon very often. However, in Georgian and Victorian times the specials were often on duty. They did not, of course, wear a uniform but were usually equipped with a warrant and truncheon and sometimes an armband. The special police had their greatest moment in 1848 when the Chartist mob – reckoned by some to number as many as a million –gathered at Kennington on the south side of the Thames from London. Over 200,000 citizens of London enrolled as special constables, with the Duke of Wellington taking command. They were so successful in their organisation that the rioters dispersed without attempting to invade London.

Some Helpful Definitions
of Police Equipment

Truncheon	Wooden club usually carried by a constable.
Tipstaff	Symbol of authority to carry out a particular function – usually associated with the early police. Made of wood or metal and usually surmounted by, or tipped with a crown. Can also mean the person invested with the office.
Stave	Normally around six feet in length, this was the forerunner of the truncheon. The early watch were usually armed with staves and many of the local constables at the end of the 18th century had both long and short staves.
Beadle's stave	The type of stave carried by a beadle was often surmounted by a carved or painted decoration showing his authority and parish.
Wands of office	These were carried by the governors of a number of the London hospitals. They are usually thin and approximately six feet in length.
Nightsticks	Carried by the night police of the 18th and 19th centuries, these were often longer and heavier than truncheons.
Staffs of office	Unlike long staves, these are often only 24-30 inches long. They are of a uniform thickness and have no handle. They often have painted details of the office at both ends of the staff – sometimes, apart from a handle area the complete shaft is decorated.
Swingle	Particularly dangerous flail-like weapons, usually made of two pieces of wood joined by a length of metal chain.
Bludgeon	Intended to be carried in the pocket – usually composed of a handle at one end and of a round ball of wood at the other, the two parts being connected by rope or, in some cases, chain. Bludgeons were occasionally used by the police and there are examples of decorated ones.
Life-preservers	Usually about ten inches long, they had weighted ends, often made of lead, which were connected by either a length of bamboo or whalebone. They were usually covered with finely knotted string which was waxed. These were carried by both members of the public and police; when used by police they were occasionally decorated with badges.
Bâton	Derived from the Norman French for a truncheon and now generally held to be a symbol of office. The word is used in both the Channel Islands and in Canada.

CHAPTER TWO

Truncheons

Very fine Parker, Field truncheon. This shows the typically bold decoration to be found on truncheons from this company. Author's collection.

When I show my collection to visitors who are not familiar with truncheons, they are always surprised by their great variety of shapes and sizes and usually comment on the very fine decoration with which many of them are painted.

There is no certainty as to when the painting of truncheons and staves started, but it probably goes back as far as the 13th century. We know that constables and tythingmen were carrying staves even before this date and, when Richard I's bodyguard of sergeants-at-arms was formed, the mace they carried as their authority for making an arrest was probably decorated with the royal coat-of-arms. No examples from these early days seem to have survived and therefore we shall never know for sure whether the staves of the ordinary constables were decorated in any way.

From the 17th century onwards the decorating of truncheons became more common and, by Georgian times, it could be said to have become the accepted practice. However, as with tipstaves, there were no set rules for identifying truncheons and very often the inscription or the coat-of-arms used was entirely up to the owner.

By the time of William IV the decorating of truncheons had become standardised by the use of the royal crown and cypher, and in many cases the designs were very elaborate.

The firm of William Parker of Holborn is the one most usually associated with the manufacture and distribution of truncheons in the 19th century. The firm acted as the main agent for Hiatt's (sometimes spelt Hyatt) of Birmingham who was also the major manufacturer in the country for many other items of police equipment, including handcuffs and lanterns.

The truncheons of parish constables and of those for the smaller towns would have continued to have been made in their own areas by local craftsmen; on appointment, the new constable would probably go to his local carpenter and have an individual truncheon made. This accounts for the many variations found in size and design since, as with tipstaves, the owner would be able to give free rein to his imagination. Having had the truncheon made, he would then have to find someone to decorate it. This local approach shows up clearly when a number of truncheons are looked at together. There will always be some which are so crudely painted that they have obviously been copied from a standard design, while others are works of art in their own right and display heraldic designs of first rate quality.

One interesting fact which did come to light recently concerns the baluster type of truncheon which was common in the Manchester area – these are usually 12–15 inches long, with a shaped handle and a cylindrical end of two or three inches set between raised ridges. The decoration is always on the rounded section at the top. A George IV example, which had been damaged at the top end, demonstrated that the elaborate design of the royal coat-of-arms was, in fact, printed on a piece of paper which had been stuck down in position between the ridges. This particular example was still in black and white, but it would seem that the intention was for the local craftsman to buy some of these black and white strips to fix around the top of the truncheons he had made and these could then be painted over in colour – an early form of 'painting by numbers'. This may not have been so in every case and could only apply to this type, but it would certainly account for the excellent and uniform designs which are on so many of these baluster truncheons. Needless to say, it took a damaged one to reveal this short cut.

The painting and decorating of truncheons was more than just ornamentation – by having the royal crown and cypher and, in many cases, the royal coat-of-arms, it clearly showed that the constable was acting under the authority of the Crown. The further identification of his town or village, very often by the local coat-of-arms, would serve to identify his area of authority, while his name or initials would prevent unauthorised use and identify him personally. Constables prior to 1829 did not wear a uniform, nor did they carry a warrant card which only came into general use in the mid-1880s. Even if they had carried one it could not have been read by the majority of the population, most of whom were still partially or totally illiterate. *Therefore, the painted truncheon was the constable's badge of office – and the painted details supplied all the information to the public necessary for him to execute his duties.*

Since so many of the truncheons, swords and tipstaves which the general collector is likely to come across date from the 19th century and were supplied by the firm of Parker, Field and Sons, the following details will prove helpful in establishing a date. Fortunately their truncheons were always stamped at the very bottom with the firm's particulars which varied according to different periods in the development of the company. Whilst only dating articles to within certain periods it, nevertheless, is a very useful guide.

Name on truncheon	Made between
Parker, Holborn	1796–1841
Parker, Field & Sons (sometimes only 'Field')	1842–1877
Parker, Field & Sons 59 Leman Street or 122 Leman Street	1877–1883

Baluster truncheon for George IV – showing the stuck down printed paper coat of arms and cypher. This was probably intended to be painted in colour. Author's collection.

Right: A. *Arms used by Geo. I, Geo. II and Geo. III. After 1801 the three fleur-de-lys in the top right quartering were taken out.* B. *Coat of arms in use from 1801 to 1837.* C. *The arms brought into use for Queen Victoria and which with some variations are still in use today.* D. *The arms as in B but which were actually used from 1801 to 1816. These show the electoral cap of Hanover set above the middle shield.* E. *After 1816, when Hanover became a kingdom, the electoral cap was changed to a crown and this coat of arms was therefore in use from 1816 until the death of WmIV in 1837.* Pilgrim Press.

A

B

C

D

E

Another quite accurate method of dating truncheons to a definite period is by the royal coat-of-arms. From the time of George I (1717–1727) until 1900 only four coats-of-arms were used:

1 **From 1714–1801** The shield has in the top right hand corner three fleur-de-lys. This coat-of-arms was used by George I, George II and George III.
2 **From 1801–1816** The fleur-de-lys were discontinued and a lion rampart in the top right hand corner substituted. There is also a further coat-of-arms in the centre of the four main panels, with an 'Elector's Cap' above it to represent Hanover. (As this is an ermine-tipped crimson cap, on coats-of-arms look for the white band around the cap in the middle of the shield.) This coat-of-arms was used only by George III.
3 **From 1816–1837** The coat-of-arms remains the same but the electoral bonnet becomes a crown in honour of Hanover becoming a kingdom. When identifying coats-of-arms, look for five curved rows of pearls on the top of the crown – I often find that these are the easiest parts to pick out on faded paintwork since they show up as lines of dots. This coat-of-arms was used by George III, George IV and William IV.
4 **1837–1901** Queen Victoria's coat-of-arms dropped the centre shield, and looks similar to the modern arms; it therefore became easier for artists to depict it on the small curved surface of truncheons.

Another means of partial date identification is by the crown which is often painted at the top of truncheons. Many of the Georgian crowns are shown as being quite soft in their curves and perhaps with only a slight swelling at the top section. With William IV the crown became more angular at the top and took on a more definite shape, with the top part being generally more pronounced than the lower section, whilst with Queen Victoria this shape became even more exaggerated and distinctive.

Only two books have previously been published concerning truncheons: *Truncheons – their Romance and Reality* by E. Fenn Clark in 1935, and *The History of Truncheons* by E. R. H. Dicken in 1952. Both of these were limited editions and have long been out of print. The authors' collections have been broken up and during my research I have been able to identify many examples from both, listed in museum collections. I have a number of items in my own collection which were illustrated in the above books. This, of course, is what happens to collections when someone dies, unless measures have been taken to keep them intact by presentation to a museum. Even then, with the great shortage of space which seems to be a standard feature for most of the larger museums, there is no guarantee that the pieces will ever go on show to the public.

The following sections describe a number of truncheons and their styles which may be typical for a particular area. With the great variety that exists it will, however, never be possible to list descriptions which could identify all truncheons.

Truncheons of hundreds and tythings

When the office of high constable was finally abolished by Act of Parliament in 1869, it marked the end of an important era in English policing. His area of responsibility had been the old hundred and under him had come the tythingmen, or headboroughs, each responsible for his own group of families of ten men – although in later years this was usually more. Additional to the tythings, the high constable was also in charge of the petty constables, or as they became, the parish constables.

Generally, hundred truncheons are rare, with probably the greatest number being for the hundred of Whalesbone, or Brighton – this was due to new office holders being given a presentation truncheon. A number of these have been recorded and they are usually for the period 1830–1850. The name Whalesbone is really a corruption of Wellesborne which originally was the name of a stream running in the hundred. The truncheons are all of a similar design; the one in my collection is 20 inches long with a black painted body – the Victorian crown has below it a large royal coat-of-arms and the wording 'Hundred of Whalesbone'. In a panel beneath this are the two dolphins of Brighton and finally the date 1841 and the name 'Wm Jolly'. The reverse of this truncheon has a red shield bearing a white cross with a red rose in the centre, and some initials at the bottom which are partly obliterated, but which look like 'T.F.'. At the very bottom of the truncheon we find 'J.G.' cut into the wood, and as these initials are also on most other Whalesbone truncheons, they obviously refer to the maker. I have a further hundred truncheon which could come from the same area and is 21 inches long, of uniform thickness with a carved ring handle. The shaft is painted black with the words 'Constable of the Hundred of Brightford' and a carved crown surmounting it.

Probably the most interesting example of a hundred truncheon in my collection is 17 inches long with a plain ebony handle and a 9 inch brass barrel which ends with an elaborate decoration of moulded acanthus leaves and an acorn finial. The barrel is engraved 'Constable of the Hundred of Bradford 1798' and it is a most impressive piece. I have seen a description of a similar one also for the area, so it may be a design which was popular in the district.

Tything truncheons can be even rarer than those for the hundreds since by the time it was general for truncheons to be decorated the parish constables had taken over many of the functions of tythingmen. I have one 15 inch specimen with the barrel painted blue and the cypher 'GR' and 'Tyg. 85' below.

I have no idea where this particular example originated from, but there is also another interesting one for Melksham in Wiltshire. This has an unusual shape, having two brass-bound rings at the top, with four turned wooden rings underneath and then a tapering shaft with a shaped handle. The overall colour is black and below the rings is the cypher 'GIVR' and the words 'Melksham 1829'.

Truncheons of parish constables

The parish was, and indeed still is, an area within the jurisdiction of a church forming a division within the local bishopric or diocese. When petty constables came to be appointed, the parish was the ideal area for them to be based on, since in most cases the manor court and the church worked together. The petty constables, or as they later became, parish

constables, were usually drawn from within the ranks of tythingmen and, of course, whilst there could be many tythingmen within a parish, there could only be one parish constable, since he had specific jobs to perform.

We are conditioned to think of a constable fulfilling those same functions as he has today, but two or three hundred years ago his duties were quite different. While he had to arrest wrongdoers, put them before a magistrate and, if necessary, convey them to prison, a parish constable also had the duty to collect a number of local taxes which varied according to the legislation in force at the time. However, records still existing from the 18th century show that it was not unusual for a constable to have £100–200 a year passing through his hands and, of couse, account books had to be kept. This amount of money, translated into modern terms, would be in the region of £10,000. Generally, should an incident occur where an arrest had to be made which was not as the result of a 'hue and cry', the victim would have to go before a justice of the peace to have a warrant sworn out and, in turn, would have to approach the parish constable and pay him a set fee to have the arrest made. The constable would also earn sums of money for conveying prisoners and for the execution of other warrants, particularly those for debt.

Since the job was so onerous and the fees not great, it was quite common for the constable to pay a deputy and so be left to get on with his business. Unfortunately this often resulted in people of poor quality being appointed.

Of the many types of truncheons which a new collector will come across, those of parish constables and special constables are probably the most numerous, although only as a general type. Each parish truncheon is likely to be different to any other, since the painted name made it unique to its parish of origin. The styles and decorations will also vary enormously, but unfortunately many parishes were not fully identified in the decoration and have, therefore, to be classified as unknowns.

The parish unit, of course, also applied within cities and towns. There exist a number of 19th century truncheons of London parish constables many of which are identified only by initials. For example, the parish of St. Mary's Islington will be identified on the truncheon as 'St. M. I.' whilst St. John Hackney is 'St. J. H.'. Only a few seem to have been spelt out in full and I have found that often these are for 'WIVR' (King William IV). In the case of special constables' truncheons, it is not unusual to find the numbers, generally painted at the bottom, to be quite high since, during the many riots in London, it was often necessary for large numbers of special constables to be enrolled. Another common one marked for William IV is from the parish of St. Martins which, of course, is in Trafalgar Square. This truncheon is usually a Parker of Holborn.

Top left: *Five parish constables' truncheons.* From left: *1. Croydon, with arms for 1801–1816. 2. Leigh (Wilts). 3. Mortlake (Surrey). 4. Orgrave 1791. 5. Standard parish constable's truncheon produced by Parker, Field for the Northampton Constabulary and issued by them to parish constables.* Authors collection.

Left: **Seven London truncheons.**
From left: *1. 'St.MI' No. 19 and the 3 swords of Middlesex (St. Mary's Islington). 2. '1868 St. George'. 3. 'VR St.M.N.' (St. Mary's Newington). 4. 'WIVR. St. Martin's (St. Martin's-in-the-Fields). 5. Hackney B29' – probably Chartist Riots, although some attribute these truncheons to the Bread Riots of later years. 6. 'WRIV St. Pancras. Middx 296'. 7. 'St.M.I.90' (also St. Mary's Islington). Author's collection.*

Six truncheons of different styles.
From left: *1. Plain polished wooden truncheon with silver band engraved 'Constable of the Fountain Club' (I believe that this was a well known gaming club in York in the early years of the 19th century). 2. Very unusual truncheon which with its ornate decoration probably served also as a tipstaff of office. Made of oak, the upper band contains the royal coat of arms and the cypher GIIIR, while in the painted band immediately beneath this is a shield with the Welsh griffin, sheaves of corn on either side and above the shield the figure of a man carrying an old corn threshing flail. The truncheon is lead weighted at the top and was probably carried by the Constable of the Corn Exchange in either Swansea or Cardiff. 3. Interesting and unusually shaped truncheon. The top part representing an open lattice-style bridge and then in descending order around the truncheon the initials 'BW. Police No. 3' 'IV W.R' and finally the name 'T. W. Inman Esq., 1836'. 'BW' stood for Bridgwater in Somerset and this truncheon is described in the book by E. R. H. Dicken. 4. Green painted truncheon for the Wincanton Town Police. It is interesting that the cypher has been altered to read 'VIR' whereas originally it was painted for WIVR. The alteration has been made by scraping off part of the W to make it a V and the V from IV. Alterations of this kind were quite common when a Sovereign died and shows that truncheons were too valuable in those days just to throw away. 5. Possibly the head of an original long stave. This is an unusual truncheon as it bears the name 'Caterick' (Yorks) and on the reverse side has the following detail. 'AN REGT, LIX GEO III' This is the only truncheon or stave which I have come across with an attribution to a military regiment. 6. WmIV truncheon in oak, with a well made brass cap. Author's collection.*

Public office truncheons

Each of the public offices, which in 1792 amounted to eight, had a complement of three magistrates and six constables. However, at Bow Street there was not only the force of detectives who became known as the Bow Street Runners, but also the Bow Street Patrol. Truncheons of the public offices are quite rare nowadays and, apart from those recorded in the collections at the Bramshill Police College, the London Museum and the Horniman Museum, there do not seem to be many still in existence. Generally, they are only identified by the initials of the public office and for this reason can be easily overlooked for their original issue.

After the Bow Street Horse Patrol was reformed in 1805, it was issued with truncheons, swords and pistols and a number of these truncheons are still in existence. They can vary slightly in length but are usually around 21 inches. The style of decoration is quite easily seen to be by the same hand, although the actual placing of the decorative components can vary between truncheons. Basically, starting from the top there is the crown surmounted

Left: **Bow St. Horse Patrol truncheons.**
The one on the left is for Geo. IV and has the wording in the red cartouche 'Bow St. Night Police-20'. The middle and left examples are for Geo. III and both have the wording 'Bow St. HP' (Horse Patrol). The middle one has the number '9' on the reverse and the right hand one the number '106' also on the reverse. The generic style of these truncheons is very obvious and this was in fact carried through on the constables' truncheons at the other police offices for this period.
Author's collection.

by a lion, the royal arms within a garter underneath. Below is the cypher 'GR' and the words 'Bow St.' and 'HP', while on the back is usually found the number of the truncheon; I have examples numbered 9 and 106.

The reorganised Horse Patrol proved so successful that a further body of one hundred men was formed in 1821 both to provide a foot patrol and also as a training section for the Mounted Patrol. I recently acquired one of their truncheons and, unlike the previous examples I have seen which actually say 'Unmounted Horse Patrol', this one proved to be identical in size and design to the one numbered 9 mentioned above, but in place of the wording 'Bow St. HP' this has the cypher 'GIVR' and the wording 'Bow N.P. Street' in a shield with a red background – 'N.P.' in this context stands for Night Patrol or Night Police.

City of London Truncheons.
1. Well painted example with the number '23'. This is similar to the second one. These were possibly Special Constables' truncheons. 3. This is an early type and was probably issued for special constables at the Chartist riots. 4. A Parker, Field truncheon of the pattern issued to the City Police in the mid-19th century. Author's collection.

Interesting wooden truncheon with the arms of the City of London and a carved crown. At the bottom this truncheon is incised 'Robert Sedgwick 1779'. The cautionary and unusual verse cut into the truncheon reads as follows:

'A caution here let it be mine
So may it be my brother thine
Rest here my staff then learn be time
To live like men commit no crime
For hark here whoost the law doth say
You must be just you must obey
T'was so ordained we know of old
Then learn be wise don't swear nor scold
Don't do no wrong to friend or foe
Lest you for this to prison go
My office is to keep the peace
Then see you do from quarrels cease
If not then blame yourself not me
If you the inside prison see
Yet if you will be thus advised
You neer by me will be surprised.'

London Museum Collection.

City of London truncheons

The great variety to be found in the patterns of the City of London truncheons is due mainly to the fact that there were 26 wards within the City, each of which appointed constables. Generally, their truncheons bear the coat-of-arms for the City and the name of the ward. These continued after the establishment of the City of London Police in 1839 and tend to have a very good decoration with a bold coat-of-arms surmounted by the dragon's wings, which is one of the symbols of the City. There is another pattern of City truncheon which is particularly plentiful and this is marked 'Parker', meaning that it is pre-1841. The barrel is painted black and at the top is the white shield of the City with the sword in the top left corner. Their apparent numbers and approximate date could indicate that they were originally made for the Chartist Riots and issued as special constables' truncheons.

Truncheons of the Metropolitan Police, 1829–1900

I have described the first pattern of Metropolitan Police truncheon under **Tipstaves,** since I feel that it was intended to have a dual function. However, its life was obviously short and gave way to a more standard shape of truncheon which usually had a crown, the cypher 'VR' and the initials 'M.P.'. Later truncheons, probably from the 1890s onwards, were not generally decorated but were die-stamped – usually with the initials

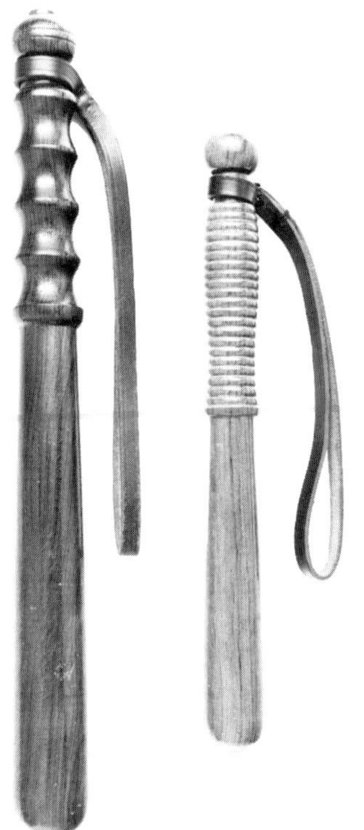

Examples of two modern truncheons
The one on the right is of the C.I.D. pattern and is also carried by Inspectors, whilst the larger one is the standard constable's issue. Both are made of rosewood and are very much lighter in construction than earlier truncheons. Author's collection.

Metropolitan Police Officers' pattern short truncheon which came into use when the belt tipstaff was withdrawn in the 1870s. The right-hand example is for the Manchester Police and dates from the same period. Author's collection.

'M.P.' and also, very often, with the division and divisional number of the constable. The early ones were made of teak, ebony or lignum vitae, all particularly hard woods which will not float in water. Nowadays, the modern issue truncheon is made of a much lighter wood, which does not have the same density or strength as the old ones. However, many of the original plain truncheons are still in existence and are often still issued on division. I remember that my own truncheon was of lignum vitae and was at least 80–90 years old.

After the withdrawal of tipstaves, superintendents and inspectors carried a short truncheon by Parker, Field and Sons which was very highly decorated. The barrel had a black background with the crown at the top and the royal coat-of-arms within the garter underneath; lower down, within a red cartouche, were the initials 'M.P.'. These truncheons were made of boxwood and the decoration was of a particularly high standard. The officers would have had to buy these themselves and I have seen advertisements in almanacs of the turn of the century showing that they cost originally two shillings and sixpence. A superintendent's truncheon/tipstaff of similar pattern was available to the Manchester Police, but the boxwood was even lighter in weight.

Beadles' staves and truncheons

The office of beadle is a very old one and is usually associated with functions carried out within a parish. During the early years they were often in charge of the Night Watch, but later this duty was taken over by the parish constables. A beadle, in most people's minds, is associated with the parochial duties carried out by Mr. Bumble in *Oliver Twist* but, in fact, the overseeing of almshouses was just one job of many, which could also include acting as a general officer for the parish.

A different type of beadle also existed who was appointed by the courts; there are many ward beadles' truncheons to be found from the City of London.

The beadle's staff of office could be either long, usually over six feet, or could be a short staff or truncheon. Tower Hamlets Library Service had, some years ago, a number of silver-headed staves among which was one dated 1672 for the beadle of the Liberty of Norton Folgate. Many beadles' staves were surmounted by a figure or other device typical of the local area, and these were usually carried in ceremonial processions. The beadle would, of course, generally carry his staff to show his authority. I have an interesting long example the top figure of which is missing, although there is a filled-in part on the rounded head to show where it had been fixed. Below the head, which is slightly larger than a cricket ball, is the crown with the cypher 'GIIIR' and 'Westrow 1777' underneath. I believe this is from Bury St. Edmunds in Suffolk.

I have a further short beadle's truncheon, painted black with an overall length of 18 inches. At the top is the cypher 'GIVR' and crown and, in a circular band running down the truncheon, the words 'Harborough Beadle' with the date 1805 and a number of painted lines underneath. George III was still reigning in 1805 and the 'IV' in the cypher shows up as newer paint than the rest of the truncheon – it was obviously added when

Five long staves and an early patrol officer's walking stick.

The five examples on the left are all at least 5ft 6in high.

From left: 1. Governor's Wand of Office for Christ's Hospital – City of London. 2. Very rare, silver crowned white wand of office carried by the functionary at the Houses of Commons called 'White Rod'. This was an office which existed until the 1890s and he was generally a deputy to Black Rod and saw that the galleries were cleared and the doors within the Houses of Parliament secured. 3. Beadle's Stave. This one is for Geo. III and has the name Westrow (near Bury St. Edmunds) and the date 1777. When first made there was probably a carved figure surmounting the ball. 4. Well painted constable's stave of office for Hemel Hempstead. The details are:

> *'GIIIR*
> *Peace Proclaimed July 21 1814*
> *I.Ollif*
> *Constable*
> *Hemel Hempstead'*

The wording and date are interesting in so much that they probably commemorate the abdication of Emperor Napoleon. 5. High Constable's long stave from Cambridge – presented by the mayor – Wm. Bishop in 1845. This stave was originally in Fenn Clark's collection and is illustrated in his book. 6. Patrol Officer's walking stick – probably from Birmingham. The decoration is a lion surmounting a crowned helm with the cypher VIR. This dates it between 1837 and 1844 when the figure '1' for '1st' seems to have been dropped. When constables walked fixed beats many Midland police forces gave their patrolling sergeants and inspectors an iron ferruled stick such as this which they would tap on a street corner at night and the surrounding constables would come into them for instructions. The tradition of carrying a walking stick still persists with many of these forces but early examples such as this are extremely rare. Author's collection.

University truncheons.

Dating from approximately 1805 this interesting crowned truncheon has the badge for University College Oxford. It would have been carried originally by constables appointed by the Proctor's Office.

Right: *Cambridge University truncheon for 1854. Below the royal coat of arms for Cambridge University. This was a standard pattern truncheon for Cambridge University and there are a number of examples in existence. Author's collection.*

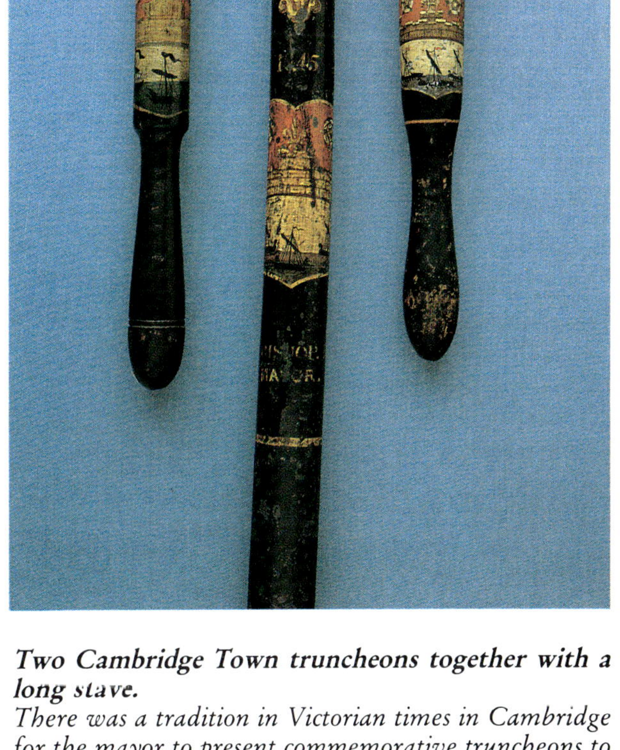

Two Cambridge Town truncheons together with a long stave.

There was a tradition in Victorian times in Cambridge for the mayor to present commemorative truncheons to the constables and painted long staves to the two High Constables. The fronts of these always carried the royal coat of arms and the arms of Cambridge (three sailing ships). The reverse usually has the details of the mayor and the date of presentation. The two truncheons illustrated here are (left) '1832 J. Purchas, Mayor.' and the one on the right for 'C. F. Foster Esq., Mayor 1862.' The long stave was presented by Wm Bishop, Mayor in 1845. (This shows more detail of the painting than the illustration of this stave under long staves.) Author's collection.

George IV became king. This overpainting is not uncommon with both truncheons and tipstaves since they were valuable objects and continued in use over periods of many years.

University truncheons

Both Cambridge and Oxford had separate establishments for policing the towns and universities. The designs of the university truncheons in Cambridge are straightforward – bearing the crown, royal coat-of-arms and the university coat-of-arms underneath. Oxford, however, had a number of long staves in addition to truncheons and these can be seen in the proctor's office. The Ashmolean Museum in Oxford also has a good selection of local truncheons and staves.

Truncheons for the city of Cambridge are usually well decorated and fairly numerous, since it became a practice in Victorian times for the outgoing mayor to present truncheons and long staves to the high constables and constables. This practice continued until after the First World War. I have two such truncheons: one dated 1862, given by Mr C. F. Foster the mayor, and the second one, dated 1833, given by the mayor, Mr J. Purchas.

There were two high constables and approximately 30 parish constables within Cambridge. The high constables carried staves of office approximately five feet long and these were also painted with the royal cypher, the coat-of-arms under the crown, the date, the coat-of-arms for Cambridge and the name of the presenting mayor. I have one for 1845 presented by Wm. Bishop.

Railway truncheons

One of the first truncheons that I remember buying was for the Manchester and Leeds Railway Company which existed only between 1839 and 1847. The body of the truncheon is painted red and the name of the Company is cut into it along the length of the body. Only later did I discover that, in the early days, railway police also acted as signalmen and guardians of the track – it was not until some twenty years after the first railway opened that the system of signalling was invented. The police were stationed along the line and would signal with their truncheon to the train driver to indicate if the way ahead was clear.

Following the tradition of Victorian truncheons, nearly all railway truncheons are highly decorative. However, they are not only very hard to find, they are also often difficult to assign to a particular railway. The following table will be helpful in identifying the various companies and the initials which were painted on many of their truncheons.

Special constables' truncheons

Prior to 1800 the services of special constables were only very occasionally called upon but, with the many riots of the 19th century, they came to play an increasingly important part. Throughout the country there were

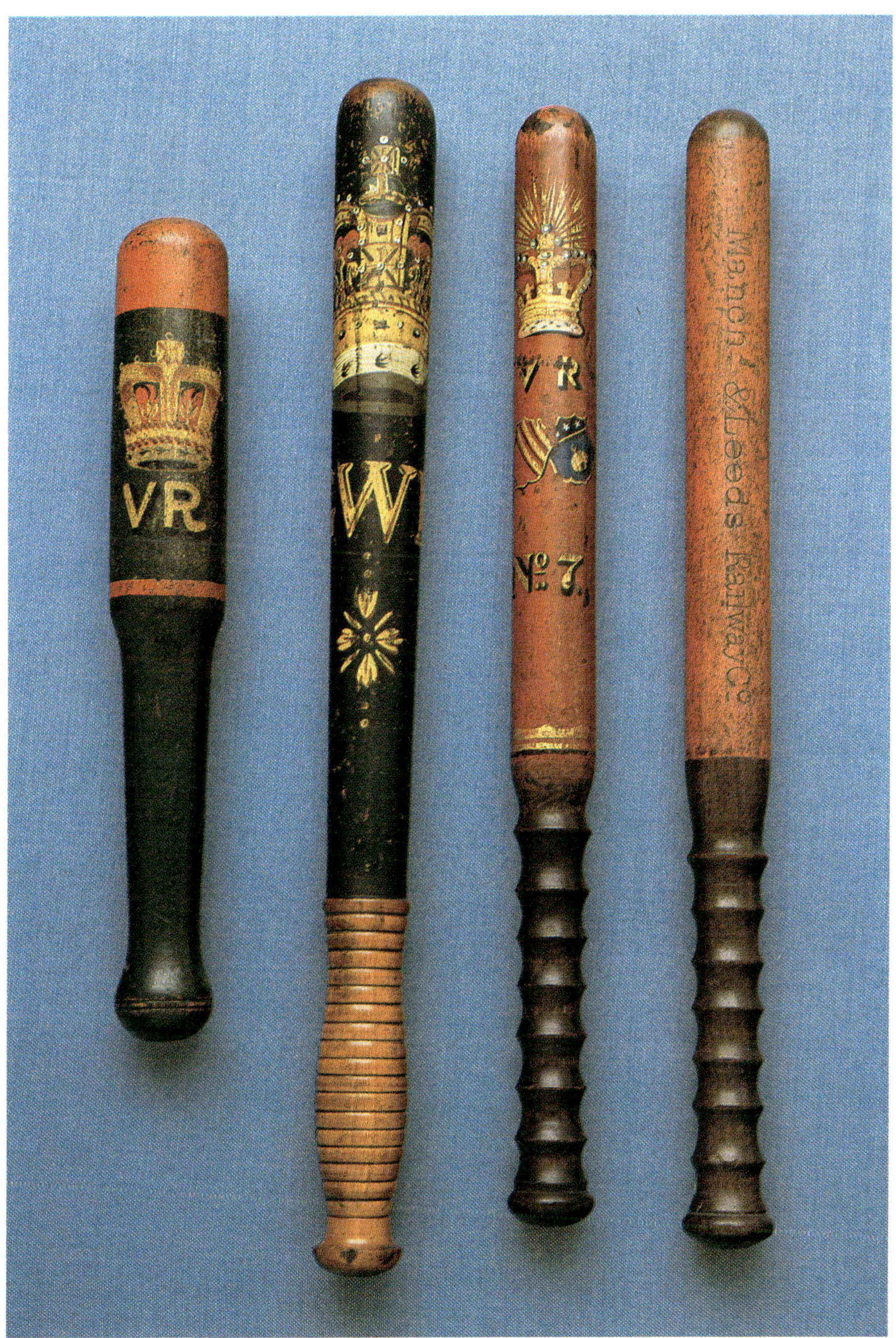

widespread disturbances for a number of different reasons and, even after the formation of proper police forces, provincial districts were still hard pressed to cope with the numbers involved in the demonstrations.

Special constables were normally drawn from the ranks of the middle class and employed artisans, and were sworn in for their specific duty by the justices of the peace. Sometimes they were issued with truncheons, as in the case of London parishes such as St. Pancras, whose truncheons can have very high numbers. However, often the special constables had to supply their own truncheons and these were usually very crude, being

THE EARLY RAILWAYS

London & Birmingham Railway	Incorporated		1833
Amalgamated with Grand Junction Railway	Partly opened	18th July	1837
and Manchester & Birmingham Railway to			
form the London & North Western Railway –	Amalgamated		1846
later London Midland & Scottish			
London & Croydon Railway	Incorporated		1835
	Opened	5th June	1839
Bristol & Exeter Railway (B & ER)	Incorporated	19th May	1836
Run by Great Western Railway between 1841	Fully opened	1st May	1844
and 1849			
Amalgamated with Great Western Railway	Amalgamated		1876
South Eastern Railway	Incorporated		1836
Afterwards became South Eastern & Chatham			
Railway and later Southern Railway			
North Midland Railway (Derby to Leeds)	Incorporated		1836
Amalgamated with Midland Counties	Opened	11th May	1840
Railway & Birmingham & Derby Railways to	Amalgamated	May	1844
form Midland Railway (MR) later London			
Midland & Scottish			
Midland Counties Railway	Incorporated		1836
London & Greenwich Railway	Incorporated	14th December	1836
Leased to South Eastern Railway	Leased		1844
West London Railway	Incorporated		1836
Incorporated under the title Birmingham			
Bristol & Thames Junction Railway. Later			
owned by London & Birmingham and Great			
Western Railways and title changed to West			
London Railway.			
A new line was opened in 1863 under the title			
West London Extension Railway			
Eastern Counties Railway	Incorporated		1836
Name changed to Great Eastern Railway in	Opened	18th June	1839
1862	Renamed		1862
Northern & Eastern Counties Railway	Incorporated		1836
Leased to Eastern Counties in 1844, finally	Part opened	15th September	1840
amalgamated with Great Eastern Railway in			
1902			
Became London & North Eastern Railway	Amalgamated		1902
(LNER) in 1923	Renamed		1923
London & Brighton Railway	Incorporated		1837
Name changed to London Brighton & South	Opened	21st September	1841
Coast Railway on amalgamation with London			
& Croydon Railway – later to be known as	Amalgamated		
Southern Railway	& renamed	27th July	1846

THE EARLY RAILWAYS

Manchester & Bolton Railway	Opened	29th May	1838
Name changed to Manchester & Leeds Railway in 1847	Renamed		1847
Great Western Railway (GWR)	Opened	4th June	1838
Opened to Maidenhead 1838	Opened	30th June	1841
Opened to Bristol 1841	Opened		1841
Birmingham & Derby Railway	Opened	5th August	1839
Amalgamated with North Midland Railway & Midland Counties Railway to form Midland Railway 1844	Amalgamated	20th May	1844
Manchester & Leeds Railway	Opened in	4th July	1839
Opened in sections	sections	and	
	between	1st March	1841
Birmingham & Gloucester Railway	Opened	24th January	1840
Later amalgamated with Midland Railway			
South Devon Railway	Incorporated	4th July	1844
Opened Exeter to Teignmouth	Opened	30th May	1846
Opened Exeter to Plymouth	Opened	2nd April	1849
Amalgamated with Great Western Railway	Amalgamated		1878
Eastern Union Railway	Incorporated		1844
Amalgamated with Ipswich & Bury St. Edmunds Railway	Amalgamated		1847
Taken over by Great Eastern Railway (which later became London & North Eastern Railway)	Taken over		1862
East Lincolnshire Railway	Incorporated	June 26th	1846
Leased in perpetuity to Great Northern Railway in 1847	Leased		1847
London Tilbury & Southend Railway (LT & SR)	Opened to Tilbury	13th April	1854
	Opened to Southend	1st March	1856
North Eastern Railway	Amalgamated		1854
Formed by amalgamation Earliest lines were those of York & North Midland Railway partly opened in 1839 and completed in 1840			
North Eastern Railway became part of LNER in 1923	Merged with LNER		1923
Pembroke & Tenby Railway	Incorporated		1859
Amalgamated with Great Western Railway 1897	Amalgamated		1897

Special Constable's truncheons.
The greater majority of special constables truncheons are not identified by town or county and this can often make it very hard to identify either their date or their origin. 2. From the left has the date 1868 whilst, 3., (which is a Parker, Field truncheon) has the wording in the cartouche 'Surrey Special Constable'. 4. Has 'Special Police KCC' and the word 'Constable' this was for Kent County Constabulary. Author's collection.

little more than turned pieces of wood, or shaved down chair legs. Sometimes they would hand-paint their own designs onto the truncheons in imitation of the regular police truncheons and this accounts for the very amateurish workmanship often to be found. Since the Chartist Riots were in the early 1840s, it is worth remembering that even these crude specimens are now over 140 years old and a few are, therefore, worth keeping in a collection – even if only as curiosities. I have one interesting example which still has the original warrant appointing the bearer as a special constable. This has been pasted to the truncheon and the wording reads 'Cornhill Ward Mr. Chas Hudson, Special Constable 16th Division under the direction of Mr. Linford L. Wilson of Royal Exchange'.

City of London Chartist riot Special Constable's truncheon (1840s).
The City arms have been drawn in ink at the top of the truncheon. This speciman is highly unusual in that the original warrant of appointment has been stuck to the wood. It reads:

*" 'Cornhill Ward'
Mr. Chas Hudson
Special Constable
    16th Division
under the direction
Mr. Linford L. Wilson of
    Royal Exchange"*
Author's collection.

Important riots and civil disturbances

for many of which special constables' truncheons were made.

Name	Date
Gordon riots (London and the South)	1780
Bristol Bridge riots	1793
Spa Field riots	1816
Kent Swing riots	1830
Warminster farm workers' riots	1830
Bedfordshire riots	1830–1831
Reform Bill riots	1831–1832
Bristol riots	1831
Cold Bath Fields riot	1833
The Rebecca riots	1839–1843
Potters riots (Staffordshire)	1842
Torquay bread riots	1847
Chartist riots	1848
Bread riots (centred on Bermondsey)	1855
Second Torquay bread riots	1867
Fenian riots (Lutterworth)	1867–1868
Blackburn riots	1878 (May)
The Great Strike	1926

Truncheons of hospitals and almshouses

These are rare truncheons but since examples do exist, there has to be a strong possibility that other specific ones would have been made and are still awaiting discovery.

The London Museum has one painted with the words 'Royal Free Hospital' within a shield and, on the reverse, the royal coat-of-arms.

I have one in my own collection from the city of Coventry but, despite having the name of the hospital and the initials of the constable to whom it was issued, neither I, nor the Coventry Museum, have been able to find its original location. The description is as follows: it is 15 inches long, has a ringed handle, black-painted body with the Coventry elephant and howdah and underneath the initials 'J.Mc.D.'. The reverse has, from top to bottom, a staff and entwined serpent – usually the badge of the medical profession.

The Hospital of Poor's Portion in Plymouth had a most elaborate type of truncheon/tipstaff and I have actually described this under **Tipstaves**. There are a number of these in existence and it would seem that they were either issued yearly, or whenever the office holder changed.

There is another type which, although it is a wand of office rather than a truncheon, has direct links with a number of the City of London hospitals.

This group of truncheons includes (from left) 1. GPO truncheon. 2. Westminster truncheon probably for a parish constable, with the Arms of 1801–1816. 3. Truncheon in its original leather holster or carrying case. This has a king's crown so is either for Edward VII, or early Geo. V, and is probably for Birmingham as it has the crest of the lion above a crown. 4. This truncheon has in the red cartouche the wording 'GJC Company' which probably stands for the Grand Junction Canal. Canal truncheons are extremely rare and apart from this one, and one in my own collection, which is not attributable to a particular Company, I do not know of any others. 5. This is for the 'Royal Hospital' which must give it a semi-military background since this is the Royal Military Hospital at Chelsea. (Nos. 1, 4 and 5 are all Parker truncheons and show very clearly the standard style of their decorations.) Collection London Museum.

All these are of a similar design, being approximately six feet long and quite thin – they were painted overall and at the top usually had the City arms and the initials of the respective hospital. I have one with 'C.H.' which stood for Christ's Hospital. One also finds 'St. Bh' for St. Bartholomew's, 'St.Th' for St. Thomas', and Mr. Dicken, in his book, mentions having seen examples for Bridewell and Bethlem.

Above:
The front and back illustrations of this unusual truncheon show clearly on the front the Elephant and Howdah which is part of the badge for Coventry. Below this are the initials 'J.McD' and underneath No. '11' – whilst on the reverse is the medical staff with the entwined snake. Research has failed to locate the origin of this truncheon but it would seem likely that it is for an early Bedlam or mental hospital. This would make it one of the very few hospital truncheons known to exist. Author's collection.

Four very interesting pieces from the collection of the Plymouth Museum.
They are (from left): 1. Mace/tipstaff for Hospital of Poor's Portion (Arms of Plymouth, Arms of Hospital, Initials 'J.W.' and date 1837). 2. Tipstaff for Hospital Poor's Portion – arms of the hospital are as for Plymouth, but with a beehive in the middle of the cross and bees. 3. Borough of Devonport Truncheon for 1837 marked '162'. The museum also has '163'. 4. Short truncheon for Hospital of Poor's Portion. Arms of Plymouth, royal arms, Hospital arms and initials 'WS' & date 1833. Originally issued to Mr. A. Saull. Photographer J. Hill. Plymouth Museum.

Canal truncheons

During the early part of the 19th century and before the network of railways had taken over, canals played a very important part in the transportation of goods from one part of the country to another. There were – as with so many organisations of those days – many companies involved in the running of canals and a number of these appointed their own constables.

The truncheons which these men carried are today very rare and I only know of two examples. One is in the London Museum and bears the initials 'G.J.C.Company', for the Grand Junction Canal, and the second – in my own collection – is of a most unusual shape, having a knob at the top with the crown and cypher 'VR' and 'l' and, in a band immediately between the top and the shaft, the word 'Canal'.

Truncheons of dockyards

Many of the dock companies had their own police or Watch, and there are a number of their truncheons still in existence.

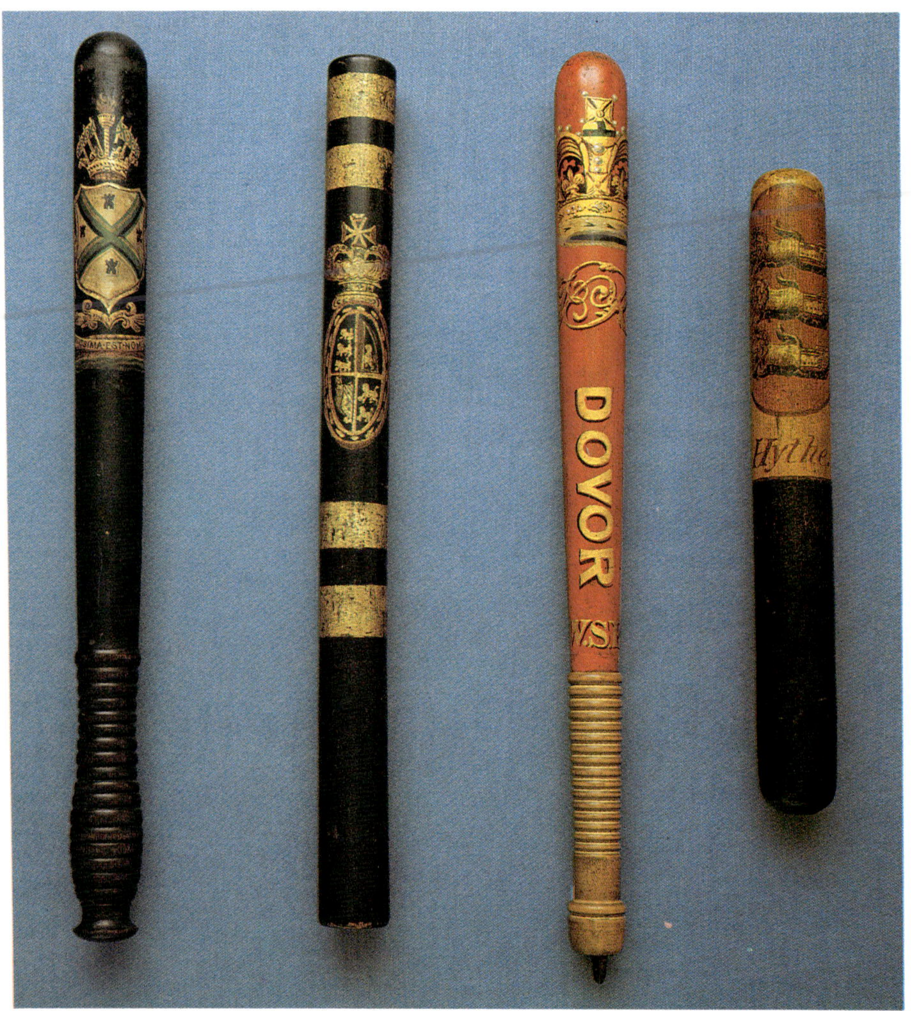

Above: *Very rare canal truncheon with an unusual shape. The word canal is on the band beneath the cypher VRI. The date is probably between 1837 and 1844. Author's collection.*

Coastal Towns and Ports.
From left: *1. Truncheon for the City of Plymouth. 2. Early Victorian Brighton truncheon. 3. Victorian constable's truncheon for Dover – with the original spelling. The constable's initials 'WSF' are just above the handle. 4. Short truncheon, or tipstaff, for Hythe. This was one of the Cinque ports. Mr. Dicken identifies, in his book, this pattern of truncheon as of the type carried by port reeves in the Cinque ports. Author's collection.*

The Plymouth Museum has a typical mace/tipstaff which is inscribed 'Plymouth Dock Watch 1768'. Portsmouth Dockyard and also the Royal Clarence Victualling Yard both had truncheons of very similar design. They were approximately 12 inches long and for Portsmouth I own one with the following details: 'Po.D.Y. 1843' and the fouled anchor with, on the reverse, the crown (1) and cypher 'VR'. The one for the Royal Clarence Victualling Yard had 'R.C.V.Y.' and the date set in a panel and underneath the admiralty fouled anchor. The two examples that I have seen have been for William IV and Victoria. The City of Portsmouth Police also carried a truncheon of similar design, but whether the naval one was copied from the city, or vice-versa, I do not know. The 'P.O.' on the example for the Portsmouth and the Royal Clarence Victualling Yard (which was at Gosport) stands for Portsmouth.

Additional to the London Dock Company tipstaves which I have described separately, there are truncheons in existence for the Hull Docks Company and the East and West India Dock Company.

There are also a number of truncheons for the Cinque Ports. Generally they can be identified by a coat-of-arms bearing on the left of the shield, the heads of the three leopards of England and, on the right, ships' sterns as the rest of their bodies. The Kent Police Museum has a number of examples for these and I have two in my collection.

Prison truncheons

Many prison truncheons were never identified as such, while some carried small cryptic illustrations of items connected with prisons, such as a key or handcuffs.

I have a very fine short stave or truncheon which is 24 inches long with a ball end. The decoration is as follows: 'GIIIR', crown, coat-of-arms within garter and stripes similar to Manchester's coat-of-arms. The clue for its identification as a gaoler's truncheon can be found on the back: a small painting of the old type of handcuffs with a bar running through and the padlock at the end.

The Plymouth City Museum has a truncheon which is identified by the word 'Prisons', and there are others to be found around the country.

Two highly individualistic truncheons.
Both of these have obviously been made as 'one offs' to the design of their owners and the one on the left is unusual in that it is the only truncheon I have ever come across which has been given a name. Beneath the cypher GIIIR and the royal coat of arms is a panel with a further crown and in a wreath above this the words 'The Peace Maker'. Some damage marks made by its use at some time as a hammer. The strangely shaped truncheon on the right is probably a gaoler's since, on the reverse, is an old pattern pair of shackles with a bar and padlock. The Hanoverian bonnet within the coat of arms dates this from between 1801 and 1816 and the diagonal bars on the decoration near the base of the truncheon are reminiscent of Manchester. Author's collection.

Scottish truncheons.
This representative collection of seven Scottish truncheons shows the variety to be found in their decoration.
From left: 1. Early Victorian constable's truncheon – probably for Glasgow. 2. Victorian truncheon for Partick. 3. Standard pattern of crown and cypher. 4. Special Constable's truncheon for Edinburgh. This is further identified by the fouled anchor on the ermine chaplet. 5. Marked 'City Police' – this could be Edinburgh Police – number '52'. 6. Is a very well decorated 'Neath Boro Police' – King's crown. 7. City of Aberdeen. Author's collection.

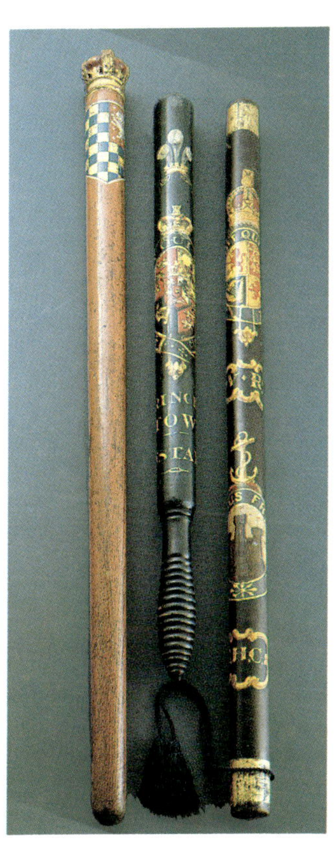

Scottish truncheons

Scottish truncheons and staves come in a variety of shapes and sizes. Edinburgh particularly has great variety. These are staves of approximately two feet which were all well decorated with the castle of Edinburgh and its Latin motto and can be further identified by the letters 'E.H.C.' which stand for Edinburgh High Constables. We also find magistrates' bâtons and, after the paid police were established at the beginning of the 19th century, the more conventional truncheons. With Edinburgh it should be remembered that a cabled anchor forms part of the badge and is often painted on truncheons – this should not be confused with the English admiralty's fouled anchor.

Later Victorian Scottish truncheons tended to be of a larger pattern than those found in England and were generally left as plain wood with the decoration applied directly on to this. Usually it was only a crown, the cypher 'VR' and sometimes the identification of the relevant town.

The Society of High Constables for Perth followed the pattern for the Scottish short staves and theirs were painted at both ends. While one end has the royal arms with a crown above, the other end bears the arms of Perth – a lamb with staff and cross – and the banner of St. Andrew within a shield surmounted on the breast of an eagle with two heads. The Latin motto for Perth is *Pro rege lege et grege*.

The manufacturer's name 'McNaughton' is often found on Scottish truncheons.

Regional styles of truncheons

There is not sufficient room to describe all of the different patterns of truncheons which could be found about the country, but the new collector will find it helpful to know that there are one or two basic designs which

Top left: *Exceptional for their quality and condition this illustration shows two staves and one long truncheon.*
From left: *1. High Constable's staff for Lewes in Sussex (dated between 1813–1820). 2. Truncheon for Princetown WMIV (1830–1837). The Prince of Wales feathers are beautifully painted at the top of the truncheon followed by the Royal Arms and the wording 'Princetown Constable'. 3. Long stave with the royal coat of arms, cypher VR and the coat of arms for Edinburgh. Within a wreath beneath this are the initials 'E.H.C'. These stand for Edinburgh High Constables.* Bramshill Police College Collection.

Bottom left: *Three Long Staves.*
From left: *1. Edinburgh High Constables, with the number 57 – this is decorated at each end. 2. A long staff for the Society of Perth High Constables. This has at one end the royal coat of arms and at the other the double-headed eagle badge of Perth with the wording within a garter of 'Pro Rege Lege et Grege' (No. 'A.20'). 3. This staff has within a ribbon running around the barrel the wording 'Bermondsey Special Constable' with above it the crown and cypher GIIIR. The number '73' is just above the handle.* Author's collection.

are typical of particular areas. For example, the Manchester area favoured baluster style truncheons, but not exclusively, and there are also many examples of the more standard shapes. Usually the crest of Manchester – a shield with three diagonal bars – will be painted on the body of the truncheon.

Liverpool truncheons tend to have a distinctive handle and often a slight waisting above this. The badge of Liverpool is the so-called 'Liver Bird' which is, in reality, a cormorant with a piece of seaweed in its beak.

For Birmingham there are some really beautiful examples in existence. The more highly decorated ones are almost entirely covered with heraldic

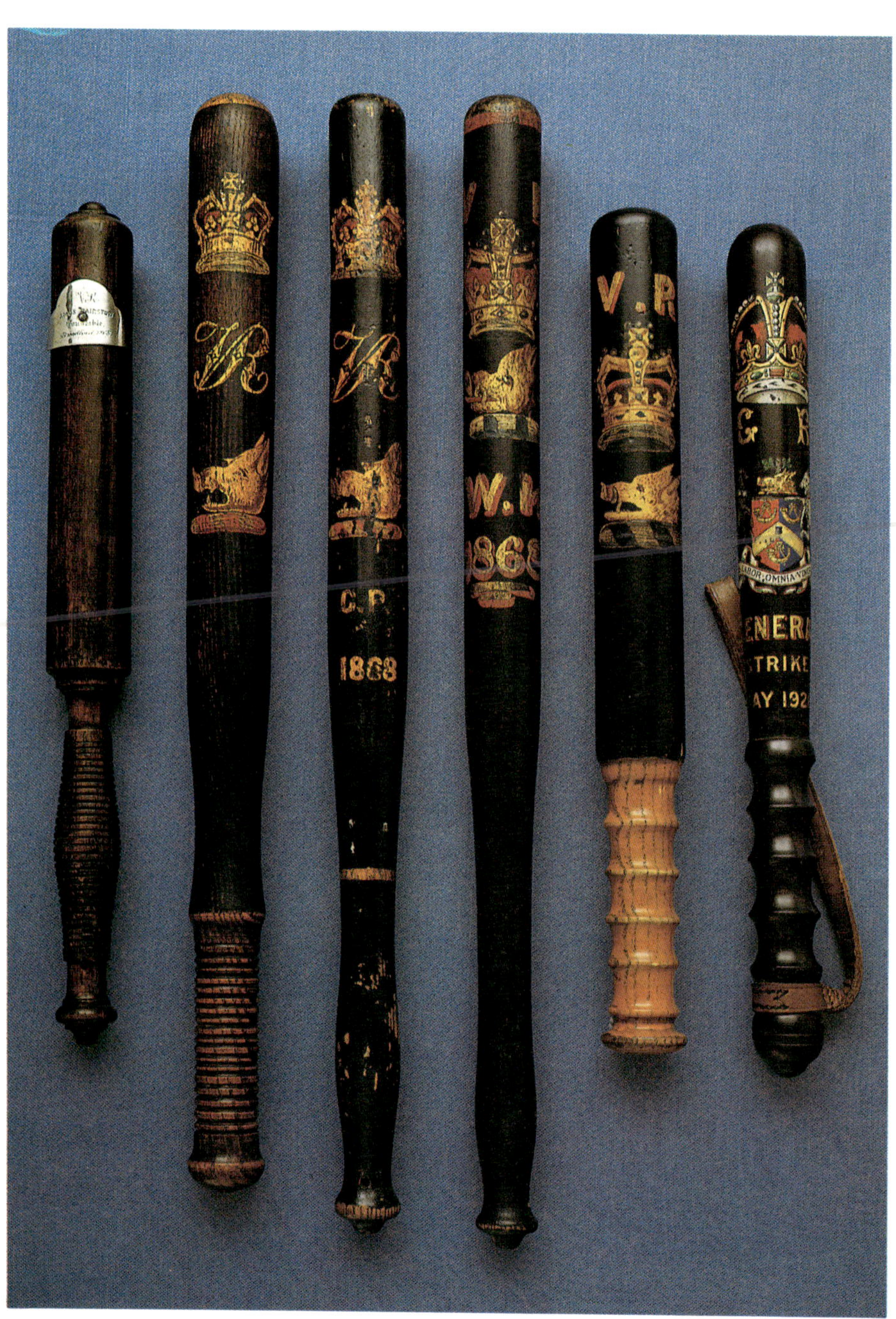

City of Bradford truncheons.
The badge of Bradford is a boar's head on a red and white chaplet and this is to be found on most of the truncheons for the City. The most interesting example in this collection is probably, 1. the plain one with the silver badge which has the wording 'VR Amos Bairstow. Constable. Bradford 1868'. I have found reference to Mr. Bairstow but have not been able to track down his exact office – he may well have been the High Constable at this time. 3. and 4. Commemorate Bradford reaching borough status in 1868 and there are a number of these in existence. 5. This is of the pattern issued only to officers. 6. This is not painted, but carried a transfer and has the wording 'General Strike May 1926'. The condition of this is particularly good. Author's collection.

Manchester truncheons.
From left: *1. Example of an early Geo. III baluster truncheon with a finely executed coat of arms. It has the initials 'G.K.' 2. Probably a parish constable's truncheon from the Manchester area and is decorated only within the baluster section at the top. 3. Early Victorian truncheon. 4. A Commemorative Manchester truncheon from 1914–1919 with the additional information 'Smith, Leader'. Many of the Midlands forces issued these to War Reserve Constables as mementoes and the decoration is nearly always a transfer. (Nos 2., 3. and 4. all show the diagonal bars of the Manchester Coat of Arms.)* Author's collection.

Liverpool truncheons.
From left: *1. Victorian Liverpool constable's truncheon with the word 'Liverpool' above the gold painted representation of the 'Liver Bird'. This bird is in fact intended to be a cormorant holding a piece of seaweed in its beak. 2. Geo. III and with the wording 'Township of Everton' and the constable's initials 'G.H'. There is also a representation of the Liver Bird. 3. Plain oak truncheon with the number '177E' stamped into the wood. However, there is a silver band just above the handle which has the wording 'Liverpool City Police Riots. August 1919'. I have seen one other example of a truncheon with this band around it, so it was probably made as a souvenir for police officers in Liverpool who did not go on strike and who served through the ensuing riots in 1919.* Author's collection.

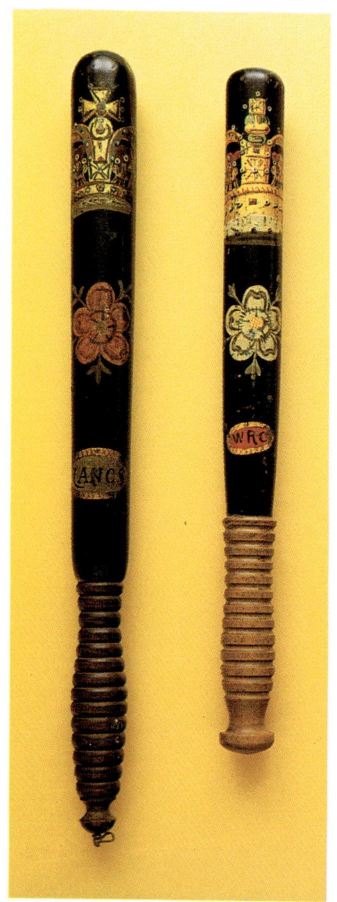

Far left: *The truncheon on the left is for Lancashire and has the red rose. The truncheon on the right is for the West Riding Constabulary (W.R.C.) and has the white rose of Yorkshire.* Author's collection.

Centre left: **Two Birmingham truncheons.** *The one on the left is for Geo. IV and shows the Birmingham coat of arms under the royal cypher and the number '2'. The truncheon on the right is a War Reserve commemorative truncheon dated 1917–1919.* Author's collection.

Left: **Exeter High Constable's truncheon.** *This has silver caps at top and bottom and the lower one has the inscription 'W. Ferris Oct 8th 1827'. The royal arms are above the city arms of Exeter.* Author's collection.

Far left: **Staffordshire truncheons.** *1. and 2. Both are inscribed 'Staffordshire Constabulary' and have the Staffordshire lovers' knot. The one on the left is an earlier pattern. 3. has the cypher VR within the Crown, the Staffordshire lovers' knot and 'W124'. 'W' in this case standing for Worcester. The torpedo shape is a common one for the Staffordshire area.* Author's collection.

Left: *Well decorated parish constable's truncheon inscribed 'W. Hare. Newton Popplewell'. This is in Devon and the Hanoverian bonnet dates it between 1801–1816.* Author's collection.

From left: *1. Truncheon for Gamlingay. On the reverse 'J. Wagstaff'. Constable. 2. Hull Police truncheon. This has every appearance in the decoration of being a Parker, Field but the handle is of a different construction. Possibly the original large knop was damaged at some time and was then re-shaped to a smaller size. 3. Constable's staff for Dover. Cypher GRIV. The painting at the top is a representation of St. Martin on horseback before a portcullis, giving his cloak to a beggar. There is shipping as a background. 4. Most unusual truncheon carved from the branch of a tree and still bearing a branch junction. It is well painted with a crown and cypher GRIV. Apart from the rough work on some Irish shelaleghs this is the only painted English truncheon which I have ever seen left in its original shape. 5. WMIV constable's truncheon for Dover with the alternative spelling and No. '64'. 6. Parker, Field truncheon with finely executed royal coat of arms and within the cartouche 'Coventry Police'. 7. Truncheon of similar style to the London police offices truncheon. This one is for Geo. IV and has the wording 'Hamlet of Ratcliffe 12'. Mr. Dicken mentions in his book that this was one of the few truncheons ascribed to a Hamlet which he had come across. The Hamlet of Ratcliffe was situated on the River Thames immediately to the left of Tower Bridge and the Tower of London. The public or police office for Shadwell actually took over this area and therefore this must have been the parish constable's truncheon.*

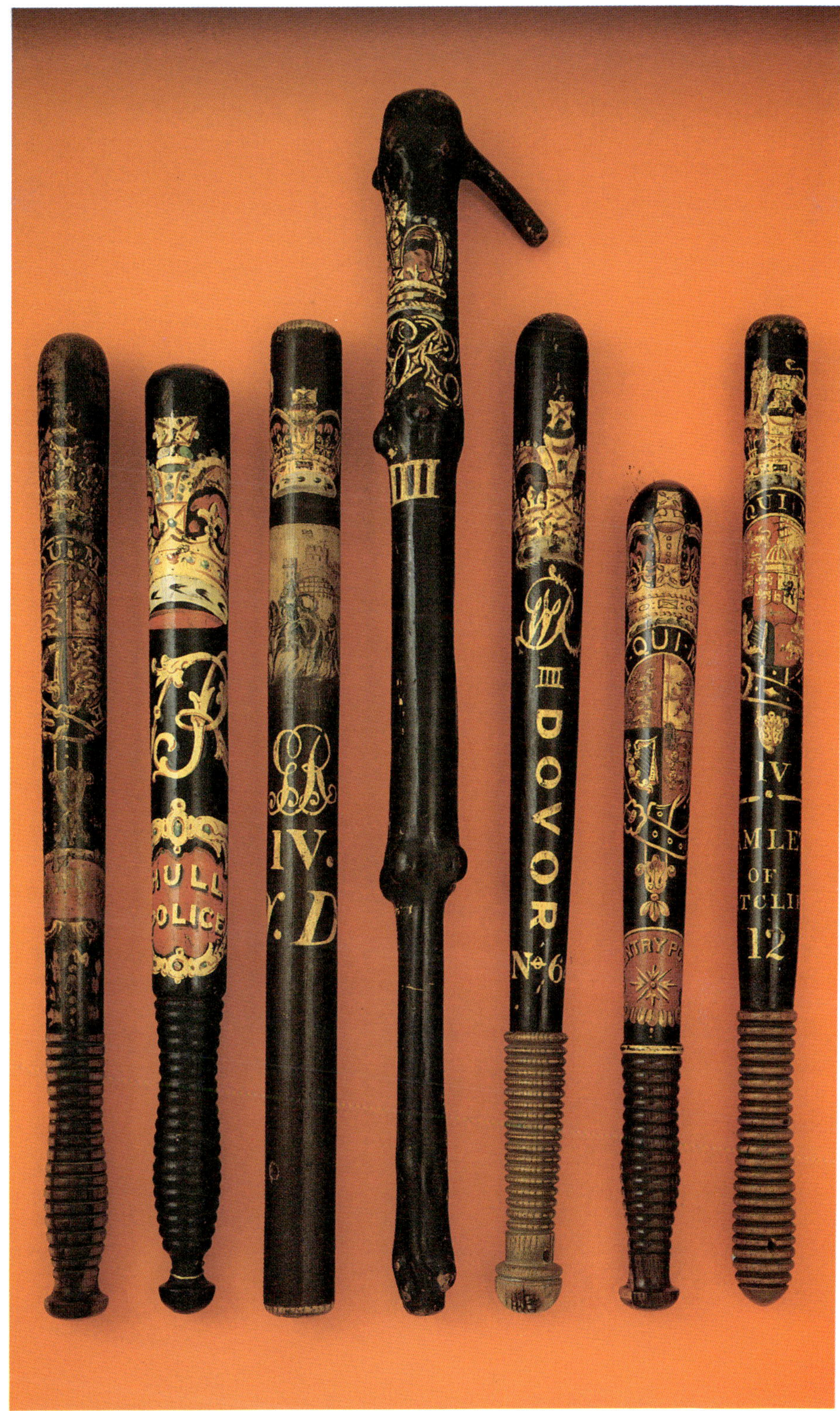

Bramshill Police College Collection.

designs, the royal coats-of-arms and cyphers and, usually, the coat-of-arms for Birmingham. This is a shield in four quarters with the top right and the bottom left having a pattern of diagonal lozenges and the top left and bottom right panels being a zig-zag of alternate colours. There are many examples of these in the Birmingham Art Gallery and Museum. Needless to say, there are very few of the more highly decorated ones outside of museums or collections.

Bristol truncheons and those for the immediate vicinity are usually of brass and are of a very heavy and solid construction. The area of their authority is usually engraved on the barrel.

West Country truncheons often have a round shaft with the top finishing in a boxlike construction of four sides – all of which are painted. Usually immediately above the square section is a short extension to the shaft with a knop above this.

Staffordshire truncheons are often of an Indian club shape where the handle – usually quite long and carved in small rings – runs straight into the body of the truncheon which swells at the top into a torpedo shape. The lover's knot is the badge of Staffordshire and this will be found on many truncheons both for county and for the main towns.

Many Oxfordshire truncheons finish with a round knop on the top, whilst the early Dorchester truncheons have a very definite club shape with a slight waisting at the top and above this a distinct knoblike end.

Exeter truncheons for chief constables usually have silver ends; I own one very interesting example dated 1827.

Irish truncheons are rare, with the exception of some of the Victorian ones issued to parish constables. These are usually of Bogoak and carved with shamrocks and Irish harps.

Miscellaneous types of truncheons

The keen collector will soon find that there are many types of truncheons outside of the more standard painted ones and many of these are well worth including in a collection. During the later Georgian period and extending into the time of Queen Victoria, a number of metal truncheons were made, sometimes with blades concealed in their bodies. One such example in the Carlisle Museum and Art Gallery has eight sharpened blades projecting from the body of the truncheon which has a conventional handle. The bottom of the handle has a metal attachment which could obviously be put on to a chain and swung round violently – the purpose for this was probably to clear rioting crowds. The museum has two further examples of plain truncheons with enclosed metal hilts – rather like swords. I would think that these were intended for issue to special constables at times of rioting.

I have in my own collection a plain wrought-iron truncheon which is only 12 inches long but weighs 3lbs – a very formidable weapon. I also have a 15 inch wrought iron truncheon which has a threaded hollow under the handle and was obviously intended to be put on to the top of a pole so that it could be used like a pike. At the side of the truncheon is a small knob and when this is pulled upwards a four inch blade – similar to the old style cut-throat razor – projects half-an-inch along the body of the

Parker, Field patented truncheon case, together with truncheon marked 'VR DB' (Dewsbury Police). This pattern of case was similar in design to the Parker, Field tipstaff case and also the larger model they made for mounted horse patrols. All three types have a spring covered with a leather button at their base and when the top of the case is released the truncheon springs up ready to be grasped. Bramshill Police College Collection.

Top left: *Two parish constables' truncheons from Ireland. These are made from a wood commonly called Bogoak and are heavy and black in colour. They are carved with Irish motifs of shamrocks and harps. There are a number of these in existence and it would seem probable that the central authorities had these made for distribution to appointed parish constables. (Alternatively a standard design may have been established to be copied locally – as in Jersey.)* Author's collection.

Top right: *Isle of Man special constables' truncheon – this one has the cypher VR, the three legged symbol for the Isle of Man, the initials 'SC' and underneath '1.T.L.'. This truncheon is very similar in design to those issued to parish constables.* Manx Museum & National Trust.

Bottom left: *Metal truncheon with eight projecting sharpened blades. These can be retracted and the shackle on the end shows that in a riot situation this truncheon could be attached to a rope, or a piece of chain and swung like a flail to disperse rioters.* Carlisle Museum & Art Gallery.

Bottom right: *Two interesting wooden truncheons which have metal handguards. These were probably issued in the Carlisle area as riot truncheons and, apart from one in York, are the only ones I have seen with a basket hilt of this shape.* Carlisle Museum & Art Gallery.

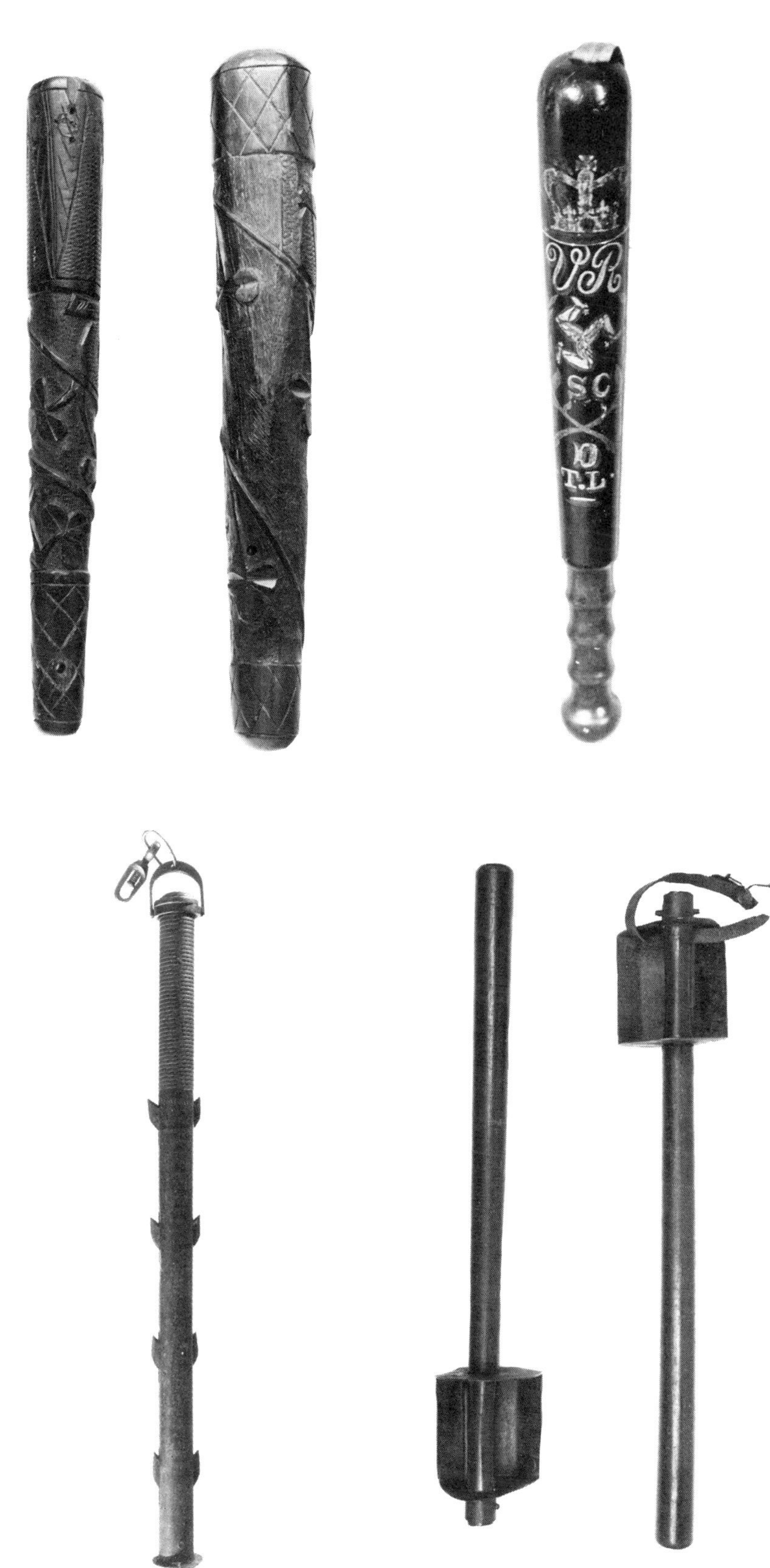

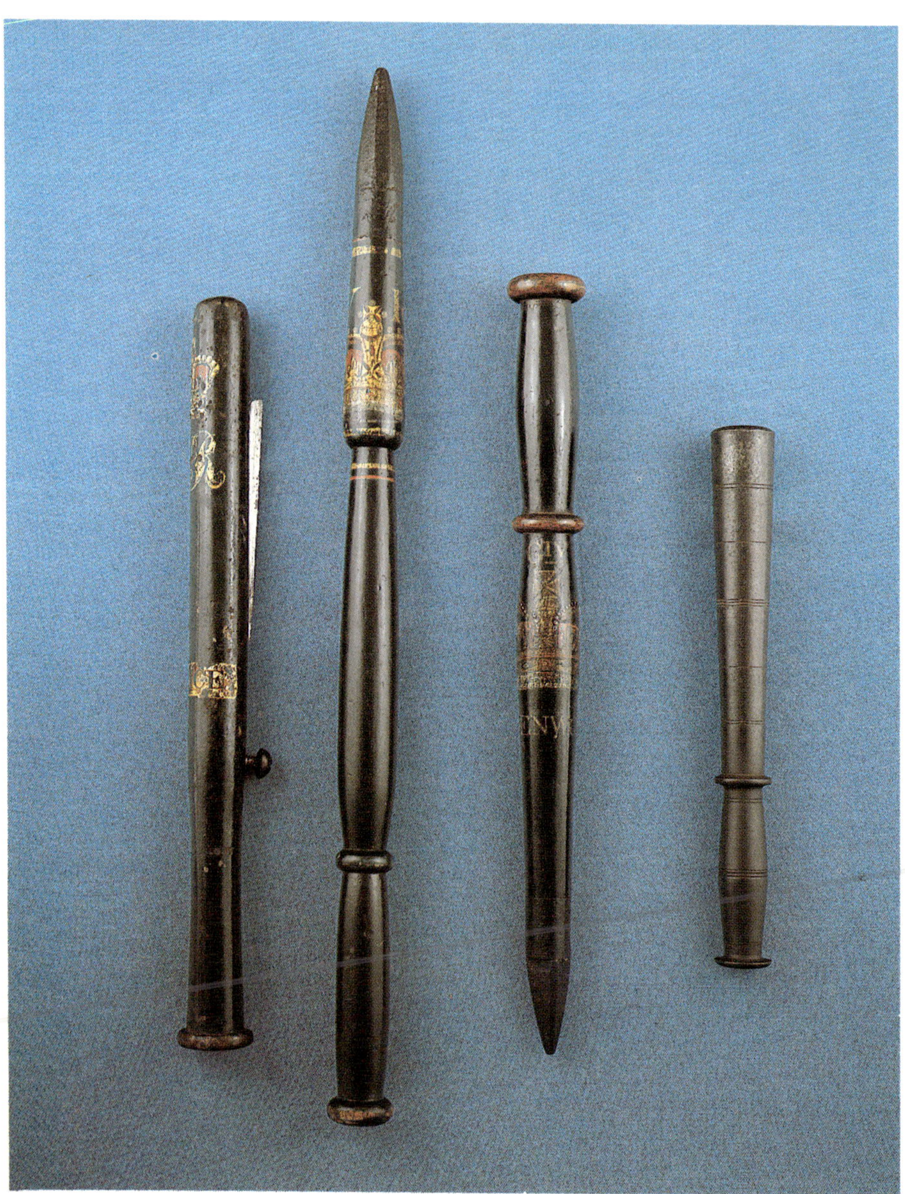

Metal truncheons.
From left: *1. Very rare cast-iron truncheon with painted decoration of crown, cypher 'VR' and the word 'Police' in a lower band. A projecting blade some 4 inches long can be moved out from the side of the barrel by means of a small knob. The base of the truncheon is hollow and threaded – obviously intended to be mounted on a pole for keeping crowds back in a riot situation. 2. Wooden and metal truncheon marked 'VR' with the crown and on the reverse 'Burcott'. The top is a metal-spike which gives considerable weight to the truncheon. 3. This resembles a naval marlin spike and is painted with the cypher 'GIVR', the crown and 'Henwood'. The metal spike is at the bottom and there are two possibilities for the shape of this truncheon (a) It is a marlin-spike which has been acquired and painted for police use or (b) with the spike at the base it was intended to be stuck in the ground for official occasions perhaps to mark a boundary. 4. Wrought iron truncheon without decoration and which weighs in excess of 3 lb. This is probably an experimental model.* Author's collection.

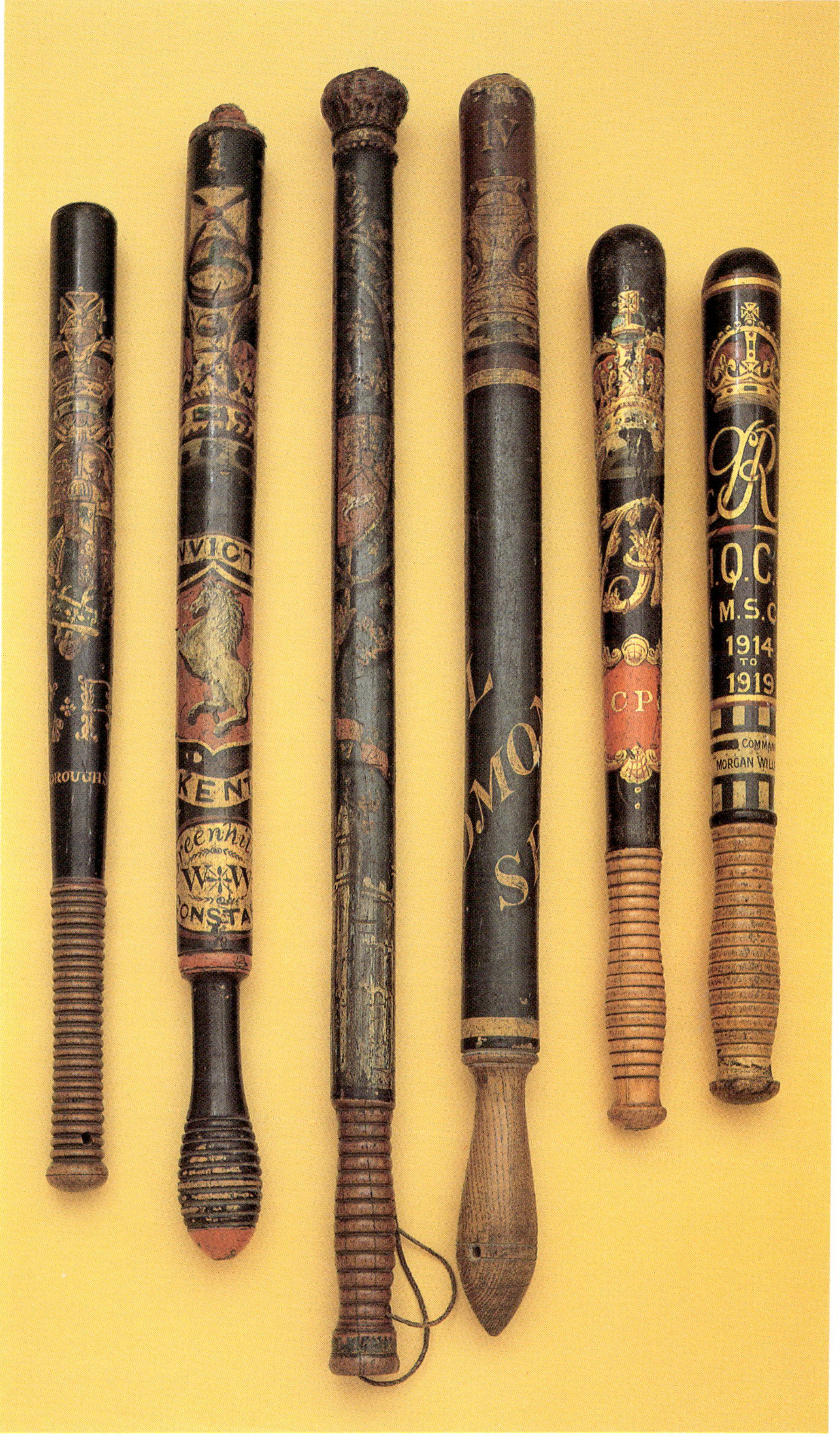

From left: *Geo. IV truncheon with royal coat of arms for Marlborough Street in London. 2. Early Victorian truncheon for Kent, with a badge just above the handle for 'Greenhythe Constable W & W'. W & W stood for Watch and Ward. 3. This is an unusual and rare truncheon – the Arms are pre-1801 and there is a carved representation of the Crown at the top. Painted on the barrel of the truncheon above the handle is the White Tower from the Tower of London. There are one or two other truncheons and tipstaves in existence which also have the White Tower represented on them and these are usually associated with the Constables of Bethnal Green. 4. Edmonton Special Constable. 5. Parker, Field truncheon of typical design with the initials 'LCPC' within the cartouche. The meaning of these letters is not known. 6. Parker, Field truncheon which has been decorated to make it a commemorative truncheon. Decoration is the king's crown for Geo. V and cypher GR' followed by the initials '"HQCD' (M.S.C.) 1914–1919' and painted within a band at the bottom, which has been made to look like a constable's duty arm-band, is the wording 'Commander Morgan Williams', on the reverse of this are the initials 'WD' and a broad arrow. I can only guess at the meaning of these initials but would feel HQCD probably stands for Headquarters Civil Defence, M.S.C. could be Middlesex Special Constabulary and Commander Williams probably the officer in charge. I suspect that his men gave him this on his retirement in 1919. Collection London Museum.*

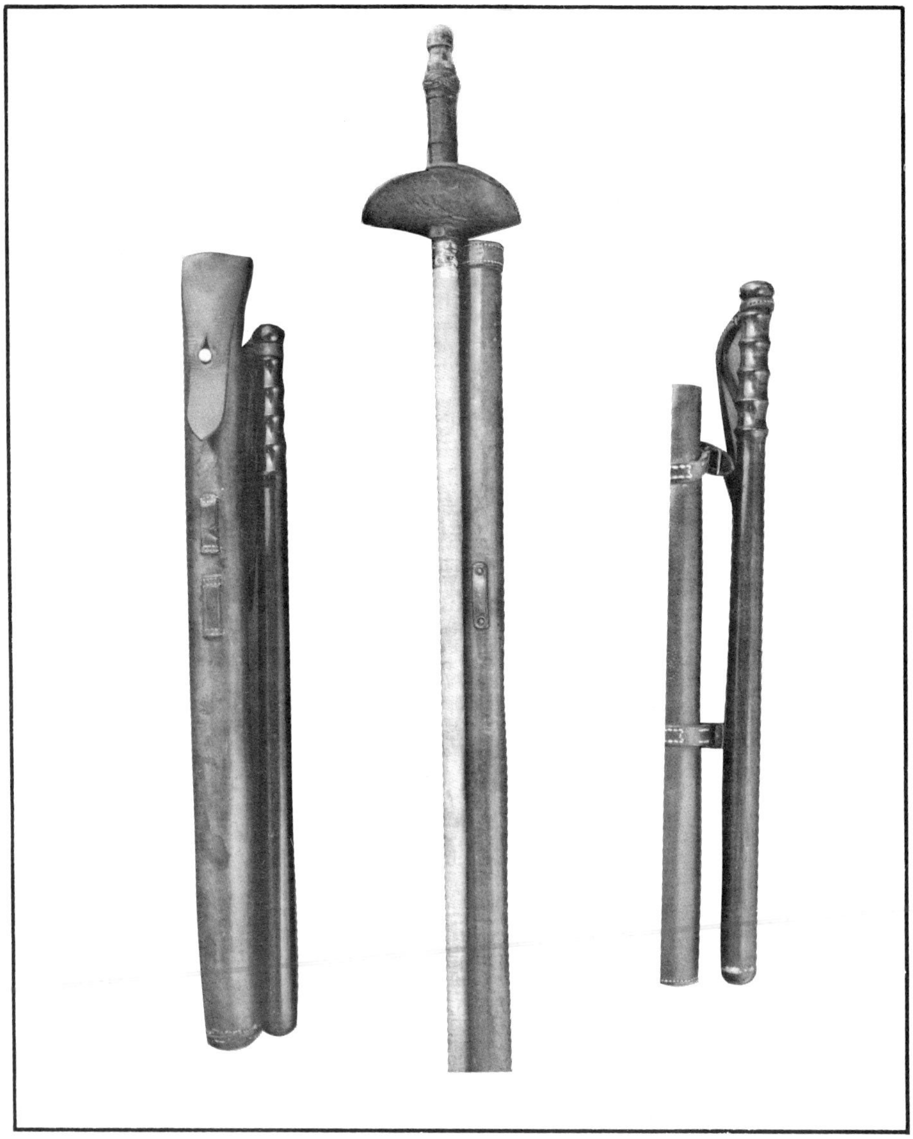

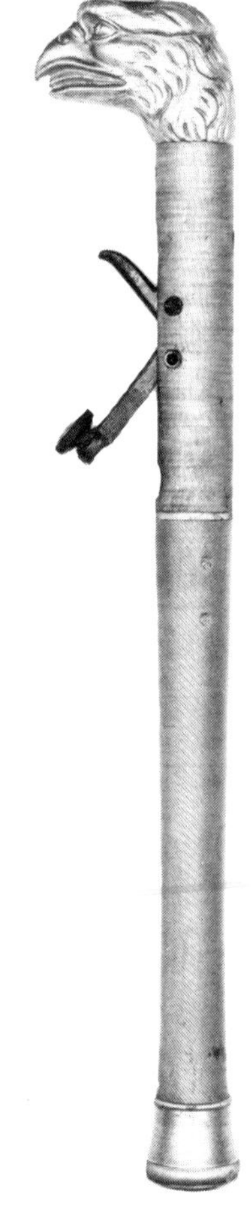

Mounted Police truncheons.
These three examples are from left: 1. A fine teak truncheon, nearly 30 inches in length with its original Parker, Field patented truncheon case. 2. 'Sabre' from the Metropolitan Police. This was an ash stick finely bound with waxed twine. 3. Similar to the type used by both the British South African Police in Rhodesia and also some Midlands forces. Author's collection.

Day's patent truncheon pistol.
Dating from the mid-19th century this unusual truncheon combines a blunderbus barrel with an under-hammer percussion action. The bird's head detachable pommel contained three shots – the screw-off pommel-cap is inscribed 'Day's Patent'. The overall length is 16 inches. This rare truncheon came up for auction with Parsons, Welch and Cowell in 1984 when it reached the exceptional price of £800. Parsons, Welch and Cowell.

truncheon. This bears a transfer for the royal crown and cypher 'VR' and at the bottom the word 'Police'.

There are also many examples of bludgeons, flails and life-preservers in existence and these frequently come up at sales. Bludgeons were particularly dangerous since they had the same action as flails – being a separate body and head usually joined together by rope – and were intended to be carried in tailcoat pockets. Life-preservers were again intended for the pocket and usually have lead-weighted ends. Whilst both types were often used by police, they rarely have any identification.

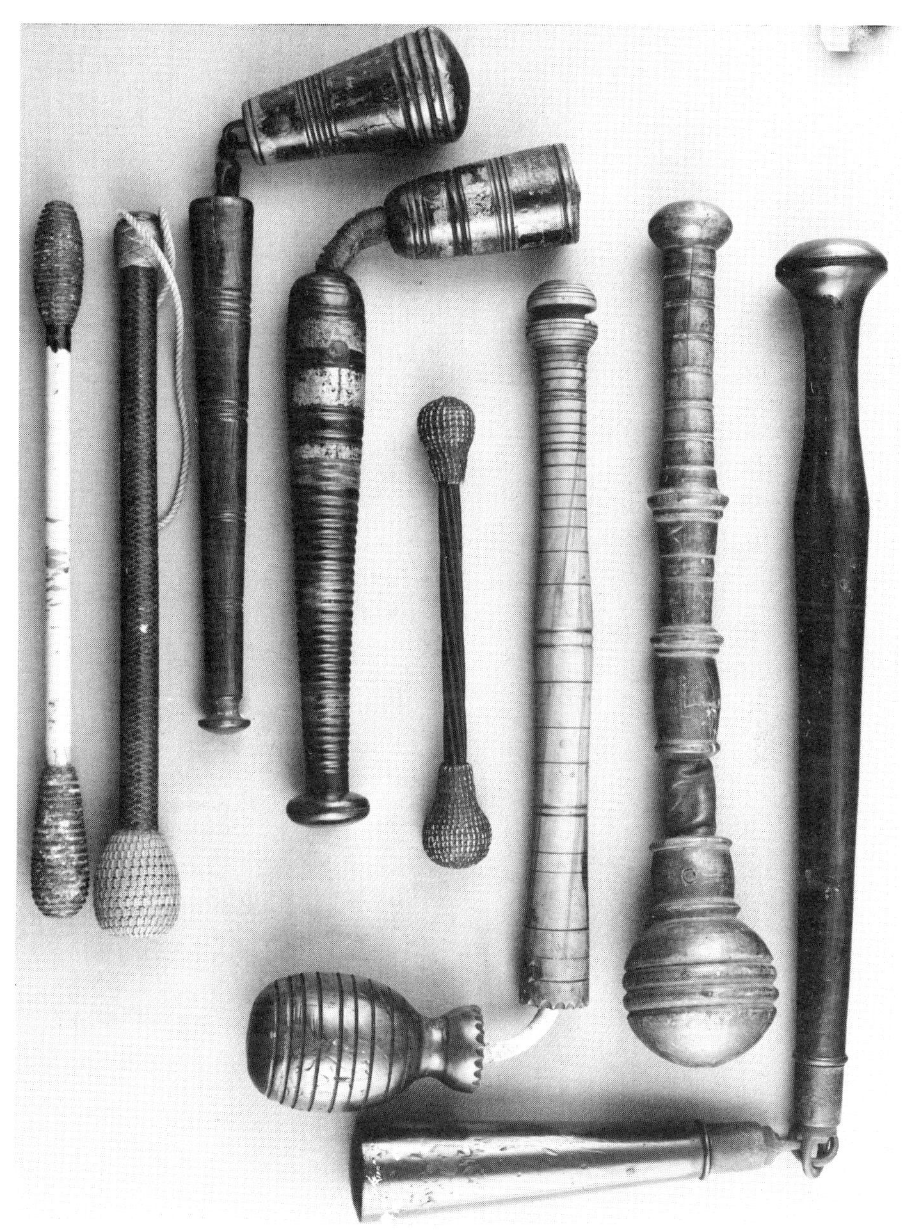

Flails, bludgeons and life preservers.
From left: *1. White painted bamboo life preserver with solid lead ends. 2. Life preserver with weighted lead end mounted on a bamboo stick – the whole carefully covered in string knotwork which has been waxed. 3. and 4. Bludgeons which have had a police use. Both are inscribed GIIIR and have the crown painted on them. 5. Whalebone life preserver with lead ends. 6. and 7. Bludgeons of typical design, with ball heads joined by leather covered rope. 8. Carved flail with the two parts joined by a metal link.* Author's collection.

Commemorative truncheons

There are a number of truncheons which were produced to commemorate special events. The most common of these are ones for the Midland forces and were given to reserve war police constables who had served during the First World War. Usually of plain teak (ie. the standard truncheon of the time), they were decorated with a transfer of the royal cypher, the coat-of-arms for the presenting town and the date 1914–1919. There are also a number of truncheons which were produced to commemorate the Great Strike of 1926 and although some of these are hand-painted, many are again transfers.

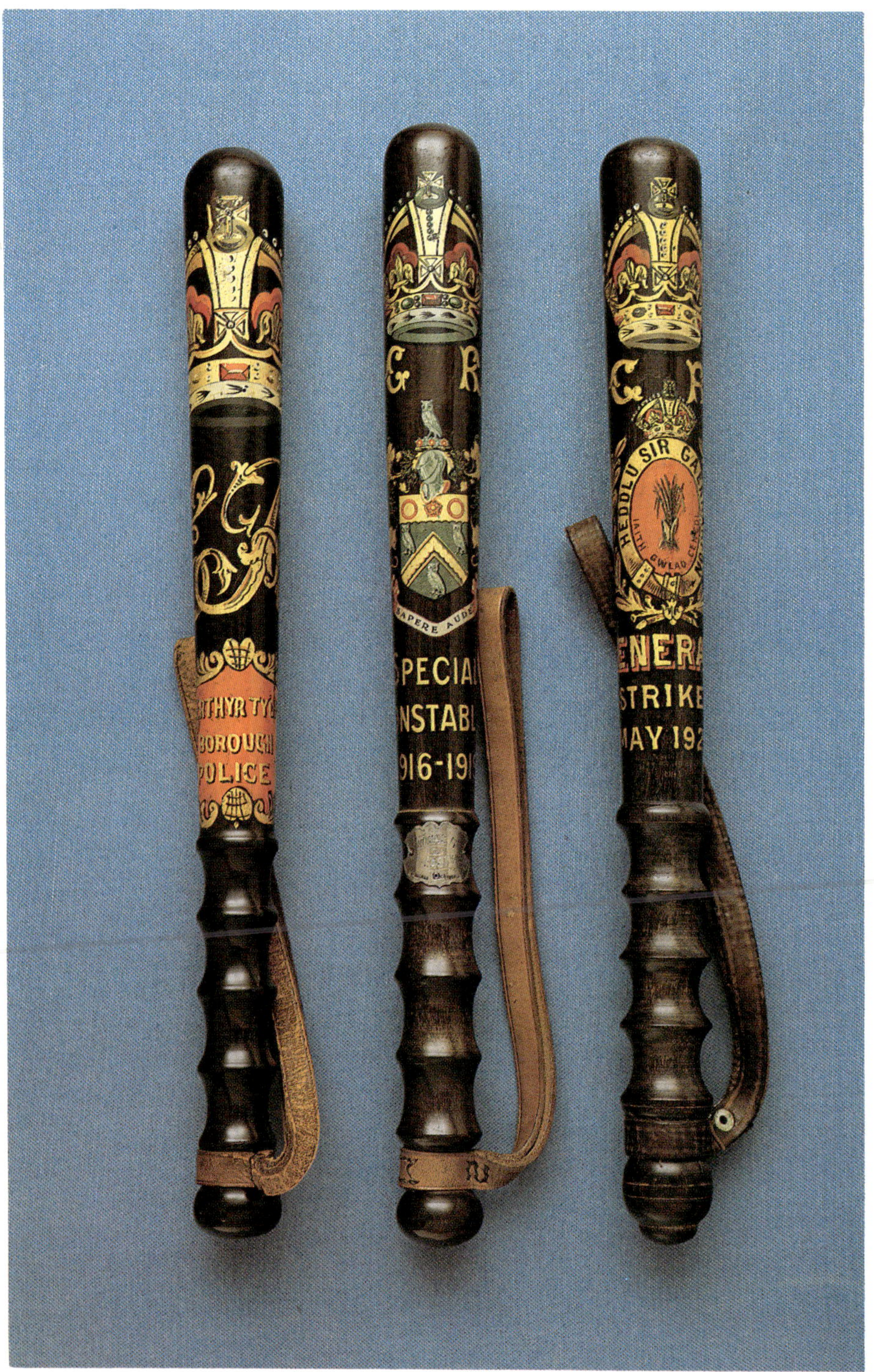

Commemorative truncheons.
Three very fine examples of commemorative truncheons From left: 1. Edward VII truncheon with the wording within the cartouche 'Merthyr Tydfil Borough Police'. A number of these were made for presentation to senior officers in Merthyr Tydfil following a visit to the town by Edward VII in 1908. 2. War Reserve commemorative truncheon 1916–18 for Oldham City Police. This one is unusual in that the recipient has had a silver plate made to be mounted on the handle which bears his name – 'Thomas A Eastwood'. 3. George V commemorative truncheon inscribed 'General Strike May 1926' with the arms of Caernarvon above this. This particular truncheon was presented by the Watch Committee to the Chief Constable following the strike. Author's collection.

Commemorative truncheons were also often made when there were royal visits to a particular town. Also, even into modern times, truncheons have been decorated by individual police forces for presentation to visiting VIPs. These are naturally quite rare and a good addition to any collection.

Hints on Collecting

One of the questions I am most often asked is 'Where do you find items for your collection?' The simple answer to this is – everywhere!

I have already pointed out that there are more police-related items in private ownership than in the public and police museums and, therefore, the possibility exists that your own friends and relatives will either have pieces, or perhaps know the whereabouts of some.

Obviously local antique shops and auction markets are possible sources and there are specialist collectors clubs such as the Police Insignia Collectors Association – although I believe membership for this particular one is limited to serving and ex-police officers. Why not form your own local club – I will always be most willing to help with advice.

Apart from local dealers as a possible source of material there are in addition some specialist shops in London who may be able to help with advice and also to locate items for you. I have always found Mr C. Bowdell at Stand 123 and Mr C. Seidler at Stand 120 – both in Grays Antique Market in Davies Street, W1, (off Oxford Street) helpful in this respect. I give their names only as London starting points and would hasten to add that I have no connection with either of them.

Another question which is often asked is 'How much should I pay?' I have deliberately not gone into the question of prices because supply, demand and rarity all play a part and we are dealing mostly with – individual items. However, as a rough guide, Victorian painted truncheons in good condition have been selling at the time of writing (1985) for between £60 – £80; swords for between £50 – £100, depending on whether they have a force's name engraved on them. Tipstaves – even more than truncheons – tend to vary according to the material they are made of and the attribution on them. A wooden tipstaff in good condition has been priced in the region of £80–£100 but, of course, silver or ivory ones will be higher.

Prices will unfortunately rise in the future as more people start to collect and also, perhaps, as a result of the survey in this book, which shows how comparatively rare antique police equipment is. However, lanterns, rattles, whistles, some uniform and handcuffs should continue at more moderate prices and I see these as useful fields for new collectors in the future.

Always keep in mind the quantities of equipment from past years – the amounts still to be discovered must be enormous.

During 1857 there were 327 official police forces in existence in England and Wales. I am indebted to Mr R. H. Hale and Mr S. Marriott, members of the Police Insignia Collectors Association, who have been carrying out research into the number of police forces which existed up until recent times *outside* of the jurisdiction of the Home Office. They have found that over the past 150 years, there have been 350 railway police forces, 12 canal police forces, over 60 dock police forces, 10 airport police forces and between 50-60 assorted other forces – including a colliery police force.

Obviously not all of these were large enough to have their own different equipment and badges but, considering this remarkable total of official and private forces, there should be sufficient material still left to fill many new collections.

Two unusual truncheons. These were possibly inn truncheons which would account for their excessive size and weight. The one on the left is carved in an exact representation of an early 19th century naval telescope, even to the rope bindings along its length. Possibly a retired naval officer – used to carrying his telescope as a badge of rank – had this made when he took over an inn. The second example is carved from the branch of a tree, the upper part still has the bark. Author's collection.

CHAPTER THREE

Tipstaves

Truncheons have always been far more numerous then tipstaves since the latter generally conferred legal authority from the Crown and therefore far fewer of them were in use. Unfortunately, once warrant cards were introduced throughout the country during the 1880s, people generally forgot the purpose of a tipstaff – although a painted truncheon would still be recognised – as a result, many tipstaves were disposed of without being appreciated for their historical value.

One of the problems of any early people living in localised communities was how to give authority to, and designate the position of, their senior person. This goes right back through history even to ancient Egypt where it was common for minor officials to carry a wand of office which would mark them out to people visiting the community – since one can assume that their own people would know them. Even today there are many societies around the world who mark their chief citizen by the carrying of a stick or other symbol of authority. In Great Britain, for instance, our mayors, chief justices and officers of parliament still have an ornate mace carried in front of them – symbolizing their authority from the Crown.

A tipstaff is exactly what its description says – a staff or stick, tipped usually with metal. However, there are records as far back as Anglo-Saxon times – which means that the tradition is probably much older – of officials carrying a stick tipped with horn or a bull's horn. For a small rural community this would seem sensible use of an easily acquired commodity, since in those days worked metal was expensive. Later, metal would have been substituted for the horn, particularly as the early tipstaff was also used as a weapon.

Gradually the carrying of a tipstaff grew to signify that the bearer had authority from the Crown; it was usually carried by a constable or some other person who had official duties or functions. That it was intended in the early days to be a weapon of offence, or defence, is clearly shown in one of the statutes of Henry VIII who specifically exempted any of his officials from retribution should they, in the course of their duty, strike any person 'with any staffe commonlye called a Tippstafe'.

Over the years there have been many categories of people who have been allowed to carry a tipstaff in addition to the traditional law keepers. A partial list of these would include constables, ward beadles, water bailiffs, marshal's men, inspectors of pavements and sewers, railway officials, rate officers, Thames river police and, of course, magistrates and judges.

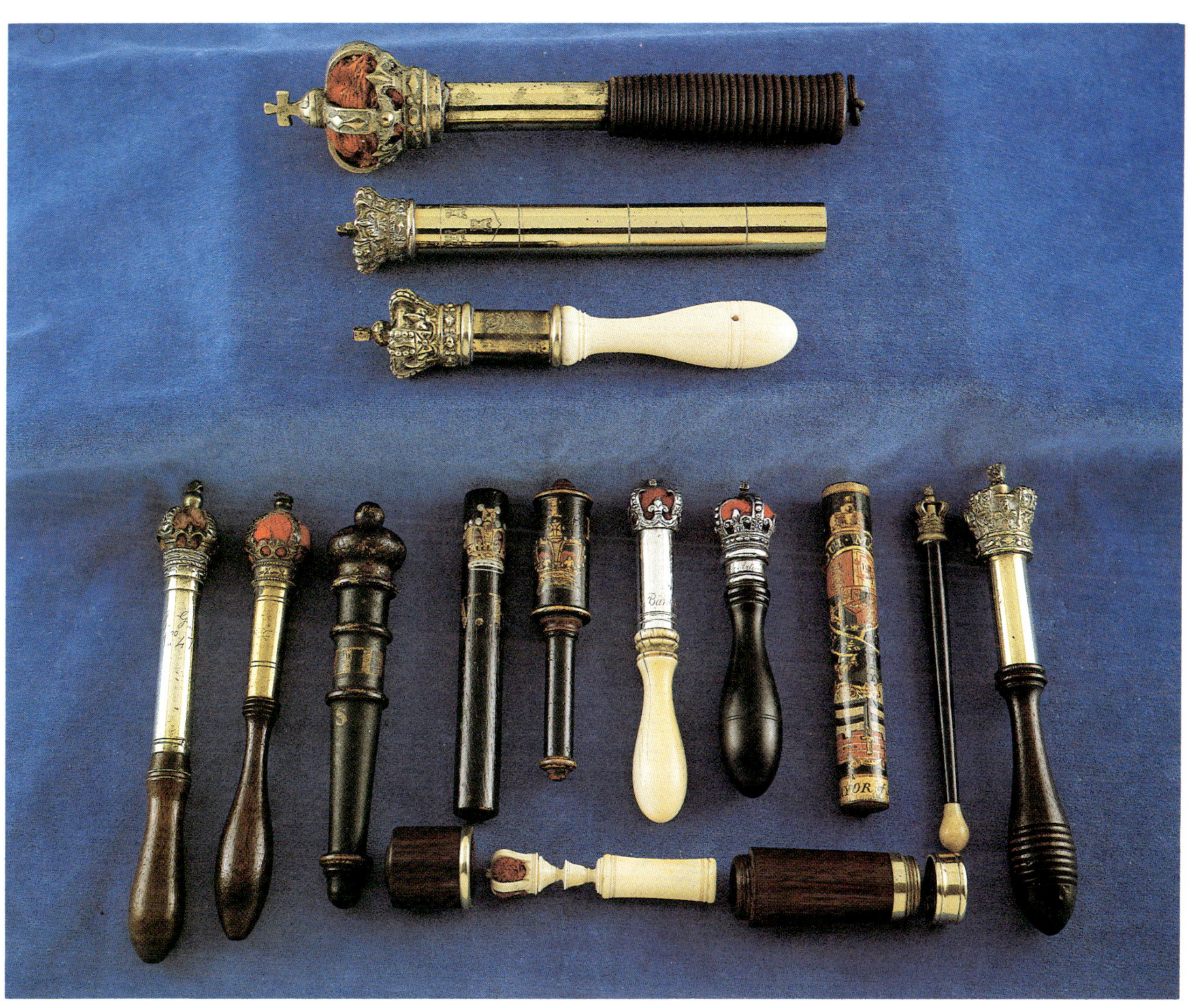

This interesting group of tipstaves shows clearly the variety in shapes and styles. The three at the top are. 1. George III tipstaff, probably from the Midlands but exact provenance unknown. 2. Plain Brass tipstaff with Victorian crown and the badge of Newcastle. 3. Ivory and brass Victorian tipstaff probably carried by the bailiff of Hungerford and with the Berkshire crescent and star. The lower tipstaves are from left: 4. George II or George III tipstaff inscribed 'BG No. 47' B.G. could well stand for Bethnal Green' and this tipstaff still has the original cloth insert. 5. Decorative tipstaff (no provenance). 6. Wooden tipstaff for Geo. IV with cypher 'GIIIR' and 'S' painted around the lower part of the barrel. 4. and 5. Pocket tipstaves probably for inspectors of railways who very often carried them in waistcoat pockets. 6. Hallmarked silver and ivory tipstaff for 1805 inscribed 'James Banting'. 7. Ebony and silver tipstaff inscribed 'Hon Artillery Company' – probably for 1777. This of course was within the City of London. 8. Painted wooden tipstaff with the royal arms and the arms of the city of Bath with painted within a band at the base of the tipstaff the wording 'Mayor of Bath'. This is probably for about 1810. 9. Slender tipstaff with an ivory filial, ebony shaft and silver-gilt crown. No origin. 10. Brass and ebony tipstaff. 11. This beautiful ivory tipstaff, which is only 2 inches long, fits within the walnut case (as shown in this expanded view) which in turn could be fitted to the top of a walking-stick. Author's collection.

One of the first differences that a newcomer notices between truncheons and tipstaves is the very much greater variety of shapes, styles and materials used in the latter. In my own collection I have examples made of wood, brass, brass and wood, brass and ivory, wood and ivory and silver and silver and silver and wood.

From medieval times silver had been reserved for officers of the king and by the 1250s these men carried silver maces less as weapons of battle and more as emblems of their authority. During the time of Richard I a personal guard of royal sergeants-at-arms was formed – the word sergeant generally meaning a well-armed soldier below the rank of knight – and these men carried their maces (which must have been decorated in some way) both as weapons and as their authority from the king if they had to make an arrest. During the 14th century permission was granted by the king for officers of the City of London to carry silver maces and it is probably from this time that silver gradually came into use for the tipstaves of men in important positions.

Not only were many different materials used in their construction, but tipstaves also came in a great variety of sizes and shapes – and, far more than truncheons, could represent the personal whims and tastes of the person for whom they were made. For example they can range in length from several feet to the small breast-pocket size of only a few inches. However, since most of the tipstaves which are likely to be found nowadays are mainly from the 19th century, they will normally be in a size range of six to ten inches and very often they will be found to have a wooden handle and a barrel of brass or other metal with a crown at the end; when of this construction, the metal parts and the wooden handle are usually of the same approximate dimensions. They nearly always have a crown and can range from the very plain to the extremely ornate. There are, of course, regional variations to style and it will often be found that Devon and Cornwall favoured square-ended tipstaves, which had four sides with a crown on top and a shaped handle. These were, in fact, very similar to the truncheons of those areas while, in Bristol, tipstaves would usually be of brass and shaped to have either a round knop at the end or else an acorn finial. The Bristol tipstaves are some of the very few which I have found to be without the crown at the end. Since all tipstaves marked an official position held by the owner, some of these men obviously sought to enhance their standing by making their tipstaves very elaborate. Others preferred them plain – not necessarily dictated by taste, but probably because they had to pay for the tipstaves themselves from the money that they collected in fees and dues.

From the collector's point of view the greater the detail and amount of inscription the better, since there is more chance of identifying the origin. Similarly, a hallmarked silver specimen will allow for its issue to be exactly dated. However, there are times when this can prove confusing as, for example, when an inscription with a date is found to differ from the original hallmark; this can probably be explained by the fact that a silver tipstaff was an expensive item and was usually handed down from one office holder to another. There was probably a ready market for second-hand ones and it is usually when there was a change in function that the date varies from the hallmark.

Many of the older tipstaves will be found to be hollow, usually

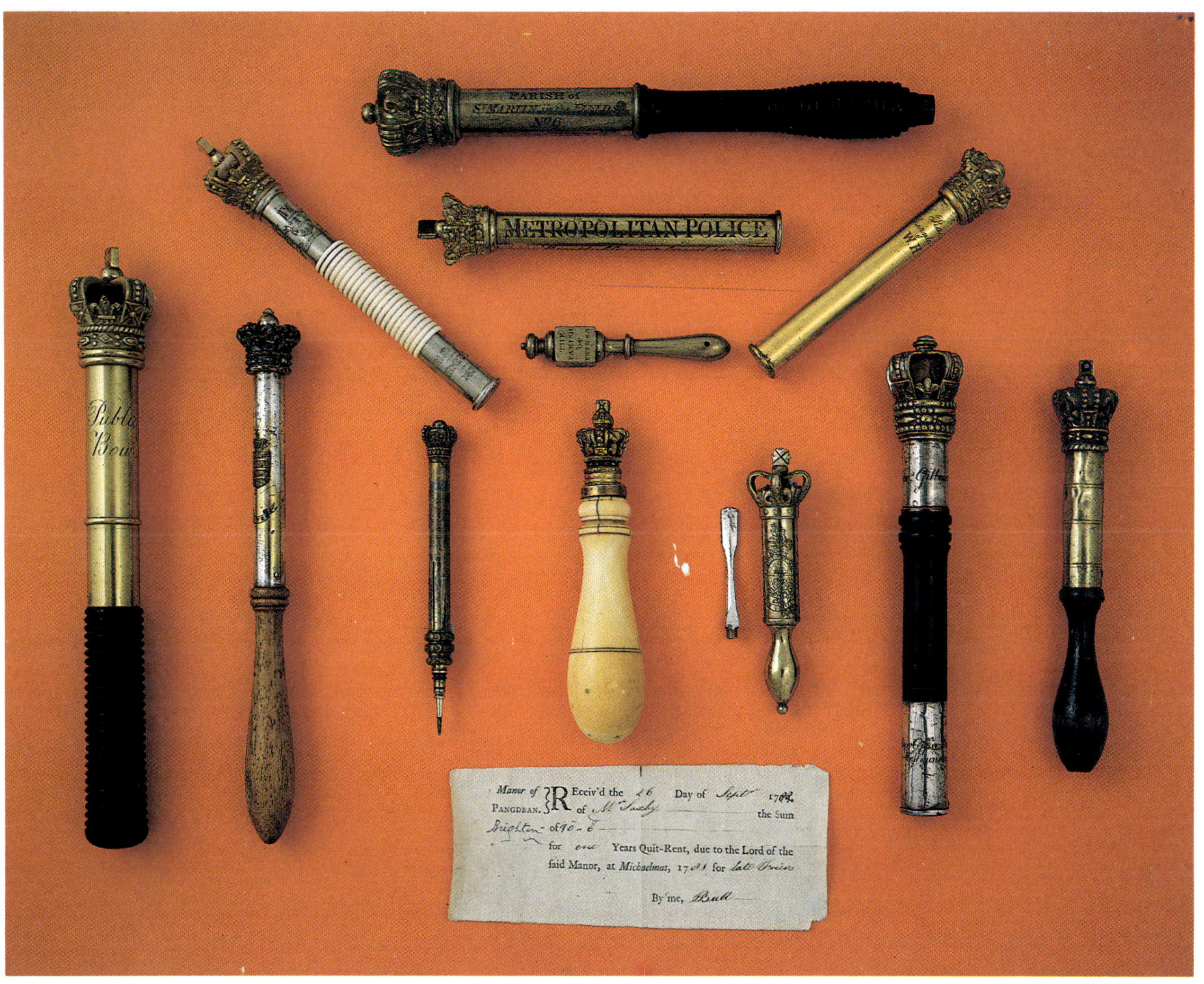

Rare collection of tipstaves, mainly from the original Dixon collection now held at the college.

These are (starting at the top) 1. Silver, gilt and ivory Parker, Field tipstaff engraved with the Arms of Cambridge and the wording 'presented to the High Constable of Cambridge'. 2. Brass and wood tipstaff inscribed 'Parish of St. Martin's-in-the-Fields – No. 6'. 3. Victorian tipstaff engraved with the wording 'Metropolitan Police Constable employed in plain clothes'. 4. Small brass parish constable's tipstaff fot Totness in Devon. 5. Plain brass tipstaff inscribed 'J. Rackel. St. Marylebone W.H.' W.H. stood for Watch House.

From left in the lower section of tipstaves: *6. Public Office Bow Street. This is the standard design for most of the early public offices. 7. Oak and silver tipstaff for the Port Reeve of Rye. This official was in fact the Harbourmaster and the tipstaff has the badge of the Cinque ports. 8. Unusual Brighton tipstaff of silver gilt which also serves as a propelling pencil. It bears a crown at the top and is engraved 'John Bradshaw High Constable'. 9. Ivory handled tipstaff for the Manor of Pangedean with underneath it the receipt mentioned in the text of this chapter. 10. Brass admiralty oar with beside it the silver oar normally carried inside but which can be screwed into the top of the crown in place of the cross. 11. Ebony and silver tipstaff inscribed at the top 'Jas Gilmor' and on the lower band 'Police Office Queens Square Westminster'. 12. Brass and Wood tipstaff – without attribution – but reputed to have belonged to 'Townsend' the famous Bow Street Runner. Originally in the Dixon collection.* Bramshill Police College Collection.

unscrewing at the crown or in the middle and, in the case of ones made entirely of metal, sometimes at the end – it is really dependant on their construction. The hollow shaft was often intended to contain a warrant – although this was not so in every case and many examples of the later Victorian type had a hollow barrel merely as part of the construction.

Warrants were of two types, the first being specific for the office for which the holder was appointed, and the second – and this was often applicable to those carried by a constable or officer of the court – was that issued by a justice of the peace or a judge, for the arrest of a named person. Unfortunately, it is almost unheard of nowadays for a warrant to still be with the tipstaff and the only ones that I know of are in museums. Both the London Museum and Bramshill Police College Collection have one or two examples of warrants issued for constables to wear plain clothes. During later years the authority for this particular duty came to be engraved on the barrel of the tipstaff. The collector will find that even many of the earlier examples of tipstaves were of solid construction –the mere possession of one bestowing sufficient authority.

The latter part of the 19th century saw an increasing trend towards the standardisation of tipstaves, instead of them being individually crafted to the design requirements of office holders. The reason for this was the proliferation in the number of officials who had become entitled to carry a tipstaff. Manufacturing firms such as Parker, Field and Sons of Holborn were quick to take advantage of this demand. There are, however, still many 'one offs' of this period to be seen.

Many tipstaves are found mounted with an open crown; whilst this may have been intended in the original design, red or purple velvet was usually put in to fill the space. This, of course, is a copy of the Cap of Maintenance which is within all royal crowns. In my experience, many museums were not aware of this practice but, since some tipstaves in my collection have the original cloth in place, there can be no doubt on this point. Crowns intended to be filled are usually of rough finish on their insides.

According to some published opinion, many tipstaves – particularly the silver ones – were given as commemoration pieces on retirement. Whilst I agree that this may have been so in some cases, it should be remembered that the carrying of a tipstaff was often necessary to exercise the authority of the office and, therefore, where one was given as a presentation, it was usually on the appointment, and not on retirement.

Silver and ivory tipstaves of good design and workmanship seem to have been made in greater numbers around the beginning of the 19th century than at other periods. In my experience, by using these materials the holder showed that he was a gentleman of some wealth and importance, even if the office for which he was having the tipstaff made did not seem to justify the material. For example, as it was possible at that time to purchase positions in the livery companies and in the Common Council of the City of London, a man who had made money in his chosen profession could buy himself an appointment which would entitle him to carry a tipstaff. He could become a ward beadle for the City of London, for instance, in which position he would also be a constable and, using his wealth to enhance the office, would perhaps have a tipstaff of better quality than those made for a similar post in the past.

On rare occasions tipstaves were made for purposes other than to show

Mr. G. R. Baber, Official Tipstaff to the Supreme Court of Judicature at the Royal Courts of Justice in the Strand London. He is seen wearing his official uniform and carrying the tipstaff. This one was made during the reign of Queen Victoria. Photographer J. Manwaring.

Chief Constable's Badges of Rank on a 1930s Chief Constable of Edinburgh dress tunic. Particularly note the crossed tipstaves within the laurel wreath. Author's collection.

authority; there are several on record which were used in annual ceremonies. One, which was previously in the collection of Sir Arthur Dixon and which is now in the Bramshill Collection, has a large ivory handle surmounted by a small crown. This unscrews and inside is the original receipt reading:

'Manor of Pangdean, Brighton.
Received the 26 day of Septr 1782, of Mr. Saxby the
sum of 10s. 6d for one Years Quit-Rent, due to the
Lord of the said Manor, at Michaelmas, 1781 for late
Friers,
By me, Bull . . . '.

There are many literary references to the use of tipstaves showing the degree to which the public knew and accepted the authority they conferred. Some even go back as far as the 14th century when we find Chaucer in his *Somnours Tale,* writing of one official:

'With scrippe and tipped staf, y-tukked hye
In every hous he gan to poure and prye
And beggeth mele, and chese, or elles corn
His felawe hadde a staf tipped with horn'.

In *Pickwick Papers* and many of his other books Charles Dickens makes mention of the use of tipstaves. In *Bleak House,* for instance, Inspector Buckett introduces himself with 'I am Inspector Buckett of the Detectives, I am; and this' producing the top of his convenient little staff from his breast pocket, 'is my authority'.

Today there is only one officer in the country who has a direct link with the past and this is the official tipstaff to the Royal Courts of Justice in the Strand. His main functions are to protect the dignity of the court, to take into custody anyone committed for contempt and, where children are made wards of court, it is his duty to try to prevent them being taken out of the jurisdiction of the court. The tipstaff – who on official occasions wears a uniform based on that of a Victorian police inspector – carries a silver tipstaff approximately ten inches long.

Finally, not many people, including police officers, realise that the badges for very senior police ranks, such as deputy chief constables and chief constables in provincial forces and commanders and above in the Metropolitan Police, include crossed tipstaves. People are so used to seeing crossed marshal's batons on the shoulders of military and naval senior officers that it is usually assumed that the police use the same insignia.

The following sections are included to help with the identification of tipstaves.

Constables' tipstaves

Very few tipstaves of any description are in existence from before the 1750s when the Fielding brothers – firstly Henry Fielding and later his brother Sir John Fielding – established the public office at Bow Street and, with it, the Bow Street Horse Patrol and the Bow Street Runners. One can still find one or two tipstaves of the Runners, such as the examples in the Canterbury Museum and at Bramshill. These have shaped wooden handles with seven incised rings half-way along at the point where the shaft narrows directly surmounted by a brass crown – there is no barrel to this particular type. Since the Bow Street Runners were the best-known policing organisation of their time, it is natural that over the years many tipstaves have been designated as belonging to them. Actually, there are very few in existence and most of the labels showing tipstaves to be such are wishful thinking.

The Wisbech and Fenland Museum, at Wisbech in Cambridgeshire, is fortunate to have in its collection a brass tipstaff engraved 'Jonathan Wild' and there is no reason to consider this not to be genuine. Jonathan Wild, it will be recalled, was the notorious thief-taker who operated at the beginning of the 18th century. The tipstaff has a brass barrel with a turned wooden handle and is surmounted by a solid crown.

The London Museum has an interesting tipstaff of six-and-a-half-inches with a turned handle, a silver barrel and a largish crown on the top. It is inscribed:

> Saml Perry
> Constable
> of St. Matthew
> Bethnal Green. 1790

Another in the museum is for Bethnal Green, dated 1803, but this is of totally different construction. It has a silver base to the wooden shaft and is surmounted at the top by a silver collar with a crown above. At the top collar is the cypher 'GR' with an outline of the White Tower (of the Tower of London) underneath and, inscribed on the bottom ferrule, is the wording:

> W. Hughes. Constable,
> Bethnal Green, 1803

The outline of the White Tower is of interest since there are several truncheons in existence which are also decorated with it.

When, in 1792, the further seven public offices were set up around London, each had three magistrates and six constables who were entitled to carry tipstaves. Whilst by no means common, there are still a number of these in existence, of which several are in the Dixon Collection held by the Police College at Bramshill. This has examples for Queen's Square, Worship Street and Bow Street and generally these are of fairly similar appearance; in fact, they are not unlike those issued to the Thames River Police who were established in 1798. As a general description, they are about 12 inches long, with an ebony handle cut into rings and a brass shaft surmounted by a crown. There is a raised ring approximately one third of the way up from the handle on the brass barrel and it was above this that the inscription was usually placed.

Another type of tipstaff can be found for these police offices which, being of silver and ebony, is altogether of very much finer workmanship than the brass and ebony tipstaves of the constables. I have always assumed these to have belonged to magistrates. On page 61 of Fenn Clark's *Truncheons – their Romance and Reality* one finds a short version for Queen's Square illustrated. However, I have one example in my collection which is 14 inches overall: it has a two-inch silver ferrule at the

Brass and wood tipstaff with the engraving 'Jonathan Wild'. There is no reason to doubt the authenticity of this tipstaff, although it is interesting to note that it is almost identical in shape and design to the one held by the Bramshill Police College and attributed to the Bow Street Runner, Townsend. Wisbech & Fenland Museum.

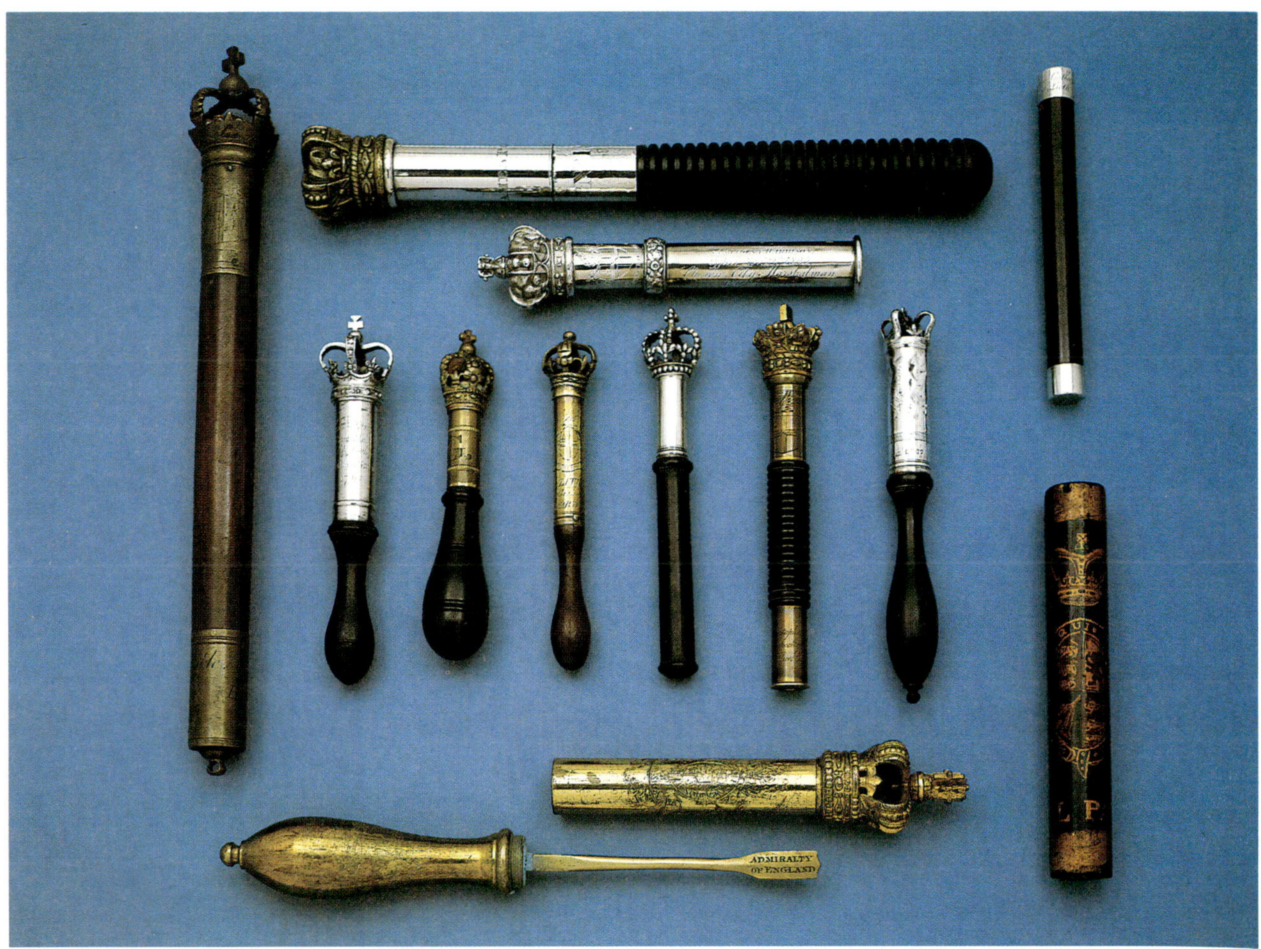

The London Museum have probably the largest collection of tipstaves in the country. This representative selection shows some of the more interesting ones. (From left) *1. Brass and wood tipstaff for GIIIR with an engraving on the top part of the Tower of London. Around the bottom brass section is the wording 'W. Hughes. Constable Bethnal Green 1803'. 2. (at top) Tipstaff inscribed 'Thames Police No. 16'. This will be recognised as being the standard pattern for the public or police offices. 3. (below 2.) Silver tipstaff inscribed with the City of London coat of arms and also the royal coat of arms together with the wording 'Anthony Harrison. Officer Novr 12th 1805. A chosen City Marshall Man Fby 27th 1818'. At the bottom are his initials 'A.H.'. This tipstaff with its two separate dates obviously commemorates important points in Harrison's career. 4. (top right) Ebony tipstaff with silver caps top and bottom, of the standard Scottish design. This one is inscribed at the top 'Alexr. Moody. Collector of the Shore Dues at Leith' and on the very top of this cap is an engraved sailing ship. On the base of the lower cap is the royal coat of arms. (Centre band of tipstaves) 5. Silver and ebony tipstaff inscribed 'Saml. Perry. Constable of St. Matthew Bethnal Green 1790'. On the reverse is the cypher 'GR'. 6. Brass and ebony tipstaff with large engraving 'G.P.O.'. 7. Brass and wood tipstaff with engraving of city coat of arms and the wording 'Robt Clitherow. Beadle Bishopsgate Ward 1788'. There is an additional engraving along the side as follows 'T. Elsam. April 9th 1801'. Since tipstaves were valuable items it is not unusual to find dual inscriptions on them, meaning that they have either been acquired second hand or passed on between holders of the same office. 8. Brass and hallmarked silver tipstaff which is interesting in that the crown is made of cut steel. 9. Parker, Field tipstaff of standard design with ebony rings and brass barrels. The top part is engraved with the City of London coat of arms and on the lower part 'Christopher Haslip. Inspector Sewers Office Guildhall'. This would probably date after 1870. 10. Silver and ebony tipstaff engraved with City coat of arms and on the side 'George Pearce. Sewers Office. Guildhall'. 11. (At bottom of picture) Brass tipstaff with beautifully engraved royal coat of arms and inside the barrel an admiralty oar engraved 'Admiralty of England'. 12. (on right) Wooden painted tipstaff and the wording 'Royal Parks'.* London Museum.

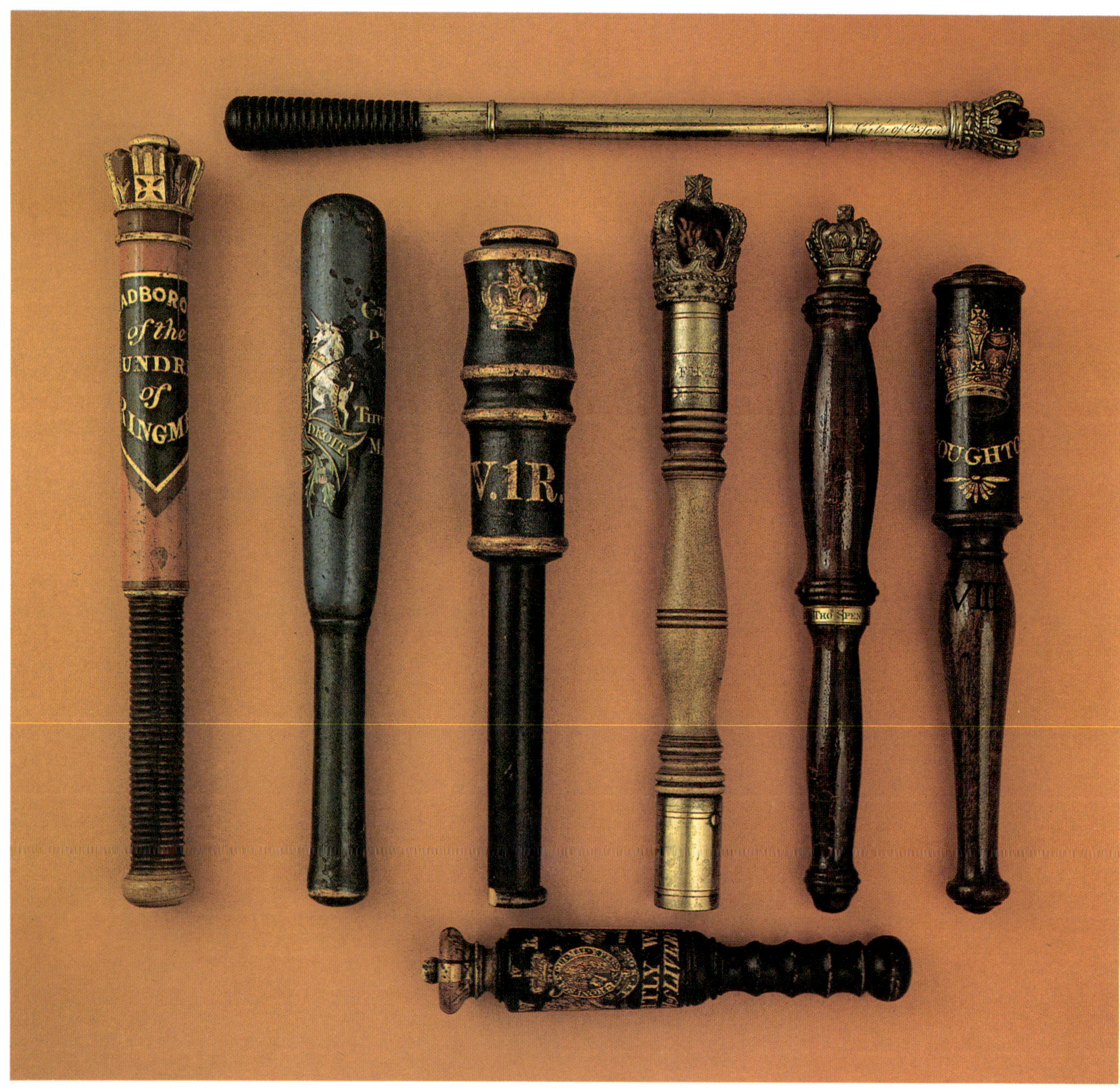

These interesting examples of tipstaves and short truncheons (which are obviously intended to have the function of a tipstaff) are part of the very large collection held at Bramshill Police College. 1. (at top) Brass and wood tipstaff with purple cloth inset to the crown. This is inscribed 'City of Oxford'. (from left) 2. Wooden tipstaff with carved crown painted 'Headborough of the Hundred of Ringmer'. 3. Wood, with black background and well painted pre-1801 coat of arms. On the back 'George Brand. Thurlow Magna'. 4. Baluster style truncheon with cypher 'VIR' beneath the crown and on the reverse the word 'York'. 5. Brass and wood tipstaff inscribed at the top 'F.H. London Police'. 6. Wood and brass tipstaff for Keighley (Yorks). This one is marked for 'Thomas Spencer 1836'. This was a standard design for Keighley. 7. Short truncheon for Wm IV and under the crown 'Broughton' – cut into the handle is the No. 'VIII'. 8. (bottom) Interesting wooden tipstaff with carved crown and painted with the details – cypher 'WIVR' royal coat of arms and on the reverse the Liver Bird and the wording 'Nightly Watch. Parish of Liverpool'. Bramshill Police College Collection.

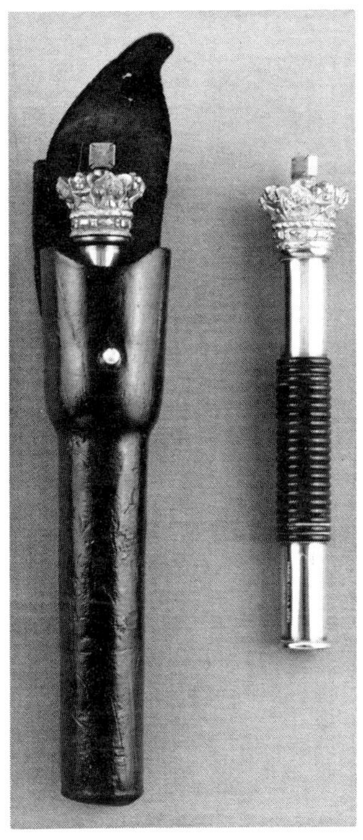

Parker, Field and Sons standard pattern of Inspector's tipstaff. The one on the left is shown within its patent leather 'pop-up' case and the example on the right can be seen to have the initials at the bottom 'WD' and in between them an arrow. This probably means that it was carried by officers from the Provost Marshall's office. Author's collection.

base, a four-inch turned ebony handle with a six-inch silver barrel above, surmounted by a very finely turned Georgian crown – still with its original purple velvet. The middle of the ebony handle unscrews and it would seem that a shorter silver top could be screwed in to replace the ten-inch one, at which time it would be identical to the one from Queen's Square. This choice indicates a dual function: the short version could be carried in the pocket while, with the longer head in place, the tipstaff could be used in court or on other ceremonial occasions. It has 'Constable of Shadwell' engraved on the silver ferrule and is hallmarked 1803. One should not be mislead by the word 'constable' in this context as, at that time, a magistrate still bore that designation.

Tipstaves of high constables

The Dixon Collection at Bramshill Police College has several good examples of high constables' tipstaves. There is one for Lewes dated 1813–1820 and a further one, in a case, engraved with the cypher 'GR IV', the date 'May 8 1824', and with 'High Constable and Headborough of Brighton'.

There are also a number of tipstaves of chief constables the latter title being, in effect, a renaming of the original high constable, of which many still remain. Those for Keighley in Yorkshire seem particularly numerous, possibly due to the frequent changes of appointment there in the 1830s. There is one such for 1836 in the Dixon Collection, another dated 1834 in my own collection and I recall having seen a further example. They have a curious shape, being of walnut with a brass band around the middle with the chief constable's details and a brass crown on the top. It is around the top of the crown that the date is usually engraved.

Metropolitan tipstaves

Whilst generally it had been the tradition for many constables to carry a tipstaff as well as a truncheon, with the formation of the Metropolitan Police in 1829 this system changed. However, inspectors and above ranks continued to carry a tipstaff in a leather case on their belt and, as may be expected, examples of these are quite common although usually without the cases. Supplied by Parker, Field of Holborn, they were seven inches long, with a lower brass barrel of one-and-a-half inches and an ebony section with turned rings of approximately two-and-three-quarter inches followed by a further barrel of one-and-a-half inches surmounted by a brass crown.

There was another version identical to this in size and design but which had silver barrels, a silver crown and turned ivory handle in place of the ebony. On both, the cross and orb above the crown could be unscrewed and the crown itself taken off so that this part could be screwed inside for easier carrying in the case. Several of the silver ones carry inscriptions; in the Dixon Collection there is one for Cambridge inscribed 'Charles Balls Mayor, 1870' and, in the Leamington Spa Library and Museum, one of identical design for the Superintendent of Leamington Police. The Commissioners for the City of London Police also carried one of this silver pattern tipstaff.

When there is no inscription, these tipstaves frequently go unrecognised as being the standard Metropolitan and City Police issue and I often find that they are offered to me with all sorts of fanciful descriptions.

The first Metropolitan Police were issued with truncheons which had a particularly interesting design. The bottom part was carved with four handgrips and the shaft of the truncheon – which appears to be approximately 18 inches long – swelled slightly at the top and had the cypher 'VR' painted around this part. Surmounting the truncheon head was a carved knop which looks similar to a flattened acorn and this had three rings incised around the lower part. This knop was obviously intended to represent the crown but could not be prominent since the truncheon was to be carried on the belt in a leather case like the tipstaves of inspectors and superintendents. I have never actually seen one and even Fenn Clark (who was born in the 1860s) says on page 98 of *Truncheons – their Romance and Reality* that he had only seen the one specimen that is illustrated in his book, the present whereabouts of which I do not know. These truncheons could only have been in use for a short time before being changed for the conventional style. Unfortunately for us, much withdrawn equipment in those days was burnt or otherwise disposed of.

City of London tipstaves

Just as one might expect, the City of London has always been particularly well endowed with silver tipstaves for its officers and officials. Many of these have come down to the present day possibly because, being of a precious metal, they were objects of value even if their historical importance was not recognised. Brass tipstaves, on the other hand, would have been regarded as of little value, especially when they were not inscribed.

The Worshipful Company of Goldsmiths is fortunate to have a small but very fine collection of silver tipstaves which was presented to it by

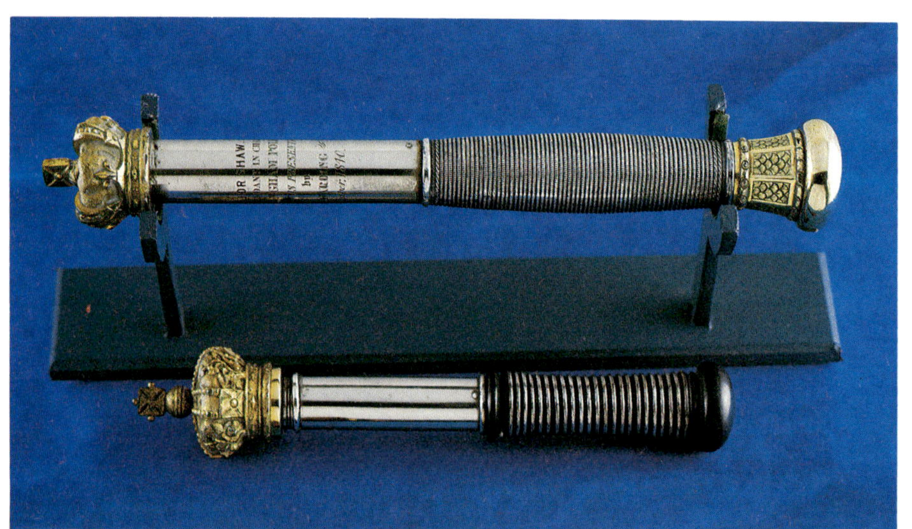

Two tipstaves with a police connection.
The one at the top is of silver, gilt and gold plating and is inscribed 'Major Shaw Superintendent in Chief, Birmingham Police This staff presented by D. Harding September 1840'
The ebony, chrome and silver gilt tipstaff underneath was carried by Mr Alfred Tyler who was the Deputy Chief Constable for Staffordshire in charge of the Worcester Police from 1889 to 1892. Author's collection.

Three exceptional tipstaves still in their original presentation cases 1. (top left) *Small wooden tipstaff beautifully painted with the royal arms beneath a painted and carved wooden crown with underneath the two dolphins of Brighton within a shield. The inscription reads: 'attended officially at the laying the first stone of St. Peter's May 8th 1824. High Constable W. Boxall Esq.' 2.* (top right) *Tipstaff in ebony and silver engraved 'Bailie George Grant Junior 1859' together with the motto 'Let Glasgow Flourish' and beneath 'Police Chambers'. Still in its original plush and leather case. 3.* (bottom) *Tipstaff for the Commissioner of Police City of London. Made of silver with an ivory handgrip and gold plated crown. The Arms of the City of London are engraved on the shaft. There is a label on on the inside of the leather case which says 'Parker, Field and Sons, Gunmakers to Her Majesty's Honourable Board of Ordnance, Honourable East India and Hudson Bay Companies. 233, High Holborn. Armourers to the Metropolitan Police Force'.* Bramshill Police College Collection.

George Lambert in the mid-1800s. Probably more than any others, these tipstaves have had articles written on them; I was, therefore, pleased to personally inspect them – with the kind assistance of their curator, Miss Rosemary Ransome-Wallis. Several are admiralty oars but there are also some examples for the City of London. They all date from the first part of the 19th century, with the latest being from 1832.

The London Museum also has some fine examples for the City of London which the serious collector will find well worth making an appointment to see.

Tipstaves of magistrates and judges

As justices of the peace acted both as magistrates and as directors of the constables within their area, they carried a staff as a badge of office. These did not necessarily have to be the tipped staves generally carried by their constables, although very often they were – the alternative was a straight staff, often about two feet long, which was usually decorated with the royal coat-of-arms and other details. With either version the stave was large enough to be clearly visible and in many cases would be placed in front of the magistrate when he was acting in that capacity. This is not to say that a magistrate would not also have a small pocket tipstaff which he could carry to show his authority at other times.

In my collection I have one very fine ivory tipstaff, two inches long and finely carved with an open crown containing the original red cloth. This is held inside a well carved walnut casing, the size of a walking-stick top, the brass ferrule of which unscrews to show a thread, indicating that it could either be screwed onto a walking stick or, alternatively, carried in the

Six Parker, Field tipstaves
These show clearly the variety of shapes and materials to be found in examples from this Company. (from left – top) 1. Silver and ivory tipstaff with royal coat of arms and cypher 'VR'. 2. Silver and ivory tipstaff with gilt crown. 3. Brass and ebony tipstaff with inscription on the top part of the barrel 'Presented by Thomas Hovel Esq., Mayor 1836 to Mr. James Smith Chief Constable Cambridge' The bottom part of the barrel has the Arms of Cambridge. (from left – bottom) 4. Brass and ivory tipstaff – no engraving. 5. Brass tipstaff inscribed 'Metropolitan Police Constable employed in plain clothes'. 6. Silver plated tipstaff with ivory turned handle and gilt crown – no inscription. London Museum Collection.

1. (at top) City of London wooden tipstaff with royal coat of arms. City of London coat of arms with the date 1755. *2. (from left)* Brass tipstaff with City of London arms and the number '1'. *3.* Rare wood and ivory tipstaff with City of London arms painted on the wooden shaft. This is particularly interesting in that the handle is made from turned elephant ivory while the crown has been carved from walrus ivory. *4.* Commemorative tipstaff for the visit of His Royal Highness Prince Leopold of Belgium in 1875. Prince Leopold was given the freedom of the City of London and the two City officials who presented the casket containing the parchment must have had these commemorative pieces made at the same time. The companion piece is in the London Museum. Author's collection.

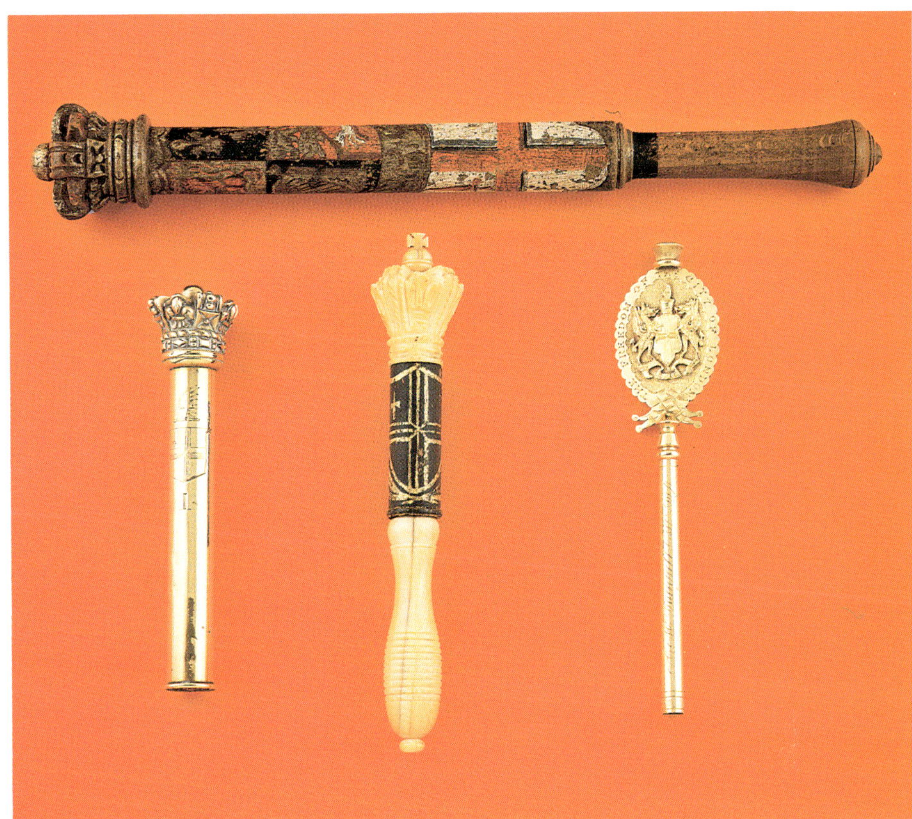

From left: *1.* Brass tipstaff engraved 'York 1824'. *2.* Ivory tipstaff with turned handle. Engraved with the royal coat of arms and cypher 'VR'. *3.* Wooden tipstaff, finely painted with royal coat of arms – pre 1801 and City of London coat of arms. This is similar to one in my own collection dated 1755. *4.* Brass tipstaff with turned wooden handle. Hollow crown with original purple cloth. Inscribed 'Wisbech Police' and underneath crossed keys. Bramshill Police College Collection.

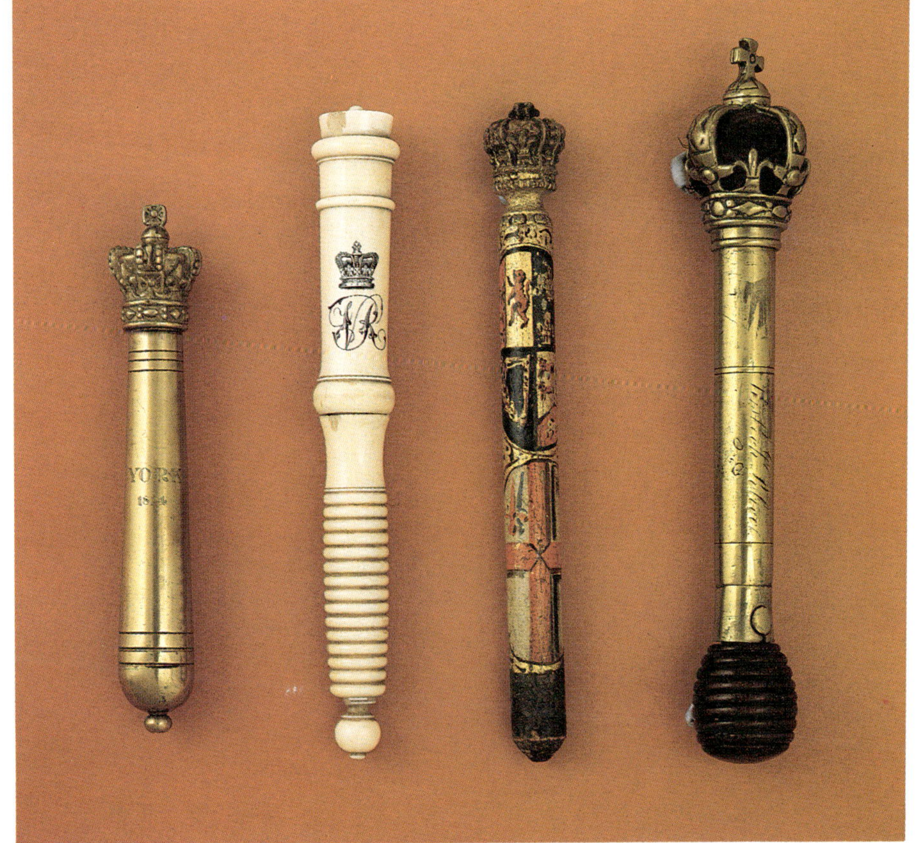

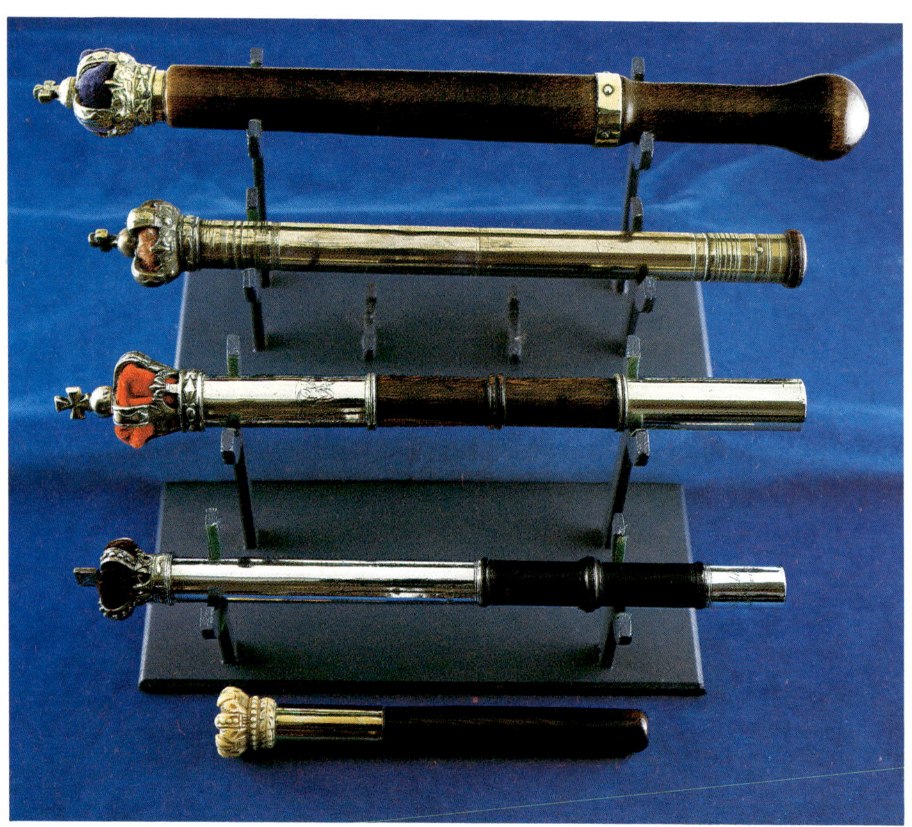

*Collection of Magistrates'
batons.*
From top: *1. Wood and
brass covered baton with
cloth insert. 2. All brass
construction with cloth
insert. 3. Walnut and silver
tipstaff with cloth insert.
Initials 'WHK' on top barrel.
4. Ebony and silver tipstaff
with purple cloth insert and
hallmarks for 1803.
Engraved on the bottom
ferrule is the wording
'Constable of Shadwell'.
The ebony handle unscrews
in the middle probably for
the addition of a short silver
barrel for pocket use.
5. Wood, brass and ivory
baton.* Author's collection.

pocket. I also have a number of well made magistrates' tipstaves of brass, or brass and wood and, in one case, of wood and ivory; these all bear a crown, although generally their size is 15–18 inches.

Some little time ago I purchased a rather battered stave of office which originally had been highly gilded. Whilst the overall condition was not good, the royal cypher for 'GIIR' could still be made out, together with the royal arms and, quite clearly, the word 'Abington' with the initials 'T.J.' and the date '1741'. Enquiry with the Abington Museum in Northampton revealed that the original 'T.J.' should have been 'J.T.' for John Harvey Thursby. He was the owner of Abington Manor where the Thursby family lived between the years 1670 and 1841. The portraits of both John Thursby and his wife, painted in 1739, were fortunately still in existence; this proved to be one of the very few occasions when I could not only place an item in my collection for date, location and owner but, in addition, could also see a portrait of the man who carried the stave – in this case, only three years prior to the making of this staff.

Judges of the various courts also carried tipstaves of office, although very few of these ever come on the market. The Victoria and Albert Museum has only three silver tipstaves in its collection; one of these is a very interesting example which formerly belonged to the Tipstaff for two of the old courts. The fact that he had his own coat-of-arms on the reverse of the tipstaff indicates that he was a gentleman of some position in his own right. This tipstaff has silver sections at top and bottom, an ebony

John Harvery Thursby of Abington. Born 1709 died 1764. This portrait was painted in 1839 by C. Philips. The Thursby family owned Abington Manor from 1670 to 1841. Abington Museum Collection. Photograph – Beedles & Cooper

Magistrate's baton – staff of office for John Thursby with the initials 'T.J.' (J.T.) and the date 1741. Only very rarely is it possible to link two items in this way. Author's collection.

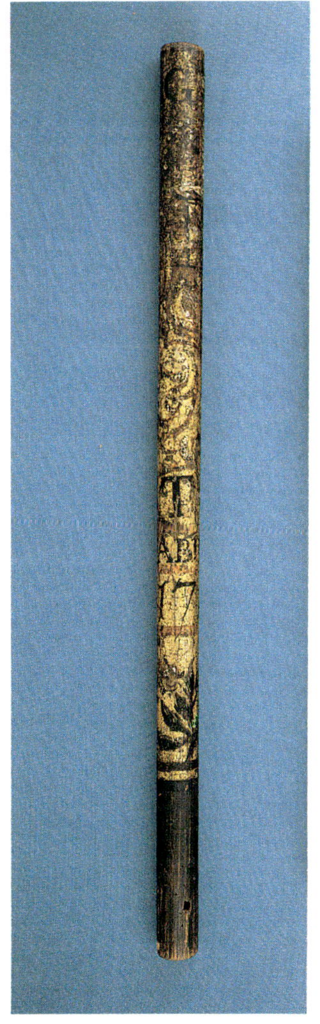

shaft and three silver rings at equal distances along the shaft – the overall length is approximately 12 inches. At the top are engraved the royal arms and the date '1795' with the arms of Davis on the reverse. The bottom of the tipstaff is inscribed

'John Davis
TIPSTAVE
to the Court of Exchequer
and
Rt. Honbl Master of the Rolls'.

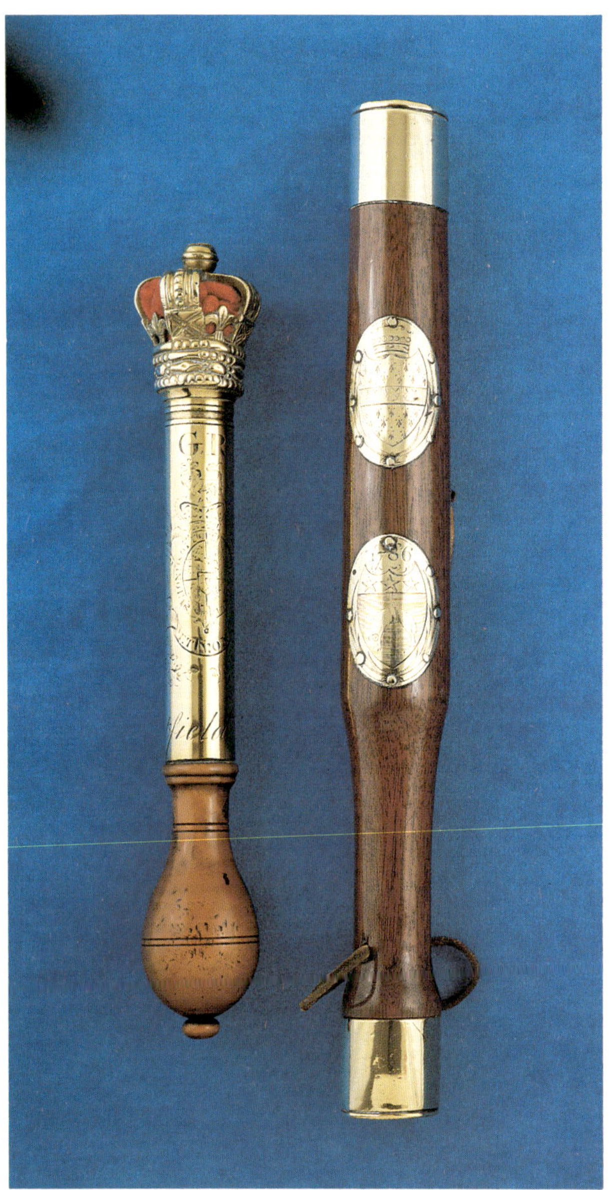

Titled families in the 18th and 19th century were often automatically made magistrates in view of their land holdings. The right one of these two tipstaves was held by the Viscounts of Leeds. The coat of arms on the top plate is their personal one, while that on the second plate is for the City of Leeds with the date 1786. The left-hand tipstaff is of brass and yew wood with the cypher 'GR'. Royal coat of arms and beneath them the word 'Hatfield 1812'. Hatfield is the seat of the Marquis of Salisbury and it is interesting that the family still hold a decorated truncheon for the same date. Both of these tipstaves would have been carried either by the Viscount or Marquis, or by their steward, when presiding at the local magistrates court. Tipstaves such as these are naturally very rare. Author's collection.

Three beautifully engraved brass tipstaves. The ones to the left and right are for the London Dock Company – the left-hand one having the date '1804'. The larger tipstaff in the centre is almost identical to an example in the London Museum which has an Admiralty Oar inside. The engraving on all four specimens appears to be by the same hand. Author's collection.

Tipstaves of dock companies

There were many dock companies around the country some of which appointed their own constables and officers and for which there are a number of relevant truncheons and tipstaves in existence. Over the years I have acquired two very fine examples for the London Dock Company which are both of solid brass construction with a shaped handle and a brass barrel of about three inches which is very finely engraved with the royal coat-of-arms (post-1801) and 'London Dock Company' underneath. One is undated, whilst the other – above the joining of the tails for the unicorn and lion – bears the initials 'J.F.' and the date '1804'. The design of both incorporated crowns filled with red cloth. The construction, engraving and the style are very similar to two other examples which I own for the same period, although their intended use was totally different. The engraving on the coat-of-arms certainly looks to be by the same hand, and serves to reinforce the view that there existed at the time a jeweller who specialised in this field.

Railway tipstaves

A number of the early railways issued those of their senior officials who came into contact with the public with tipstaves as marks of their authority. These are now extremely rare, having been produced in small numbers only. Fenn Clark illustrated one or two examples in his book and there are others to be seen in some of the railway museums.

They are usually identifiable by the engraved initials of the particular railway on the barrel. They often follow the pattern of some of the Parker, Field and Son tipstaves by having a brass barrel surmounted by a crown and a central ringed ebony handgrip. For the initials of these early railway companies, see the section **The early railways**.

General Post Office tipstaves

The General Post Office in Victorian times issued a number of their enquiry agents and post masters with identifying tipstaves. One or two of these are still in existence; they are usually boldly engraved with 'G.P.O.' on the brass barrel.

The earliest record of such a tipstaff is one from the time of the Gordon Riots in 1780. During these extremely violent and destructive riots it was feared that an attack would be made on the General Post Office in London and, to protect the building, 200 special constables were sworn in and hidden inside. From the tipstaves issued, just one remains.

Tipstaves marking civil appointments

There were not many people entitled to carry tipstaves outside of the categories listed in this chapter. There were, however, a number of governors of hospitals who carried one and probably county sheriffs could be included under this section, since by the 19th century their lawkeeping role had been taken over by others so that their function had become largely ceremonial.

Some years ago I purchased in London a very fine tipstaff of nearly 24 inches which is tipped top and bottom in silver. The construction is almost that of a mace, since it has a long straight shaft with a four-sided solid end surmounted by a short shaft and a silver cap. Each side is painted differently and there are the coat-of-arms of Exeter, the coat-of-arms of Plymouth, the crown and cypher 'GRIII' and the owner's initials 'J.S.'. A small ivory plaque mounted on one face records that it had been presented to John Sweet of Exeter in the time of George III; this had obviously been added later by the owner, his family or a museum. Since both Exeter and Plymouth are within the county of Devon, I came to the conclusion that it had probably been a sheriff's stave of office.

I later found that this particular shape is traditional to Devon and particularly to Plymouth, where there are a number of examples in the City Museum. These also have the four-sided painted square end and in Plymouth they are still described as 'mace tipstaffs'. The governor of the local alms hospital, known as the Hospital of Poors People, always carried one and there are a number of these in existence.

There is also a smaller size tipstaff which, unlike the ones with a four-sided top, has a rounded end and this is painted in four sections.

Ecclesiastical tipstaves

Whilst there are a number of church truncheons in existence, I do not know of any specific tipstaves. However, they must be considered a possibility, since the larger cathedrals in Georgian and Victorian times were usually protected by their own constables (in Salisbury, for example, he is still called the 'Close Constable') who may well have had tipstaves to show their authority.

The high ecclesiastical dignitaries of medieval days sought to establish their position by having a wand of office carried in front of them like the king and the modern equivalent of this is found in many church processions when the pastoral cross precedes the vicar. The very word 'verger' comes from the old Norman French 'verge' meaning a staff or rod, and bishops still have a staff carried in front of them.

From left: *1. Wood and silver tipstaff with metal crown at top and beneath this the initials 'WLM' standing for W. L. Marshall. Two lower bands of silver have the following engravings 'Mr. W. L. Marshall. Chief Constable of Salford 1881 Presented by W. Robinson Esq., J.P. thrice Mayor of Salford 1879–1881. 1st November 1881. W. L. Marshall'. The lower band has this engraving 'W. L. Marshall. Appointed Inspector in the Salford Police Force 8th March 1858. Promoted to Superintendentship 20th August 1867. Promoted to Chief Constableship 14th January 1880'. 2. Tipstaff in silver brass and ebony inscribed 'Thames Police No. 12'. 3. Brass and wood tipstaff inscribed 'William Rigler' Officer 12 November 1805'. On the lower band 'City Officer'. 4. Wood tipstaff with brass cap, cypher and crown for 'GRIV' and at the bottom '1829 Budle'. Bramshill Police College Collection.*

Commemorative tipstaves

These really fall into two categories: those which were inscribed and presented to mark a special occasion for a town or official body, and those which were presented to an officer on retirement, or to mark a particular event under his jurisdiction.

An example of the first would be the very fine tipstaff – identical to the standard Bow Street one and to those used later by the public offices – which is in the Dixon Collection at Bramshill. The tipstaff is engraved 'In 1765 His Most Gracious Majesty George III gave to the Magistrate of the City and Liberty of Westminster permission to distinguish themselves by wearing the arms of Westminster with the emblem of magistracy on a gold shield'. The City of Liberty of Westminster was, of course, the area of the original Bow Street Public Office and, by granting this right, George III was really giving recognition to Sir John Fielding.

The second type of commemorative tipstaff is also represented by an example in the Dixon Collection. This is of brass and ivory and inscribed:

> Presented to Mr. W. W. Homan,
> Supert of Police,
> Tredegar Iron Works,
> Monmouthshire.
> Jan 1st 1838.

From the inscription one would imagine that there must have been trouble with the workforce at the iron works that Mr. Homan, as superintendent of the local police – which in those days really meant the chief constable –

helped to suppress. Or did the iron works have their own police of which W. W. Homan was in charge? Such questions are typical of the ambiguities present in tracing the history of tipstaves and truncheons.

Bristol tipstaves

During the 17th century, Bristol was particularly famous for two things: the slave trade, until it was suppressed, and brass. Due to the existence of the brass workings it became common for truncheons and tipstaves within the Bristol area to be made of brass and, of course, they made very fearsome weapons. The Bristol Museum has the major collection of these in the country and only very rarely do specimens come on sale.

Generally, the truncheons are of solid construction with approximately six inch long wooden handles and brass tops of eight to nine inches. The truncheon head finishes in a knop which is attached to the body by a short neck. Tipstaves tend to be of similar appearance and again usually have either a knop or an acorn finial. In my collection I have one tipstaff inscribed 'St. Michael's Ward' which has a turned wooden handle of four inches with a brass top of three-and-a-half inches, finishing with the acorn.

The large truncheon which I have bears the cypher 'GIIIR' and is inscribed 'St. Mary Court Ward No. 11'. I have another very fine truncheon which again follows the standard measurements of a five inch handle and an eight inch brass top but, in this case, the top three inches from the neck are in the shape of an acorn. This one is engraved 'Bourton' and investigation has revealed that this was the name of a small parish some five miles outside Bristol.

Some authorities always list all of these brass-topped examples as being tipstaves – and certainly they are true to definition in being staves topped with metal – but as they were used by the constables, they could be considered combined truncheon/tipstaves. Generally they will have an inscription and also very often bear a date.

Scottish tipstaves

Scottish tipstaves seem to follow a standard design by being generally only five to six inches long, usually with an ebony shaft and a silver cap at top and bottom. This style has been recorded for Edinburgh, Leith, Fife and Stirlingshire. Glasgow also has a number of tipstaves on record, although these tend to be of the more conventional pattern, finishing with a crown often made of silver. Edinburgh, Perth and Dundee all had their own Societies of High Constables; it is quite possible therefore to find tipstaves both for the high constables and the general commissioners of Edinburgh Police, and also for the constables who policed the city of Edinburgh after 1805 when a paid police force was established.

The Worshipful Company of Goldsmiths has three interesting Edinburgh tipstaves all of which follow the same pattern of a cap at top and bottom with a band in the middle. One of these, which is approximately eight inches long and of thicker construction than usual has its middle band engraved 'Secretary Edinburgh Constables', whilst the earliest one is

Large presentation mace/ tipstaff in brass and ivory inscription reads 'Presented to Mr. W. W. Homan Supert of Police. Tredegar Iron Works, Monmouth- shire, Jan 1st 1838'. Bramshill Police College Collection.

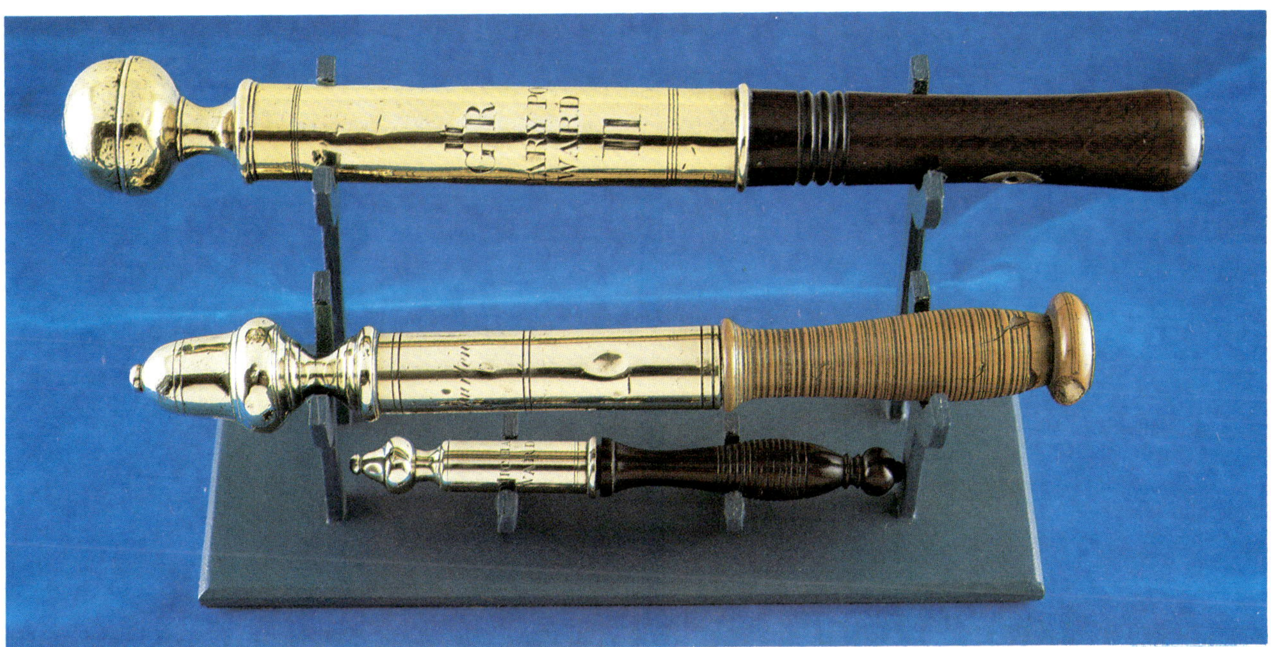

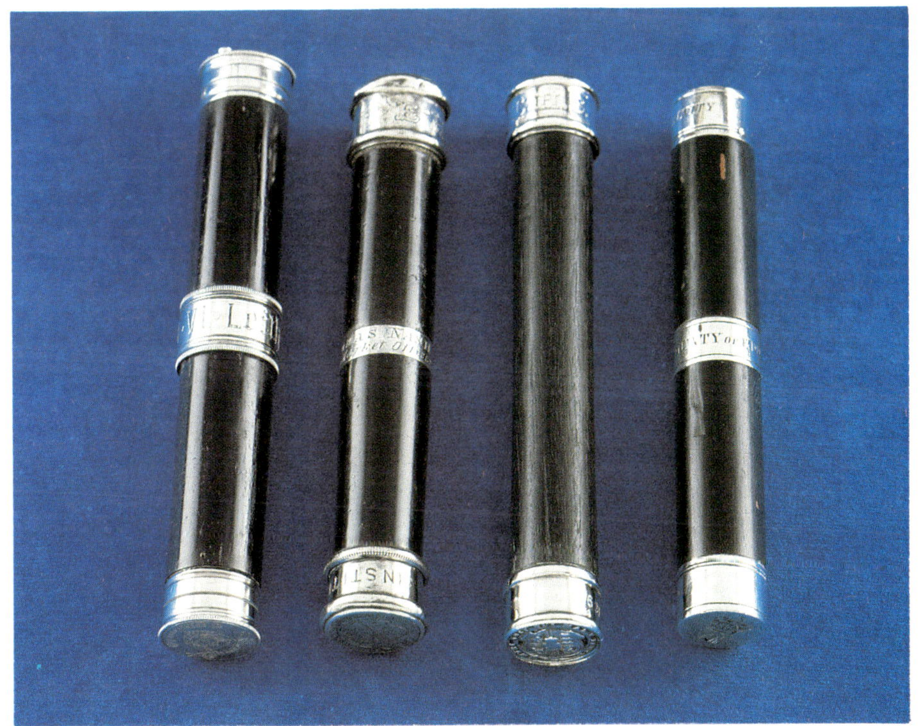

Bristol truncheons/ tipstaves.
From top: 1. Wood and brass truncheon with ball end 'GIIIR' Cypher and 'St. Mary Port Ward II'. 2. Wood and brass truncheon with acorn finial – the word 'Bourton' is engraved on barrel. Bourton is a small village approximately 5 miles from the centre of Bristol. 3. Tipstaff with acorn filial, engraved 'St. Michael's Ward'. Author's collection.

Four ebony and silver Scottish tipstaves.
From left: 1. Leith Police. 2. Edinburgh High Constables – engraved 'Thomas Nash, Corn Market Officer. 3. Edinburgh High Constables. 4. City of Edinburgh – engraved 'County of Edin' 1841 Jas Gilmour. Mary College. Trinity. Author's collection.

dated 1750 and has the royal arms and also the arms of the Earl of Mansfield. One example also has silver bands running the length of the tipstaff, as well as the circular band in the middle.

It is interesting to note that, on some constables' tipstaves, the middle band moves freely along the shaft. The purpose of this was legally significant. If the constable was obstructed whilst trying to make his arrest, he would ceremonially move the ring from one end of the tipstaff to the other to indicate forcible interruption of the discharge of his duty. In those days such an extra charge was obviously to be feared since it would carry a heavy additional sentence. But we have no description of just how, while trying to subdue his prisoner, the constable could move the ring along the shaft of the tipstaff so that the struggling man could see it!

I have four of these Scottish tipstaves in my own collection and they all conform to a standard length of just over four inches. They all have a cap top and bottom and three have a middle band. The first bears the following inscription:

Top band	*Middle band*	*Lower band*
'Jas Gilmour'	'County of Edinr.	'Mary Cottage
	1841	Trinity'

The top of the stave has a fine crown and cypher 'VR' while the other end looks as if an early Victorian silver threepenny piece has been mounted on it as this is the exact size.

The second is inscribed with:

Top band	*Middle band*	*Lower band*
'No. 47. E.H.C.'	'Thomas Nash	'Instituted 1698'
	Cornmarket Officer'	

The very top shows the castle and Latin motto for Edinburgh and on the bottom are the royal arms for Scotland.

The third has no middle band. Its top band is inscribed with 'E.H.C. No. 69' and the lower with 'Instituted 1698'. At the top are the arms and motto for Edinburgh and at the bottom the royal coat-of-arms for Scotland (pre-1801). E.H.C. of course, stands for Edinburgh High Constables whilst the date refers to their formation into a society.

On the fourth, only the middle band is inscribed – with 'Leith Town Council VI'. At the top are the arms of Leith and at the bottom a raised crown and cypher 'VR'.

One interesting point of note with these Scottish tipstaves is that, as their ends were intaglio cut into the metal, they could be used as seals on wax for official documents – although the image would be reversed.

Isle of Man tipstaves

Manx tipstaves come in a variety of shapes and sizes and there are a number in the collection of the Manx Museum and National Trust.

There is one which was carried by the water bailiff – one George Quirk – and this is engraved with his name, position and coat-of-arms for the Isle of Man. Another larger example was carried by the high bailiff; this is inscribed on the barrel with 'High Bailiff' and the arms of the Isle of Man and Douglas. It is an unusual tipstaff in that it unscrews and contains a small flask for liquid refreshment. This is the first time that I have come across such an addition and certainly it is a departure from the usual content of a warrant! Other tipstaves include one for the post mistress (this is the only case I know of a tipstaff being issued to a woman), and one made of wood and brass which is inscribed 'Thos. Cleator, Chief Constable'. Finally, there is a Parker, Field and Son pattern tipstaff of

Tipstaff, or short truncheon, for the Isle of Man. George IV. There are a number of this pattern in existence. Manx Museum & National Trust.

silver with an ivory ringed handle which is inscribed 'Head Constable'.

The Isle of Man had a further type of short truncheon or tipstaff in use at the time of George IV and there is an example of this in the Manx Museum collection. I also have one in my collection which is approximately ten inches long with the top four inches painted black. Below the numerals 'IIII' it has the crown, the cypher 'GR' and the arms for the Isle of Man. The museum example has its black paintwork extending for at least three-quarters of the shaft and has a laurel wreath surrounding the cypher and the arms, but apart from this they are identical. The wood appears to be beech, cylindrical in shape and domed at top and bottom. With the exception of the brass one for the high bailiff, all of the other Isle of Man tipstaves are post-1837 and the wooden tipstaves could, therefore, be of the type issued to parish constables at the time of George IV.

Channel Island tipstaves

The Channel Islands have a number of unusual and distinctive tipstaves and these tend to vary between the main islands.

Selection of 9 tipstaves as carried by the original Honorary Jersey Police. Jersey Museum; 'La Societe Jersiaise'.

Jersey

Records show that the Constable of St. Helier carried a tipstaff prior to 1800, but it was not until 1806 that an Act was passed which laid down that all police officers on the island, and the constables and centeniers in the parishes should be provided with their own tipstaves copied from the pattern used in St. Helier.

The basic pattern of Jersey tipstaff which the collector might be fortunate enough to find nowadays is of wood, probably walnut, and is approximately ten inches long. The tapering handle is of ringed design with a small knop at the end, whilst the black painted barrel is three inches long and has three leopards on a red shield, surrounded by the words 'Jersey Police'. Above these are two carved rings surmounted by a crown two-and-a-half inches in depth. This is finely carved and painted and gilded. One example in my collection unscrews between the handle and the shaft, obviously for easier carrying in the pocket. There is also a smaller type of tipstaff more traditional in design – which has a swelling carved handle surmounted by a brass crown. This is only some four inches in length.

Guernsey

There would seem to be three main patterns of tipstaves which have been used in Guernsey, but they are all rare and very infrequently do the smaller ones appear for sale.

The first type is of silver and ebony and is approximately 12 inches long. There is a silver mount at the base, a long straight wooden handle which swells at the top and is surmounted by a silver crown and, immediately below this, a silver shield bearing the Channel Islands arms.

The more common type of tipstaff was that issued to parish constables and, although there are variations in the trimmings, these all appear to be of basically the same design. The overall length is approximately six inches, of which the handle is three-and-a-half inches. This is turned so that it swells in the middle and the bottom is capped with a silver ferrule. Above the handle there is a two-and-a-half inch section which firstly swells out like a barrel and above this is a round section carved to roughly give the outline of a crown, although without any protrusions. It has two silver shields, each held by three silver pins and these bear the arms of the Channel Islands. The wooden outline of the crown has a strip of silver around the waist and four bands which go over the top and are pinned in the middle – this enhances the idea of the crown.

The third design is simpler and slightly shorter. Although it has a carved handle and base similar to the previous type, there is no metal ferrule and the swelling section at the top is finished only with a small wooden knop bearing a copper shield embossed with the initials 'S.P.P. – S.C. 1914' (standing for the St. Peter's Port Special Constable – 1914).

Sark

The island of Sark is so small that in earlier days the law was administered by honorary constables. These carried ebony and silver tipstaves which, while similar in shape to those of the Guernsey parish constables, were half as large again and of much better workmanship. The metal bands around the carved top were a much closer representation of a crown but the shield on the barrel of the tipstaff is of the same pattern as for Guernsey. There are ceremonial occasions even today when the Sark constables carry their tipstaves.

Unidentified tipstaves

Unfortunately, at least 50 per cent of tipstaves which can be added to a collection are without identification and, unless they are silver, it is impossible sometimes to even date them other than by general style and perhaps by the shape of the crown. One of the frustrating things is that very often the style and shape of an unmarked tipstaff will almost exactly match one where the full history is known – and one which may have been associated with important office holders. Unfortunately, shape and style are not enough in themselves to enable one to say that the unmarked one was used for the same purpose. Many silversmiths and jewellers made tipstaves and, having worked out a pattern for one customer, they may well have used this again, either identically or with small variations, for other commissions. Similarly with brass tipstaves. Once a mould had been

Interesting tipstaves.
From left: *1. Walnut and silver tipstaff with the initials 'AM' and the date '1661'. The style for the handle is typically Jacobean. 2. Brass and wood tipstaff with interesting Acanthus leaf and acorn finial. the Brass barrel is engraved 'Constable of the Hundred of Bradford 1798'. 3. and 4. Identically patterned tipstaves from St. George's East in the East End of London. There was apparently a tradition in Victorian times for the constable to present an inscribed tipstaff to the church warden on his appointment each year. 3. is engraved 'presented to Mr. J. Stratford by J. Shirley Constable St. George's East 1848'. 4. reads 'presented to Mr. Braden by T. Scotcher Constable St. George's East 1849'.* Author's collection.

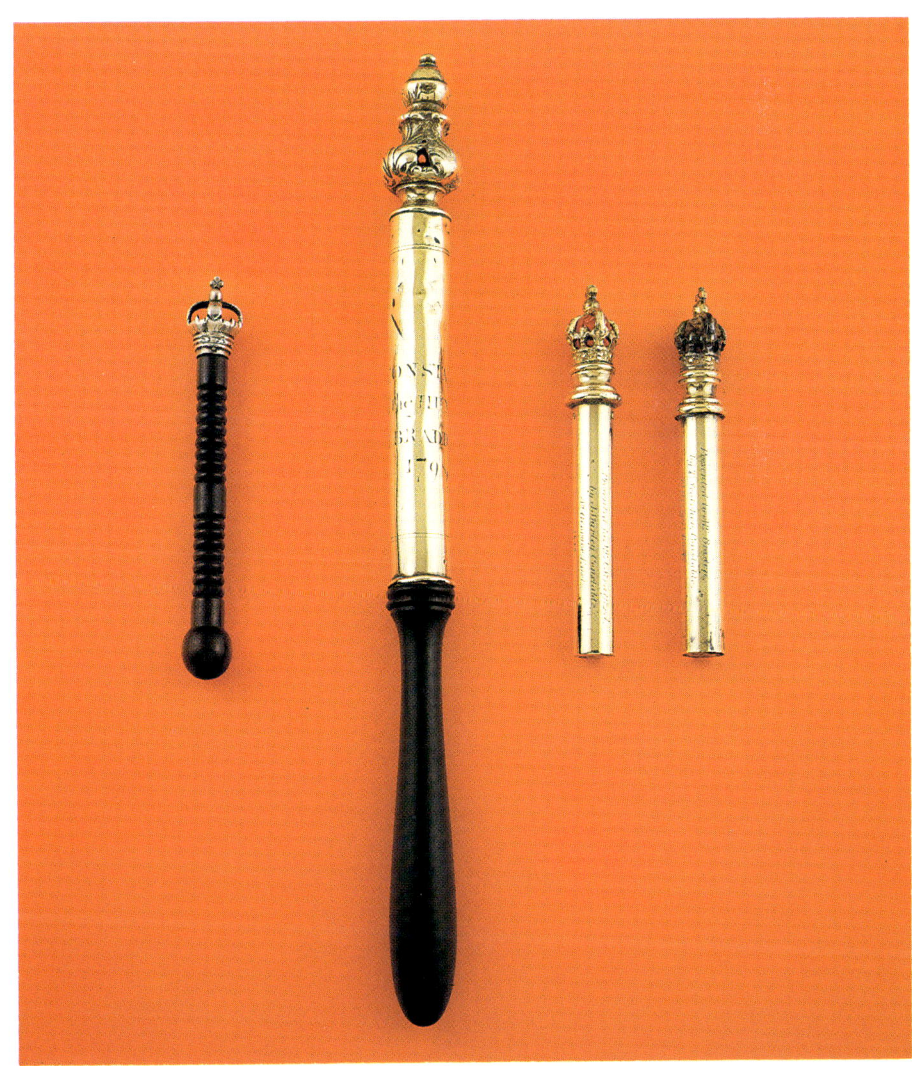

made, it would be unrealistic not to expect a number to be produced from it, and these off-the-peg tipstaves only became personalised when they were inscribed.

The most important 'unknown' in my collection is also probably the oldest. It is only seven inches in overall length and has a fine turned handle of walnut. Ending in a wooden ball, the handle has been turned in concentric rings in typical Jacobean style and is surmounted by a small silver crown which is hollow and may originally have had a cloth inset. On the crown is the inscription 'A.M. 1661'. I have no reason not to consider this to be a genuine piece since the crown is of the style of Charles II and the woodwork typical of the period. The pricked way of inscribing the lettering is also typical of that time. 1661 was only one year after Charles II was restored to the throne and we may expect that in those first few years after the Restoration many new tipstaves would have had to be made since, under Cromwell, most of the old forms and symbols of authority had been swept away. The initials 'A.M.' could have either of the usual two meanings: representing the office or the office holder. However, as staves of office for the royal household were often denoted by their initials only, my own personal feelings are that this tipstaff belonged to the 'Assistant Master of the Royal Household'. Unfortunately, it is unlikely that I will ever know for sure.

Admiralty oars

Admiralty oars can come in two forms. There are the large maces which many corporations and courts have as emblems of their authority over harbours or maritime affairs, and there are the small tipstaves which were either oars on their own or else had one concealed in the shaft. These were normally carried by water bailiffs, harbour masters and constables. They were also carried by officials of the Admiralty Courts. The possession of an admiralty oar bestowed great authority on the holder since he then had the power to board, search and seize ships within his jurisdiction and to execute warrants concerning any of them. On encountering resistance, he could call on the ships of the Royal Navy to assist him.

Most of the admiralty oars still in existence are held by major museums such as the National Maritime Museum at Greenwich and the London Museum, or by large collections as at Bramshill Police College. They very rarely come on to the open market and I therefore count myself fortunate to have acquired two examples for my collection. One is a cylindrical silver tipstaff with an open crown surmounting a hollow shaft. The crown has a red cloth insert. The base of this tipstaff unscrews and, fixed to the inside by a threaded mount, is the admiralty oar. This can be detached and placed on the top of the crown by unscrewing the orb and cross which, in turn, can be screwed into the base plug for safe carrying. The hallmarks show that this was made in 1810 and the maker's mark is 'I.C.'.

Two of the silver admiralty oars held by the Worshipful Company of Goldsmiths are of similar pattern to mine, and also bear this maker's mark. He was probably John Clarke II of Clerkenwell Green. Unfortunately, this is one of the tipstaves which has no attribution, although on the shaft of the oar are the scratched initials 'C.C.O.L.' which could just possibly represent 'Chief Constable of Liverpool'.

Four unusual tipstaves which form part of a small but important collection held at Goldsmiths.
From top: *1. Tipstaff for 1793. Royal arms. Maker's initial's 'AD'. 2. Silver and ebony tipstaff bearing the name T. Tanson. Royal arms for pre-1801. 3. Tipstaff and admiralty oar, combined with a working flint-lock pistol. Made by R & S Hennell in 1814. The crown is in mace style and the oar is carried within the barrel and screwed into a plug. This is probably the most unusual tipstaff in existence. 4. Silver tipstaff of highly individualistic design. Made of silver with an open crown, within the barrel of the tipstaff are a serrated file with dagger top and a silver admiralty oar. Immediately under the crown is the inscription 'William Levy Officer to the Sheriff of Middlesex 1832' on the lower part of the barrel are the arms for the City of London.* Worshipful Company of Goldsmiths.

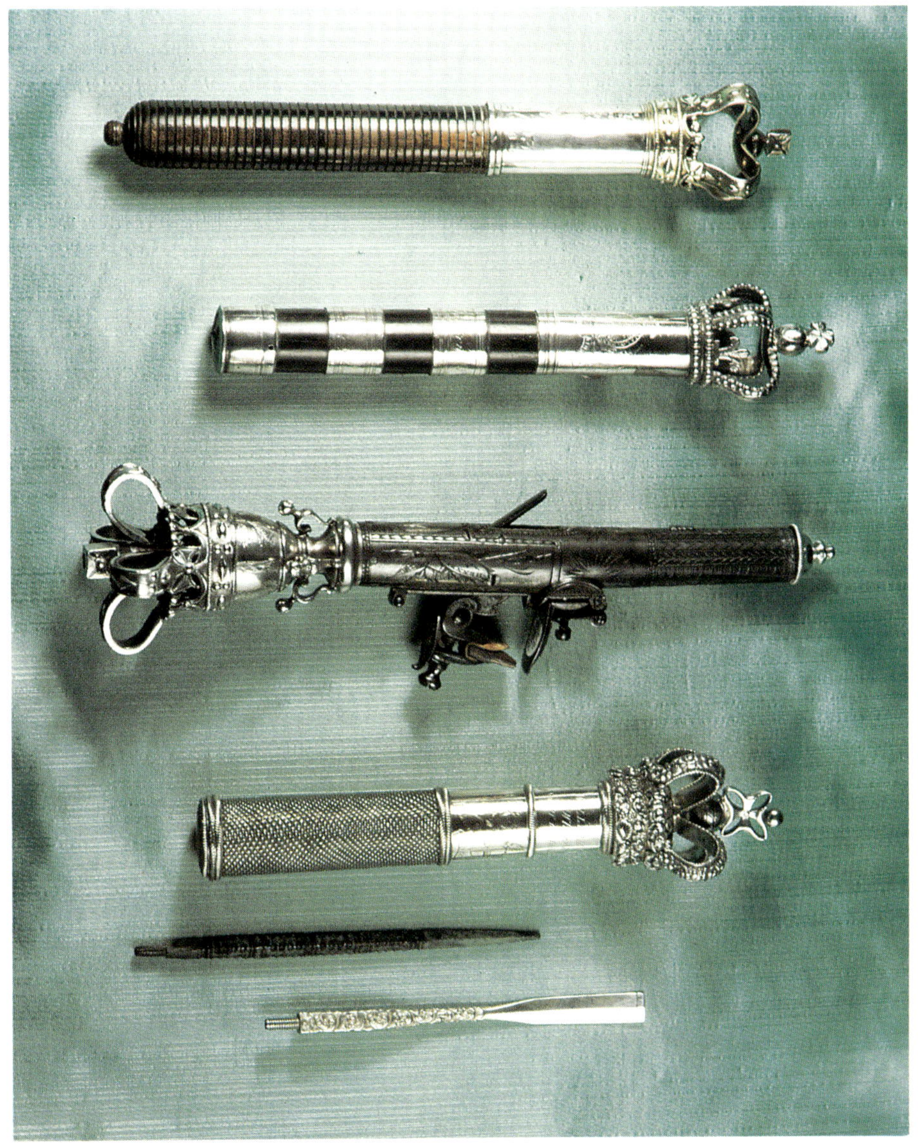

The other admiralty oar in my collection is of the type used by water bailiffs and is a silver oar of five inches with a ring at the shaft end whereby it could be hung from a chain of office around the neck. Engraved on the blade is the crown, the cypher 'GRIV' and the fouled admiralty anchor. There is an almost identical oar in the Victoria and Albert Museum but this is for 'GIIIR'.

Probably the two most famous admiralty oars still in existence are held by the Worshipful Company of Goldsmiths. One is a working flintlock pistol which was made in London in 1814 by R. & S. Hennell. The overall length is 13¼ inches and it has silver mounts. The crown is unusual in that it is in the form of a macehead and the small admiralty oar, which is normally carried in a base plug inside the pistol barrel, is screwed into the centre. The other unusual one is 12 inches overall, with a most ornate chased openwork crown, a silver barrel divided by a ropework band and a handle of a knurled pattern. The barrel is engraved with the royal arms, with

Three magnificient mace/ tipstaves.
From left: 1. *Cut glass and silver tipstaff. The origins of this are unknown but it may well have been for the Beadle of one of the glassmaking guilds. I know of only one other glass tipstaff. 2. Large silver mace with the arms of the old East India Company which was disbanded in 1701. The Latin date engraved on this is for 1650 and there is the inscription 'Tomi A. E. Smith'. On the four panels at the top of the mace are the royal arms and the crown above the thistle, the Irish harp and the rose. 3. Silver and wood tipstaff surmounted by a silver Admiralty fouled anchor. The top part of the ball is inscribed 'Clemt. Inn. Joshua Blackwell principell Trinity Terme 1717' The lower part of the ball is engraved with the Admiralty fouled anchor.* London Museum Collection.

From top: *1. Most unusual chain of office together with plate and crown with the cypher GIVR and a cock crowing. The accompanying tipstaff also has a crowing cock on the top and a pewter wrist chain. The box in which they are both contained is inscribed 'James Mitchell' and 'Crier to the Verge of the Palace 1804–1833'. No one is absolutely certain of the position filled by Mr. Mitchell but it would seem likely that he was the Official Time Caller who patrolled the Palace calling the correct time. The fact that he carried a tipstaff as his authority shows the wide uses to which tipstaves could be put. 2. Ebony and silver tipstaff. Top band with the royal coat of arms hallmarked for 1866 with the second band inscribed 'William Charles Frayling died 25. Aug. 1866' the second part of this band is inscribed 'Frederick George Frayling appointed 22nd Oct. 1866.' Whilst the original office has been forgotten, it is quite obvious that the son succeeded his father. 3. Silver admiralty oar with unusual mace head. This head is engraved with the royal arms and of the City of London and the silver oar is held in the base attached to the knop. The oar is hallmarked for 1813.* London Museum Collection.

beneath them the admiralty foul anchor. On the reverse is the inscription 'William Levy, Officer to the Sheriff of Middlesex 1832'. What makes this tipstaff particularly unusual is that one finds, held in the shaft, both an ornate admiralty oar and also a file with a pointed dagger end. Both of these could be screwed into the centre of the crown in place of the orb and cross. The file may have been intended to cut padlocks open but it is unlikely that it would have had sufficient strength. Probably it represents the whims – as with the pistol tipstaff – of a rich official who was trying a little 'one-upmanship'. The Worshipful Company also has a number of other interesting admiralty oars, mostly for the first part of the 19th century.

There are good examples of admiralty oars at the London Museum and also in the Dixon Collection at Bramshill. The National Maritime Museum at Greenwich also has two very fine admiralty oars, one for 1819 and the other for 1817. It also has a number of Admiral-of-the-Fleet batons which, while having a different purpose to tipstaves, had the same original derivation. Batons for Admirals-of-the-Fleet and Field Marshals are similar in design, usually having a gold ferrule, purple velvet covered shaft and an ornate head surmounted by a St. George slaying the dragon. Their overall length is approximately 15 inches.

Royal staves

Since all tipstaves have descended from medieval days as representing the king's authority, it is natural that within the royal household the chief officers were marked by the carrying of an official wand of office. Needless to say, they are almost unheard of in modern salerooms. However, in 1984 I was fortunate to purchase one of the original silver-sticks-in-waiting for the reign of William IV (1830–1837).

After the restoration of Charles II there was still considerable unrest in the kingdom and in 1678 it was decided that a royal household appointment should be made giving him a personal bodyguard. This honour went to the colonels of the three troops of Horseguards. These officers took turns in carrying out the duties of Goldstick – which they carried as a badge of office – when on duty they were referred to as Goldstick-in-Waiting. They were responsible for the safety of the sovereign from his rising to his going to bed, but for the night his safety became the responsibility of the Master of the Bedchamber. A further senior officer of each troop became Silverstick-in-Waiting with responsibilities to stand-in during any absence of Goldstick. When the three troops were re-organised into regiments in 1788 the appointment of Goldstick was vested in the Colonel of the Regiment and its commanding officer was also appointed as Silverstick and was in Waiting when his regiment was in London.

Both Gold and Silverstick-in-Waiting later came to provide a link between the sovereign and his household troops and often conveyed his commands to them – sometimes even acting as a military adviser to the king.

Fenn Clark in his book *Truncheons* records that in 1927 a gold-stick-in-waiting for the reign of William IV was sold at auction for £31 10s. – at a time when even admiralty silver oars were only selling for £5! This particular piece virtually disappeared from public sight and it was only recently that I discovered, with the help of the librarian of the Worshipful Company of Goldsmiths, that it was held in the private collection of Walkers, the London jewellers. Enquiries revealed that the firm had recently been taken over by H. Samuel Ltd; this famous piece is now part of their collection. Both the gold and silver sticks were made by the same London jeweller, John Linnett, in 1831 and are identical in the design of the head, including the decorations. The gold top however weighs some seven ounces. The length of both sticks is 40 inches and they were intended to be held by the neck so that the top, with its royal cypher, crown and emblems of Ireland, Scotland and England could be pushed forward to show the authority of the bearer.

The Household Cavalry Museum at Windsor holds a number of gold and silver sticks from previous reigns and, since none have been presented since Queen Victoria, the present office holders make use of these on ceremonial occasions. Silverstick is always nowadays the Lt. Colonel commanding the Household Cavalry and gold stick is held on alternate months by Colonel of the Life Guards and the Blues and Royals.

The London Museum hold two interesting silver topped sticks of almost identical appearance to silver stick, but in place of the raised cypher they have respectively GRIV and WIVR and the royal arms cut into the top. They were both held by the King's Harbinger or Crier and in previous centuries his function was to announce the arrival or presence of the King.

Silver Stick-in-Waiting for the reign of William IV. The Stick was a common design for royal appointments which could include both Gold and Silver Stick-in-Waiting and also the Kings Harbinger. Rare. Author's collection.

Cleaning old truncheons and tipstaves

I was given the following cleaning mixture by a friend in the antique trade and have used it for a number of years to loosen accumulated grime and dirt from *wooden* truncheons and tipstaves:

Vinegar

Linseed

Turpentine

Make up as a mixture using equal parts of each. Shake thoroughly before using – rub in very gently.

I have found this to be quite effective and it has never damaged any truncheons in my collection. Needless to say I always try a small amount first on a part where it will not show – just in case! Whatever you use for cleaning, a small toothbrush is always very helpful to get into the awkward parts.

The cleaning of brass tipstaves – particularly if they still have the original cloth –can be very difficult. I usually apply several coats of a patent brass cleaner to soften the verdi-gris and have found impregnated wadding helpful to bring back the polish. Both products are easily found in shops. The antique trade sometimes use a short-cut of diluted ammonia on brass or metal – but great care has to be taken not to get this on leather, wood etc.

Another way of cleaning very dirty brass is by a mixture of salt and lemon juice –but on the occasions I have tried this it seems to leave a dull finish.

CAUTION I pass these cleaning tips on for information and do caution care in their use – and a testing procedure first before application. *I can take no responsibility for their use which must be the decision of the individual collector.*

Heads of two ebony sticks of office both carried by Alderman and Colonel Samuel Wilson who was the King's Harbinger. The head of each stick has the royal cypher and coat of arms – one being for George IV, in silver, and the other for William IV in silver gilt. The office of Harbinger is a very old one and goes back to the days when the king used to go in procession around the country. His official Harbinger would go before him to announce his arrival and presence. London Museum Collection.

Police Lanterns

Within the field of police-connected collecting, lanterns certainly cannot rate as one of the more exciting subjects – however, in the overall picture of police equipment over the past years, they cannot be overlooked.

Styles of police lanterns.
Author's collection.

Side view of a bullseye lantern showing the twin carrying handles and the belt hook. This one also has a lip under the hook in order to prevent it slipping off the belt. Author's collection.

Until the advent of gas lighting and then of electric lighting, the streets of even major towns and cities were very poorly lit and, of course, the darkness gave rise to many street crimes. This is not a phenomenon which affected our forebears only; it is to be found even today, whenever there is a power failure or strike – proof indeed that things have not really changed very much and that civilisation, and the accompanying freedom which we take so very much for granted, is really an artificially imposed state.

The earliest forms of public lighting were the watch fires on street corners and the burning torches fixed by the owners of larger houses into special iron brackets in front of their doors. There are still some of these in existence in front of old houses in London. Personal lighting was by smaller torches of bound straw or wood and the earliest street watches would have carried these. This type of lighting persisted quite late into Victorian times and boys – known as 'link men' – could be hired to run in front of pedestrians or carriages to light the way. Many old houses still have a wrought-iron inverted cone by the front door in which the boys would extinguish their burning torches.

The next development was that of a wooden lantern or lanthorn with panels of thin cowhorn encasing a tallow dip. Wax candles as we know them were very expensive and used only by the very wealthy – poorer people were forced to use the quick burning type of dip which was really only a string wick dipped in animal fat and allowed to harden. The obvious advantage of the enclosed lantern was that it was not so subject to weather conditions; it acted as the the forerunner of all later forms of lanterns, up until modern electric torches.

When metal could more easily be worked, it was used for making lanterns. These had glass covers and air vents to allow the candle to burn freely without draughts.

The needs of the early watchmen and police gradually shaped these lanterns so that certain features became standard, even when made by different manufacturers. Firstly, some kind of handle was necessary for holding the lantern and even candle lanterns can often be found with twin handles on the back and, in some cases, a loop handle over the top. Secondly, as the carrier did not always want to be conspicuous, a sliding panel was made which could be brought round to seal off the light. The other main feature which I have found to be common to even Georgian candle lanterns is a metal spring projecting from the top of the lantern at the back: this was intended to allow the lanterns to be hooked over a waist belt. I always use these three main criteria when deciding if an early lantern had police or watch connections.

One important point to remember is that lanterns were the equivalent of today's electric torches and, therefore, large numbers were produced for sale to the general public. While many oil lanterns have come down to the present day, in my experience you can usually distinguish between those made for the police and for the public.

Candle lanterns undoubtedly persisted well into Victorian times and it was only the advent of greater technology and manufacturing methods which allowed oil lamps to come into general use. The bullseye lantern is, in fact, quite complicated since, apart from its outer tin shell and ground glass magnifying lens, there is usually a ceramic lamp with adjustable wick which is fixed inside. I have tried lighting one of the older ones and found that its magnified beam was approximately half the strength of a modern 3-cell torch.

These oil lamps throw out a considerable amount of heat and during the cold winter patrols must have been a source of some comfort to the old policemen! After 1829, when uniformed police began to spread across the country, it was standard practice for the lantern to be hooked over the belt which was then worn on top of a greatcoat. The means used was the sprung single lever at the back of the lantern; some models have a further projecting lip at the bottom to stop the lantern falling off when the wearer leant forward. To prevent accidental burning, a large oval leather patch was attached to the belt and the lantern hooked over in front of this. One Midlands force has a record of its men returning from night duty with black faces, having kept the lantern under a cloak to warm themselves. The fumes and soot would rise through the top of the cape, leaving a sooty deposit over their faces and necks.

Oil lanterns persisted in use until well into this century and I have one quite large example dated 1918. Probably some forces had them in use as late as the 1930s but, of course, during this period experiments were being carried out with different patterns of electric torches, of which the standard one was the Smiths Wootton lantern. This was in use in the 1930s in most police forces and, although battery powered, it carried forward many of the features of the old oil lanterns. For example, it has twin handles on the back and also the sprung hook for attaching to a greatcoat belt. The on/off switch on the top of the lantern was capable of being moved slightly to allow a partial light. These were in use until after the last war and then gradually modern type of electric torches became standard.

Inside of a bullseye lantern showing the 'deadlight' which could be turned by revolving the chimney. The lamp was of the wick and paraffin type. Author's collection.

Conditions of lanterns

Whereas it would be almost a sacrilege to try touching up or restoring a truncheon or tipstaff, I feel that, with lanterns, repainting and restoration is permitted. In fact, due to rust and general neglect, there are not many examples which a collector would want to put on his shelves without some attention first.

Types of lanterns

Over the years, I have identified eight manufacturers, but quite obviously there were many others producing their own patterns. It is not uncommon to find unnamed examples which follow the style of some of the more standard bullseye lanterns, but which differ sufficiently to show that they were made by different manufacturers. The companies I have identified as manufacturers of police lanterns are: Hyatt and Company, Dolan, Carron, J. H. Steward Ltd, Smiths Ltd, D. B. Ltd, E. Camelinat & Co. Ltd and T. Joyce.

The following descriptions of some of the different models produced by these manufacturers will help with identification but, given the variations in style and size, look for the three criteria which I mentioned earlier to ensure that yours is really a police lantern.

Hyatt & Co. Birmingham	The products of this company follow the usual cylinder pattern for lanterns, with a ground glass bullseye magnifying lens, the usual handle with hooks, moveable deadlight and sometimes a flare rim around the lens. The chimney at the top of the lantern is nearly always a raised and pointed piece of crinkled metal and this can vary in height from one to three sections, one on top of the other.
Dolan Vauxhall, London	I have seen several examples of these lanterns which usually have a plate bearing the name 'The Crescent Lamp'. Apart from the usual handles and hook on back, certain models also have an iron carrying handle from the top of the lamp. These lanterns are not round, but bow-shaped at the front and square across the back. The chimney follows a similar shape. There is also usually a striker plate for the old type of matches just inside by the oil lamp.
E. Camelinat & Co. Ltd Birmingham	I have only seen one example from this company, but it follows the standard pattern of handles and belt hook for a police oil lantern. The lantern is of the cylinder type but nearly half as tall again as most Hyatt models. It has a double crinkle style chimney.
T. Joyce London	The only example I have seen from this company is a standard cylinder shape bullseye lantern. The firm's full address of 43, Bishopsgate Without is given on a small brass plate and it would be interesting to find out if, for example, they had a contract at one time to supply the City of London Police, since they would have been very close geographically.
J. H. Steward Ltd London	The address given on this electric battery lantern example is 406 Strand, London, and the name of the particular model is 'Orilux'. Dating probably from the 1930s, the lantern has a small bullseye magnifying lens, with a brass disc set behind the lens, containing green and red lenses which can be quickly revolved into position to change the colour of the light. There are many refinements, such as an off/on switch which can be screwed down, and a further flat-topped switch which can be used to flash the lantern. The whole lantern is carried in a beautifully stitched pigskin case. I have no further information regarding this

	firm, nor have I seen any other examples and it will be interesting to see whether, in the future, any more do turn up in collections. However, in view of the neck-strap on the case and the fact that red, green and white lights can easily be used, it is hard to think of any purpose for this lantern, other than police use.
Carron Ltd Leeds	This is a much smaller oil lantern and probably intended to be carried in a pocket, providing ventilation was allowed at the top. The lens is a flat bullseye type and the oil burner very small. The usual criteria for judging police use are not present, but this particular one came with a 'pedigree' of police service.

Finally, I must make reference to three further types of electric battery powered police lanterns. These cannot be shown under the list of manufacturers as the descriptive names could apply to that particular model only. Birmingham City Police in about 1913 had in use a lamp called the 'Cyclops'. Similarly, the Warwickshire Police in the early 1920s used a 'Foster' pattern of battery hand lamp. Unfortunately, I have no further details of this – or of the heavyweight chargeable battery lamp which the Newcastle-under-Lyme Constabulary had in the late 1930s. No doubt many further examples will turn up in the future which will add to our knowledge on the subject.

Comparing these early and relatively ineffectual forms of lighting with the portable lanterns carried in police cars today – which measure their light in thousands of candle power – is just one instance of how modern technology has changed policing in such a relatively short number of years. However, the lanterns that we have discussed in this chapter cover a period of well over 100 years and are, therefore, worthy of inclusion in police collection.

CHAPTER FIVE

Methods of Alarm-Raising

Any person carrying out the basic functions of policing requires three types of equipment in order to effectively carry out the job. Firstly, a means of defence or offence, eg. a truncheon; secondly, a form of illumination for patrolling at night and, thirdly, a means of raising an alarm and calling for assistance.

The equipment itself may have changed through the years, but these fundamental requirements still remain. Guns and tear-gas are now in police arsenals, but the basic truncheon is still a police officer's first line of defence. Similarly, as has been discussed in a separate chapter, candle lanterns may have given way to advanced floodlighting techniques, but the officer on foot patrol still uses a hand torch. Modern two-way radios have certainly advanced communications – so much so that many police forces have considered seriously withdrawing whistles as an item of equipment. However, batteries can fail, buildings can obstruct the signal and many policemen, even today, owe their safety to the humble whistle. During my own years of service there were at least three occasions in which I blew my whistle to alert people during a chase or to summon assistance.

The urge to break with established tradition and to be seen as modern in approach has meant that many items of equipment associated in the public mind with policing have been withdrawn in recent years. Armbands, of course, disappeared from the Metropolitan Police in 1968 and, to my knowledge, only the City of London Police still wear their distinctive red and white duty armbands. Similarly, there are not many forces who still issue capes to their patrolling constables and we all know that in Scotland helmets were withdrawn soon after the Second World War. Apart from the threat from a number of forces to withdraw whistles, there is also talk from time to time of changing the helmet for a flat cap. Should this ever happen, it will be hard to distinguish between the uniformed police and security guards!

Traditions are something which grow with age and we have only to look at the picture of an American police officer, with all of his badges and items of hanging equipment, to see what happens when one tries to create traditions of uniform artificially.

The above observations are, perhaps, a digression on the subject of this chapter but when we consider that whistles alone have been in use for over 100 years, their importance as part of the uniform becomes obvious.

Rattles

In Saxon times when the hue and cry was being raised, attention would have been gained by shouts, the blowing of horns and probably the beating together of sticks. Over the years, local constables and watchmen obviously refined this last method until a form of rattle came into general use. Probably the earliest type would have been a handle with a projecting blade of hard wood with weights attached to cords so that, when twisted sharply, the weights would strike the blade of wood and make a distinctive noise. There is a rattle of this style in the collection at Bramshill Police College and another at the London Museum. Refinements over the years eventually led to the more traditional style of rattle, where two blades of wood, usually oak, are held in a frame and a ratchet turned – generally by swinging – to make the blades 'snap' and create a loud noise.

Early records show that the first 'Charlies' were issued with a bell, lantern, rattle and stave, so certainly by the 1660s the rattle had become an accepted and standard method for town watchmen to raise an alarm.

With the formation of the Metropolitan Police in 1829, it was logical that the rattle should be issued. However, the type generally used by watchmen had been quite large and clumsy and had been carried with the handle usually stuck through trouser waistbands. Since the Metropolitan Police were to wear a uniform, the rattle was made smaller and with a folding handle, so that it could be carried in a special pocket in the tailcoat uniforms. However, as is often found with this old equipment, there was another pattern almost identical in the head shape, but with a fixed handle. Unlike the old watchmen's rattles which normally had two 'tongues' to revolve against the ratchet, these smaller police versions usually have only one and very often are weighted with plugs of lead which help the rattle to swing easily and also be used as a weapon.

There are some patterns of the early, larger, watchmen's rattles which have a knob on the top above the ratchet; with these, it was intended that the rattle would be held in one hand and the knob turned to make the alarm sound.

Some forces stamped their initials on either the body or the handle, but most that I have come across are without identification.

During early Victorian times a policeman who used his rattle would have had to account to his superiors for its use and it could be a disciplinary offence if this was not thought to have been justified. The reason for this was that his Victorian employers did not like to be awakened at night!

The use of the rattle has given us the expression 'to spring your rattle' which, whilst not so commonly heard today, still means to become excited and create a disturbance.

The Bramshill Police Collection has a truncheon which is slightly longer than usual and has a rattle carved into its head. The ratchet is across the top end and the blades are cut out through the body of the truncheon for approximately one third of its length. How effective this would have been is hard to say and it was probably produced in only limited numbers for one of the many smaller forces of early Victorian days – there is no identification on it, however, to show which one.

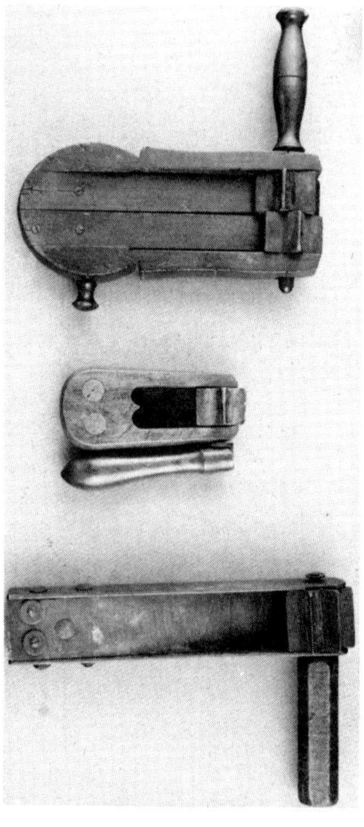

1. Watchman's rattle
2. Folding police rattle
3. Zeppelin Gas Alarm rattle from the First World War. Author's collection.

Rattles and whistles.

From the left – rattles: *1. Early police rattle. 2. Rattle of the type carried by the Watch. It was not swung but held in one hand by the handle and revolved by means of the knob on the top. 3. Another pattern of police rattle – this one had a folding handle. The lead weights can be clearly seen and this made it a useful weapon as well as giving it extra weight when swinging.*

Whistles – from left: *1. Three patterns for the Liverpool police. 2. and 3. Early patterns of police whistles which succeeded rattles. 4. Four patterns of the standard police whistle of later years showing varieties of metals. 5. (centre) Modern chrome whistle and chain. 6. A further pattern of the style of those in 4. Author's collection.*

Whistles

The Metropolitan Police used rattles for over 50 years but, by 1884, it was felt that rattles had become old-fashioned and cumbersome; also, with the increasing background of traffic noise on the street, their sound was often masked. Tests were carried out and it was found that the sound of a whistle could be heard for approximately 800–900 yards, more than double the distance that the sound of a rattle carried. It was therefore decided to withdraw all rattles and to issue whistles – and this in turn was soon followed by the other forces. However, as may have been expected, many of the older police who had carried rattles for all of their service complained bitterly about the change since the weighted rattle had also served as a useful additional weapon.

The first whistles were not of the pattern used today but were rather oddly shaped 'pea whistles'. They were made of a dull grey metal with a sharply cut out mouthpiece and a dome top with a large ring. The ball was made of cork and they sounded just like the football referee's whistle of today. There was a different pattern, perhaps for officers, which had an acorn top instead of a dome with a smaller ring; these were made of a silvery metal. The chains to hold them would not, of course, be chromed. There was no maker's name or identifying mark.

The present form of air-whistle making the distinctive 'beep' sound that we associate with a police whistle came into use at a later date; it was then that many police forces started to have their force's name engraved beneath that of the maker.

A genuine Metropolitan Police whistle will normally be engraved at the top 'The Metropolitan patent' and at the bottom 'J. Hudson and Co. 244 Barr Street, Birmingham'. However, the words which will identify it as a police whistle are 'Metropolitan Police' in the middle of the whistle and a number engraved below the sound outlets. The firm of Hudson must have produced millions of this type of whistle and obviously many were bought by householders in case of need. These were, of course, not engraved with the identifying police force, but in all other respects, including the words 'The Metropolitan', they are identical. Therefore, when collecting whistles, it is essential to look for the name of a particular police force.

When police boxes came into general use in London, constables had a key to these boxes attached to their whistles and it is, of course, very desirable to find one of these complete sets.

There are a number of early, experimental type of whistles in existence which were obviously proposed for the police although to my knowledge they did not come into general use. One of these is a combined pea and air whistle joined in the middle, the 'pea end' of which I assume to have been meant for controlling the traffic whilst the other end would have been kept for emergency use. I have another very interesting model which is fixed to a leather strap intended to be put over the hand, so that the whistle rests on the back of the hand. There is a small fan at the back which revolves and, when blown, this makes a siren-like noise.

One force which did depart from the standard police whistle was the Liverpool City Police who used a rounded triangular pattern of brass whistle intended to go into a leather loop on a crossbelt. This was of the air type and was always engraved 'Liverpool City Police'. I have seen examples in both nickel and brass.

Early type of police or watch rattle.
Instead of having a swing action this one is a hollowed out piece of wood with a wooden clapper attached – thus when twisted sharply there is quite a penetrating sound. London Museum Collection

Metropolitan Police whistle with one of the original keys for the old police boxes. Author's collection.

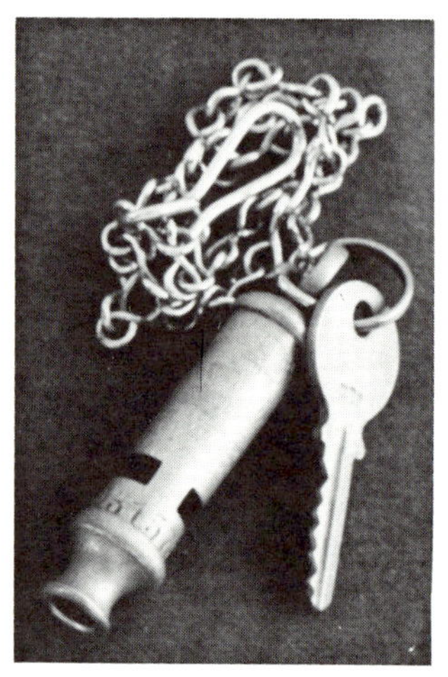

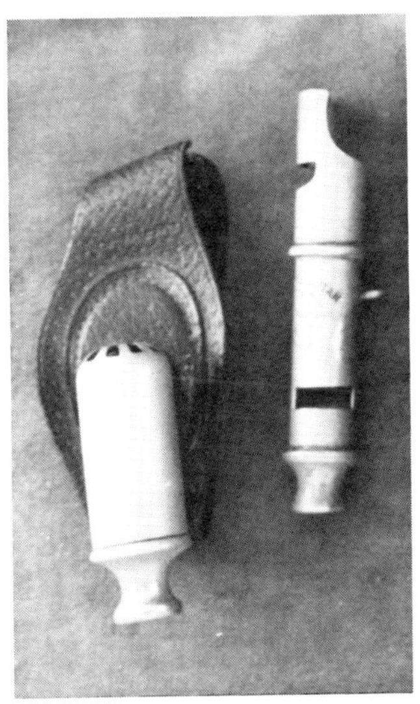

Two early experimental whistles.
The one on the left has a fan and is intended to go on the back of the hand and the second one has both a pea whistle and a wind whistle joined together. Author's collection.

Obviously, other companies apart from Hudson were producing whistles, but unfortunately they did not always put their name on the product. Two firms that I have come across are The Acme City Whistle marked on Kent Special Constabulary whistles and Dowler & Sons, 94 Great Charles Street, Birmingham on early Maidstone Police whistles.

A number of police forces have already discontinued the carrying of whistles but, as mentioned earlier, apart from their historic and traditional value, whistles can still be very useful in places where a radio is either not worn or will not work. I am sure many would consider it a pity if the general use of whistles was to end. The modern pattern of whistle now has a highly chromed chain and body, but the sound has not changed.

Other means of alarm

The use of bells is traditional in the United Kingdom for alarm raising. I believe that many of the early watchmen, as well as the first City of London Watch of 1663 who were in fact known as 'bellmen', carried a handbell instead of, or in addition to, a rattle. I have not personally come across any which have been inscribed or could be definitely associated with police activity – however, there are probably some tucked away in corners and it would be interesting to learn if anyone owns such a bell with a definite link to the past.

Although Huntley House Museum in Edinburgh has one handbell which does have a link with the police, its purpose, however, had been garbage disposal rather than alarm raising. At one time it was the duty of the police in Edinburgh to walk through the streets in the early hours of the morning ringing this bell as a signal to householders that they should empty their domestic garbage into the streets. Following the policeman came the city 'muckmen' whose job it was to rake up the rubbish and remove it. The police apparently continued these duties in Edinburgh until 1856 when the town council established a cleansing and lighting department.

Town criers have also traditionally used bells to attract attention before making their announcements and many of these were engraved with the name of the town or parish. Although this could lead to some confusion over the provenance and use of a particular bell, many of the town crier's calls would have been in connection with crimes and so would have a place in a police collection.

CHAPTER SIX

Police Swords and Hangers, Pistols and Other Firearms

This will be a short chapter since, although issued with swords for many years, the police never had a great variety of them. Examples do come up at auctions and in antique shops from time to time, but they are by no means common. Similarly, pistols and firearms were also limited in their numbers and types.

Swords

Firstly, I should make clear the difference between the two types mentioned in the title. In the police context a sword is a straight weapon, usually worn by officers on ceremonial occasions as a mark of their rank. The Thames River Police was issued with straight swords as late as 1862. These were very attractive items with polished brass handles and their blades stamped with the 'M.P.' cypher and the date.

A hanger was a shorter, curved sword, based probably on the original naval cutlass – its blade of approximately 24 inches was held in a black leather scabbard with brass mounts top and bottom. Hangers were issued to the police, to the prison service and sometimes to Customs and Excise, and since many of them did not have markings it can be very difficult to tell them apart. Some types have a greatly curved brass handguard, whilst others are more angular. All have fishskin handgrips with wire binding, and if you are fortunate you will find the original frog attached to a brass stud near the top of the scabbard still in position. Rather like a bayonet frog, this was made of leather and had a large loop and when attached to a crossbelt was then hung over the right shoulder with the sword hanging from the left hip.

Some police forces also had their name etched along the blades of their swords and I have two for Barrow-in-Furness which not only have the etching on the blade, but also have the numbers '11' and '53' stamped respectively into the brass plate near the top of the scabbard. These represented armoury numbers. I should make it clear that swords were not carried by foot patrol officers as general items of equipment but were kept within the police station for issue on certain duties.

These duties could include night patrols in particularly dangerous areas, patrols in graveyards to protect against bodysnatchers and when dealing

From the top: *1. Police hanger engraved on the blade 'B in F Police' (Barrow in Furness). The scabbard has an armoury number '11'. 2. Short police hanger engraved on the back of the hilt 'Marshall's Office, Mansion House, London No. 15'. This was for the City of London. 3. Thames River Police sword and scabbard. Brass hilt. Engraved beneath the hilt 'MP' 'Field' (for Parker, Field and Sons) '1868'. 4. Police hanger engraved on the sword blade. 'W. Parker Maker to His Majesty. Holborn London'. This pattern is identical to one shown in the London Museum as being carried by the Bow Street Patrol and in fact is probably one of their original issue. 5. Police hanger with curved 'D' hilt. This is of the pattern used in later Victorian times. 6. Early pattern of police hanger.* Author's collection.

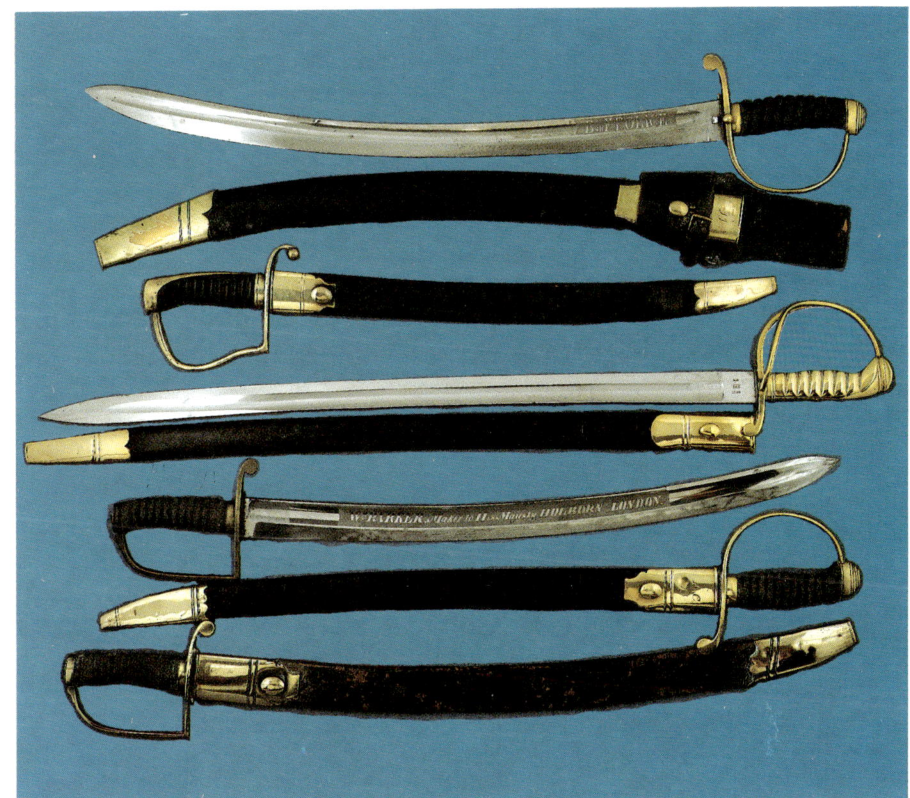

with riots they were on general issue. A body of police armed with swords was a formidable sight and there are several recorded instances when they were used to good effect at times of civil commotion in the Victorian era.

Although prison service swords – and some of the early customs issue swords – are often indistinguishable from police issue hangers, there are exceptions. I was fortunate some years ago to come across two swords in an antique shop which had engraved on their blades 'Chatham Prison'.

The main manufacturer of police swords was Parker of Holborn and the London Museum has a very fine example from this company with the initials 'H.P.' for Horse Patrol on the hilt. This is the only one that I have ever seen for the Bow Street Horse Patrol, although I acquired at auction some years ago an early Parker sword with the engraving 'Swordmaker to His Majesty the King' along the blade. This possibly referred to George III, and apart from the 'H.P.' initials is identical to the one from the London Museum; so it probably was used by the original Bow Street patrol prior to 1805.

Police swords can be expected to fetch quite high prices because of their comparative rarity and these will certainly increase where there is identifying engraving. Research with the various museums and police forces around the country has only brought to light some 300 authenticated police swords in all of the collections.

Pistols and other firearms

Police have always had access to firearms since the time of Sir John Fielding's Horse Patrol in the mid-1700s where the captains were armed

Two pistols.
The upper pistol was probably issued to the Birmingham Police and carries the number 'B7' beneath the crown. The lower twin-barrelled percussion cap pistol was probably not standard issue but is of the type commonly carried by police officers in the mid-19th century. Author's collection.

with a carbine and two pistols. Ranging from the muskets and pistols of the early days, firearms have progressed to the present vast selection of rifles, revolvers, shotguns, tear gas guns and even machine guns.

From the collecting point of view, firearms are a specialised subject and require an extensive knowledge of makers, types and styles. There is also the additional difficulty that any firearm not held to be antique, or that is capable of being mistaken for a modern firearm, or that can be converted to fire, is held to require a Part 1 Firearms Licence – and this is not granted just for the purpose of holding a gun in a collection.

With the earlier flintlock and percussion weapons the big problem is actually to identify a particular item as having a link with the police. Since only selected police stations held firearms, the requirement in numbers was quite small and they were generally bought or loaned from the army.

I have come across examples that have been over-stamped with a force identifying mark and number and, in fact, I bought some years ago a percussion cap pistol with the stamp 'B7' beneath a crown. This probably stands for the Birmingham Police and the '7' would have been its armoury number. However, the pistol also has the broad arrow showing its military origin.

Boxed presentation pistols were sometimes given to officers to mark long service or a special occasion. The Birmingham Museum has a set which was presented to Major Shaw, the Superintendent-in-Chief of the Birmingham Police for 1839–1842. I was fortunate enough to acquire this officer's silver and gold plated tipstaff – also a presentation – so he for one did not have to buy much of his own equipment!

During the 1840s a constabulary carbine was made specifically for the Irish Constabulary. This was a single shot, muzzle loading percussion cap carbine and occasionally examples do come onto the market. Some mainland police forces also probably used this gun.

The dedicated collector of firearms is obviously much more likely to find police-related items than a general collector – however, my advice is to look for identifying marks and initials on all old pistols and muskets that you may come across.

Leg Irons and Other Restraints

The earliest form of restraint was called a 'snitcher'. This was a doubled length of rawhide with both ends put through a wooden handle and firmly fixed. When restraining a prisoner the loop would be put over both wrists, the handle tightened and the prisoner could then be easily led – the obvious disadvantage being that you had to actually hold the wooden end to stop the loop coming undone.

From the 17th century onwards simple handcuffs were being manufactured by several companies. These could be closed, locked with a key for each wrist and then held together by a short chain. However, by the early

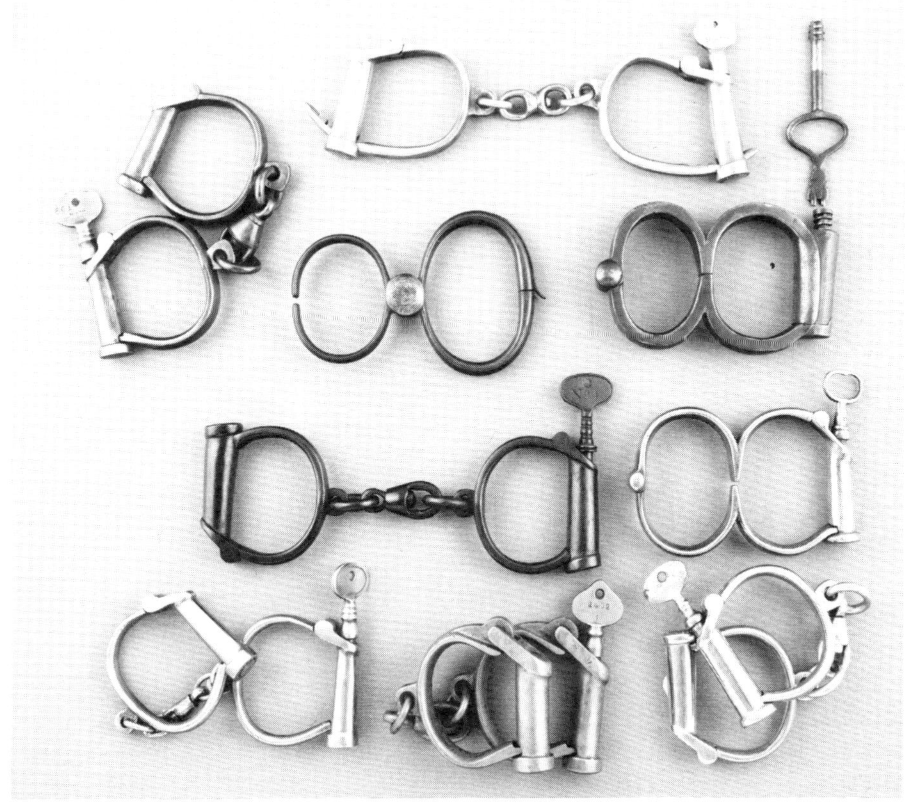

Various patterns of handcuffs which have been used by the police and prison service during the past 200 years. The right hand pair in the 2nd row from the top is a heavy duty prison issue from the late 19th century whilst the 'figure of 8' pair immediately beneath these is of the first style issued to the Metropolitan Police. Author's collection.

1800s the firm of Hiatt in Birmingham was supplying most of the handcuffs and leg irons. This company has been in existence for over 200 years and still manufactures equipment for many police forces.

The general collector is likely to come across several basic types of handcuffs, ranging from the figure-of-eight which locks at one end, to the leading handcuff which has one large loop to go over the prisoner's wrist and a smaller one which can be easily opened to go over the police officer's wrist. However, the type that is most likely to keep appearing is the standard 'D' cuff with chain, which locks individually on each side and was in general use until the late 1960s, when it was replaced by the American-style ratchet handcuff. Handcuffs are found with different weights and thicknesses since women's and children's sizes were made. Earlier models are steel or nickel and the later ones chrome.

Occasionally one can find heavy duty prison handcuffs which have a double lock, and also leg irons which are really larger versions of the standard pattern handcuffs.

Early prison restraints of interest include the ball and chain – usually a cannon ball firmly secured to a length of heavy chain which was then padlocked via a shackle around the prisoner's leg. These could weigh as much as 50 lb and greatly restricted movement.

Full body chains are also occasionally found; these were generally used for conveying prisoners to the assize courts. They consist of a network of chains which secured both ankles, both wrists and, in addition, often had two cannon balls on lengths of chain which had to be carried. They may have been cumbersome, but not too many prisoners escaped!

Pair of Hyatt Leg Irons. Author's collection.

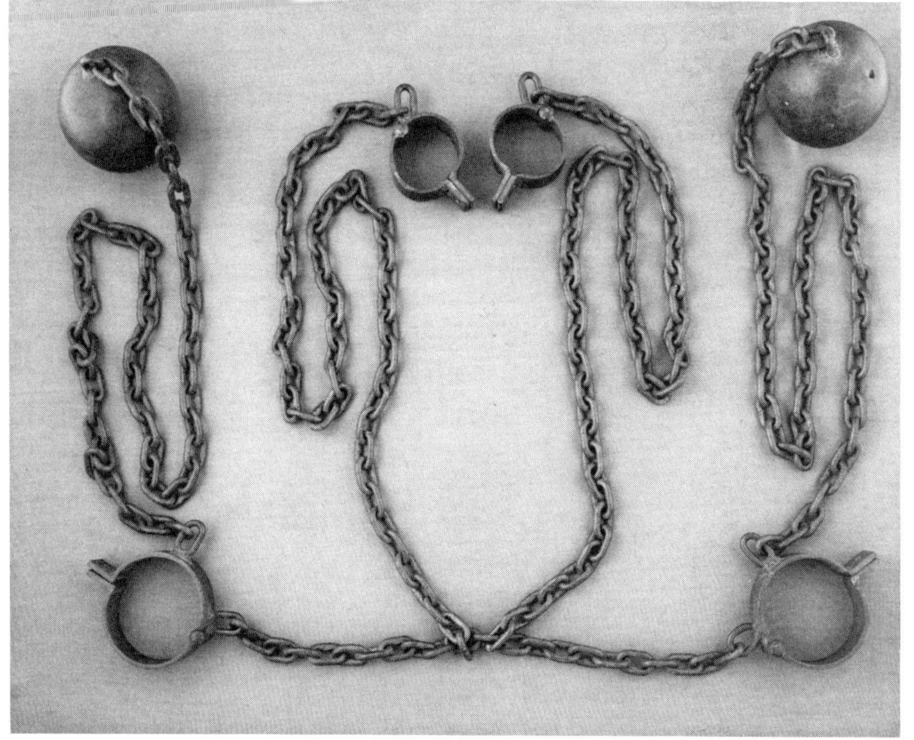

Full set of body chains – or as they were commonly called Assize Chains. They were introduced to secure both the wrists and the ankles at one common point and in addition 2 heavy cannon balls were attached to the ankle shackles with a sufficient length of chain for them to be carried when the prisoner moved. Chains such as these are now very rare and can command unusually high prices when they come up at auction. Author's collection.

Occasionally one finds leg irons which have a longer than usual length of chain between them and a large circular ring in the middle of the chain – these were transportation leg irons and the long chain was intended to be threaded through the central ring to keep prisoners in position when on board ship.

Apart from general examples such as those listed above which obviously have connections with English policing, the collecting of handcuffs has become very specialised with the existence of so many varieties and styles from different countries around the world. I know of one collector in Bournemouth whose collection runs into the hundreds, but these are obviously outside of the scope of a book such as this.

Ball and chain from Belle Vue Prison Manchester which was pulled down in the early 1890s. The ball in this case is a 28lb cannon ball and the total weight of ball, chain and shackle is nearly 50lbs. Author's collection.

CHAPTER EIGHT

Helmet Plates, Badges, Buttons and Medals

One field of police-related collecting which has gained great favour in recent years is that of badges. This is probably because of all police equipment they are the most plentiful and, moreover, badge collecting – particularly in the military context – is an established form of the collector's art in the UK.

Since this is such a big field of collecting and there are so many varieties of badges, I do not intend to go into great detail – however, I will summarise for the novice the different types of badges which can be looked for.

Helmet plates

Until the changeover from the original top-hats to the new style helmets, there was no identifying badge on police headgear. However from the 1860s onwards, each force started to design its own 'plate' to go on the front of the helmet; these vary from the very small to the large ones featuring a sunburst. They were copied from the military badge style of the time – not unnaturally, since the helmets themselves were also variations from the standard army issue. Senior officers' parade helmet plates were often made of solid silver, while the metal used for other ranks varied from

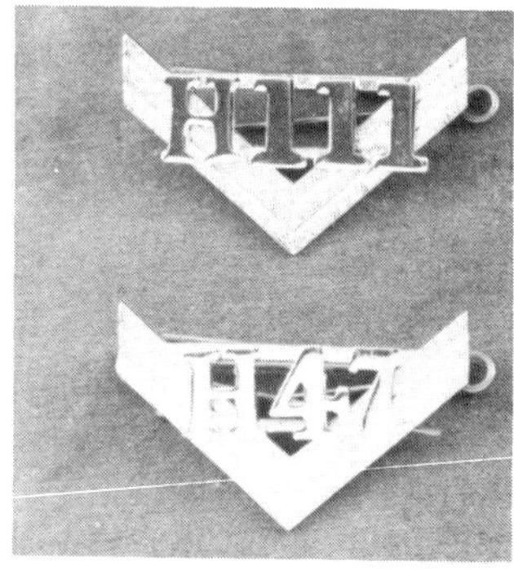

Two cape brooches from the Metropolitan Police Author's collection.

A small selection of the variety that can be found in helmet plates. These are in the top row – Metropolitan Police George VI; County Borough of Barrow-in-Furness No. '54' – reign of Queen Victoria; Metropolitan Police at the time when the Constables number was also on his helmet plate. Centre row – Manchester coat-of-arms, Reign of Queen Victoria; Sheffield City Police King's crown. Bottom row – Hampshire Constabulary. King's Crown. Cap badge – formerly belonging to the Deputy Chief Constable of Staffordshire in 1889. Bristol Constabulary, King's Crown. Author's collection.

Small variety of modern lapel badges, buttons and Inspector's insignia of rank. Author's collection.

Two patterns of breast number badges. The upper one is of the type used by Dorset and Bournemouth Constabulary, the lower one is the experimental pattern used for a short time in the Metropolitan Police. Author's collection.

brass to nickel and chrome; the decoration could include different coloured enamels, gilding and paint.

One of the main attractions to the collector is that, with each change of monarch, there is an alteration to the crown on the top of the plate and where shown, to the royal cypher. Bearing in mind the number of police forces and the fact that we have had five kings or queens since Queen Victoria, there are obviously great numbers of badges required to make a full collection.

Lapel badges

Many county forces – but not the Metropolitan Police – have additional identifying lapel badges. These usually consist of a shield showing the appropriate coat-of-arms surmounted by a crown. Many people now collect these as they are often easier to come by and cheaper than helmet plates.

Shoulder numbers

Although these are collected by some enthusiasts, they obviously do not have the appeal of the large helmet plates. The origin of these numbers goes back to 1829 when it was decided that, in order to identify individual constables, they should have the letter of their division, plus an individual number, on either collar of their frock coat. This was really an extension of the military system of regimental numbering whereby each Foot regiment was numbered and its men always wore that number.

Some county forces have had their numbers made as single units but the Metropolitan Police has always supplied separate letters and numbers with screws on the back which are pushed through the cloth and a small plate screwed on to hold them in position. This obviously makes them much harder to consider as collectables.

However, in recent years, the Metropolitan Police experimented with a chest badge showing its coat-of-arms with a space underneath for the constable's number. These experiments were short lived, but some did get into general circulation and are now much sought after. The Dorset Police still uses this new style of numbering.

Cape brooches

The older cloth capes were usually fastened by two lions' heads with a chain passing between and attaching to a hook behind one head. These were usually well cast and although some were painted black they are attractive enough to collect.

Additionally, some forces – including the Metropolitan – had the police officer's number cast in one piece for fastening to the collar and, in the case of a sergeant, his three stripes were included in the casting behind the number. These were called 'brooches' and are obviously much sought after.

Special constable's lapel badges

During the First World War so many regular police officers volunteered for regimental duty that large numbers of civilians had to be recruited as special constables. They did not wear a uniform but were usually given a truncheon, a duty armband and an identifying lapel badge.

These have become highly collectable since they were attractively made, usually of metal and enamel, showing the coat-of-arms of the particular force, together with its name. Some – particularly those intended for officers – were made of silver, eg those of Oxford and of the City of London. The Metropolitan Police lapel badges were usually of brass with different coloured enamels within the crown – ones that I have come across have been red, yellow and blue and these represent the rank of the individual.

During the early part of the war the Metropolitan Police and some Counties also issued brassards with a pewter plate for fixing around the upper part of the arm and these are usually embossed with the rank of the wearer.

During the Second World War a number of forces again issued lapel badges showing that the wearer was a war reserve constable; the Metropolitan Police had a blue and silver enamel one with the letters 'MP' in the middle and 'War Reserve' around the outside, surmounted by the king's crown.

Medals

The collecting of medals is usually a specialised hobby and, with the high prices involved, one that requires a great deal of knowledge. However, the collector of general police equipment and memorabilia is likely to be offered police medals from time to time and, from my own experience, I will detail these as follows:

Queen Victoria's Golden Jubilee
Queen Victoria's Diamond Jubilee
Edward VII Coronation Medal
George V Coronation Medal
Special Constable's Long Service Medal

These are, of course, all general service medals and not gallantry awards – however, the name, rank and divisional number of the constable is usually engraved around the rim and the earlier ones for regular police were often made of solid silver.

The customary issue of these medals to constables over a certain length of service must have died out after George V since in many years of collecting I do not recall being offered any for later reigns or coronations.

Buttons

There are different categories of buttons and, although the variety is too great to allow me to go into great detail, I will list these to help the beginner:

greatcoat buttons,
tunic buttons – large,
tunic buttons – small,
senior officers' buttons.

Varieties of pewter brassard plates issued early in the First World War. Author's collection.

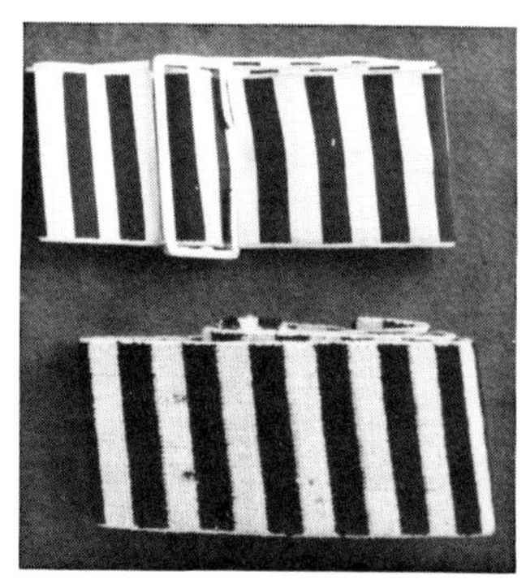

Two patterns of Duty arm bands. The lower is of the type used until the mid-1960s and the top one, the newer nylon variety which was in use until arm bands were discontinued in 1968. Author's collection.

Above: *A small variety of the various special constable's lapel badges dating from the first World War. Three patterns of the Metropolitan Police are given in the middle row. The centre badge in the first row is for the second world war Metropolitan Police War Reserve.* Author's collection.

Right: *Some relatively common police medals which may be acquired by a collector. (From left) Special Constable long service medal. Second row (top) Commemorative medal for the Police Convalescent Home at Twickenham with details of the numbers of serving police in the Metropolitan Police and City Police dated 1870 (Metropolitan Police – 604 Inspectors, Sergeants 1180, Constables 11876. Police Stations 180,* Courts 17). *Bottom. Metropolitan police 1914 long service medal. Centre. Liverpool City Police good service medal. Fourth row. (top) King George V Coronation medal (lower) reverse of George V Coronation medal. Right. Queen Victoria's Diamond Jubilee Police medal. This one has in addition a small souvenir medal of the death of the Duke of Clarence in 1892 at Sandringham. Possibly the officer was on duty at the funeral.* Author's collection.

Most buttons are embossed with the name of the police force around the outside and the crown appropriate to the monarch in the middle. Many of the Victorian examples are attractive since the shape of the crown was very distinctive.

The materials used can range from brass and nickel to the chrome of today. The older kind of senior officers' buttons were often of silver and they rarely bear the force's name – usually just a crown. These are scarce and much sought after.

Belts

Victorian greatcoat belts and those for the early part of the century usually have a fine buckle made on the interlocking principle. The centre of this is usually moulded with the appropriate crown and in many cases the force's name. These belts were substantially made from thick leather and, because of their durability, often turn up in antique shops.

CHAPTER NINE

Helmets and Headgear

When dealing with police uniforms of any description we are really only talking of a span of time covering approximately 180 years, since it was in 1805 that the Chief London Magistrate, Sir Richard Ford, re-formed the Bow Street Horse Patrol and for the first time an organised body of men wore a distinctive uniform when on peace-keeping duties.

The headgear of the Horse Patrol was a form of top-hat which must have had a chin strap to keep it in position during hard riding. I have never seen or heard of any of their uniform descending to the present day, so it must be assumed that it has all perished – not surprising since the most they ever numbered was 150 men.

Metropolitan Police

In 1829, when the Metropolitan Police was formed by Sir Robert Peel, the question uppermost in the minds of the organisers was how to prevent the force from being mistaken for a para-military oppressive arm of the government – Peterloo was still far too fresh a memory for most people. Since the military at that time wore a very distinctive shako, it was finally decided that police headgear should be based on the civilian beaver top-hat. This decision must, obviously, have also been influenced by the fact that the Bow Street Horse Patrol had worn similar headgear for the past 24 years.

The very first pattern of police hat was made of beaver, strengthened with leather side-pieces and a thick leather crown. It swelled at the top and had a cane and wire strengthening ring inside – both to give the constable protection and also for the hat to act as a step when climbing walls or fences in pursuit of criminals! This was probably a good idea in theory, but must have proved very heavy to wear, particularly in hot weather, and illustrations of the day soon show a smaller, more conventional shape of top-hat in use.

The top-hat was worn for 34 years but, in 1863, a new style of helmet was tried experimentally, based on the military helmet of that period, and from 1865 this became the standard headgear.

From left: 1. City of London Helmet modern issue. 2. Ulster Police night helmet with black badge and rose. 3. Helmet for Warwickshire Constabulary – probably Edward VII. 4. Edinburgh City Police. 5. Birmingham Police Officers' parade helmet –the helmet plate is made of silver. (centre) 6. Cocked hat worn by an Assistant Commissioner of Metropolitan Police when on official procession duty. Author's collection.

This pattern of helmet – of which to my knowledge none have survived – would have looked strange to modern eyes. Although the basic dome-shape was present, the brim was large and slightly upturned and there was a raised section running from the top to the back. These were in use for some years but, by the turn of the century, the modern shape with its rose on top had come into general use.

As needs changed, variations have obviously been made over the years to the basic shape, but mostly these have been small ones such as painting the rose black for night use and experimenting with different styles of helmet plates. Other variations have included making a smaller version with a strengthened cork lining inside and safety chinstraps for use with the old 'Noddy' motorcycles (Velocettes) and, of course, the riot helmets which have appeared in recent years.

Provincial forces

The Municipal Corporations Act of 1835 established the responsibility of towns and boroughs to set up a police force and, although many of them were slow in doing so, the larger cities quickly saw the sense of an efficient police force and most based theirs on the Metropolitan Police. Since top-hats were the pattern for London, they also became the pattern for the larger forces. Since badges were not put on top-hats, it is very difficult to identify surviving examples and establish which forces originated them.

There are, in fact, quite a number of these police top-hats in museums and in county police force museums and from time to time they come up at auction. Their description is basically the same as for London and an identifying fixture which can help to show that they are genuine is a pair of metal vents near the top, on either side of which there are seven holes. The

Left: Police top hat – probably from a provincial force. Author's collection. *Centre: Isle of Man summer helmet – Queen's Crown.* Author's collection. *Right: Glamorgan helmet – King's Crown – Probably George V approx. 1910.* Author's collection.

point that must always be borne in mind is that, over the years, film and TV companies have turned out cheap copies for their various productions and, quite naturally, these can cause confusion when they find their way on to the market.

Since the Metropolitan Police was so obviously at the forefront of policing in England in the early days, it is not surprising to find that most outside forces also changed from top-hats to the new styles of helmet at the same time. For example, the last issue of beaver hats to the Birmingham Police was made in 1862.

Personal designs

The first report by the newly established Inspectors of Constabulary in 1857 showed that there were 237 police forces established in England and Wales. Each of these had its chief constable who governed his force with the aid of a watch committee. Obviously, many of these chief constables were ex-military officers and had their own definite ideas on uniform – they could not change the basic design, but had freedom to experiment with helmets and uniform details.

This middle-Victorian period, i.e. 1860–1880, was one of great change and for the collector can cause confusion, since items which may appear in collections or for sale may be thought to have police origins but not be directly traceable from modern equipment. For example, a number of police forces, including Luton and Salisbury, had helmets made of plaited straw painted black for the summer months and in fact in Salisbury even the peaked summer caps were of woven straw! A number of forces also issued white helmets for the summer; Southend and the Isle of Man continued to do this until quite recently. The Norfolk Police had dome-shaped helmets but with a distinctive peak and no badge or rose and when I see illustrations of these I am always strongly reminded of the Boston and New York Police Forces in America of this same period. The Cheshire

P.C. James Tompkins of the Salisbury Police in 1905. The helmet was of plaited straw. This photograph was lent to me by Mr. Tompkin's son, Mr. Charles Tompkins who still lives near Salisbury in Wiltshire.

Back row: 1. Special Constable's cap – approximately 1914. 2. Modern Chief Constable's cap. 3. Inspector's Cap 1914 – Glamorgan Constabulary. 4. Edinburgh Constable's cap. 5. Superintendent's cap from Cornwall – approximately 1930. The changing shapes and styles are clearly shown in this small selection. Author's collection.

Two Police 'tin hats' from the second world war, the one at the top marked 'SC' for Special Constable. The one underneath bearing an Inspector's pips and 'Police'. Author's collection.

County Force had a shako type of helmet with a peak and the body of the helmet moulded to the shape of the head. Of course, there were many other examples of particular forces' own ideas.

The early 1900s seem to have been the time when most forces established the styles of helmets and flat caps that we can identify individual police forces by today.

Modern helmets and peaked caps

For the collector of headgear, there is enormous variety in the different styles of helmets and peaked caps worn by the many forces in England, Scotland, Wales and Northern Ireland. Basically, there are two shapes of helmet, those with a coxcomb and those without – these last can be most closely identified with the Metropolitan Police. The different ways in which these can be varied to show regional and local identification include helmet plates and the styles of closure on the top of the helmet. For instance, for the Metropolitan Police this is a rose, for some forces it is a ball and with the closure for the coxcomb this can be of different designs. Similarly, the band around the helmet can vary from an embossed metal strip to a broad plastic band and, in the case of some forces, a chromed band.

Apart from the earlier Victorian helmets which are quite rare, one of the most sought after helmets by the collector is the Glamorgan helmet of the early 1900s. This had a metal chinstrap which could be slung across the top of the helmet on to a hook at the top and, of course, was very reminiscent of Victorian military helmets. Other helmets which are very scarce are ones from the Ulster Constabulary and Scottish ones – particularly from Edinburgh, since I understand that most of their withdrawn stock was burnt in a stores fire some years ago.

Officers' peaked caps have obviously never been as plentiful as helmets and very few early examples seem to come into the sale rooms.

CHAPTER TEN

Police Uniforms

Until 1805, neither the many and varied bodies of police around the country, nor the eight police offices in London wore any standard type of uniform which would make them instantly recognisable to the public as police officers. However, in that year, Sir John Ford, who had become the Chief Metropolitan Magistrate, reorganised the original Bow Street Patrol which had been in existence since 1763. For the first time its members were issued with a standard uniform which consisted of a blue swallow type frock-coat with yellow buttons, blue trousers, black boots, white gloves, a vivid red waistcoat and a black leather hat – similar to the top-hats of the time.

Because of the red waistcoat, the public immediately nicknamed them 'Robin Redbreasts'. It was their responsibility – as it had been the Patrol's in the past – to ride in groups or posses along the approach roads to London during the hours of darkness.

The uniform was a success and when, some years later, an unmounted horse patrol of approximately 100 men was formed to act as a training branch for the mounted patrol – also to act as a night patrol on foot – the same uniform was issued. Finally, in 1822, a day patrol of approximately 27 men – also wearing the same uniform – was established to supervise on foot the central areas of the City.

1829 saw Sir Robert Peel finally passing the Metropolitan Police Act and, from this time, London had its first organised police force. One of the important provisions of the Bill was the wearing of a standard uniform. Many people tend to think that it was Peel's new police who entirely invented their own uniform – however, the similarity in detail between theirs and that of the Bow Street Horse Patrol is so great that it is quite obvious that the Patrol's uniform was used as the basis for that of the new force.

For winter they were issued with a blue swallow-tailed frock coat which originally had eight gilt buttons, but these were later changed to silver. They had blue trousers and the frock-coat had a four-inch leather stock collar. The reason for such a high stock collar was the great incidence of garrottings in London at the time – strangulations by means of a cord – the idea for these having probably originated in India where the cult of

'Thugees' was rife at that time. The high collar was intended to prevent the officer being garrotted. The 1829 uniform also had the top-hat which I have described under helmets and, as accoutrements, a truncheon in a leather case which was hung from the belt and a rattle which was carried in the pocket of one of the swallow-tails. For the summer months, white trousers of a lighter material were allowed to be worn. Since the uniform was intended to be worn at all times, the final piece of equipment was the armband to be placed on the left forearm whenever the constable was actually on duty.

This original uniform continued in general use until 1865 when the swallow-tailed coat with the white trousers was discontinued. The swallow-tails themselves were removed and the overall tunic lowered so that it came midway between the hip and the knee. Other alterations over the years included the leather stock collar being reduced from four to two inches in 1845 and this then persisted in use until 1875 when it was eventually taken out of service. Whilst the stock may have given some protection against throttling and also would have helped to keep the neck of the tunic clean, nevertheless, it must have been extremely hot to wear in warm weather and would also have restricted head and neck movements – one can imagine that its removal must have been a great relief to all who had to wear it.

After 1887 the leather truncheon case was taken out of service and from that date the truncheon was carried in a special pocket in the trousers – where, of course, it is still carried today.

1897 was an important year for the Metropolitan Police, since that was the first time a new material, serge, came into use to provide lighter jackets. The jacket had a new type of collar called a 'Prussian collar' and also had two breast pockets. This was the style of uniform which continued in use until 1949 when, for the first time, the police were allowed to wear a collar and tie together with an open style of tunic – but only for the summer months. However, it proved so popular with the men, giving them much greater freedom of movement, that during the period 1951/1952 it gradually took over as the standard daily tunic.

Victorian Police Officers for the City of Leicester – outside the Guildhall in the early 1860s. Note the tall beaver hats and the collar flashes with their numbers. Newarke Houses Museum, Leicester.

The Metropolitan Police continued to issue a uniform based on pre 1949 style for ceremonial purposes until 1971, when it was finally withdrawn. The material was a very fine Melton cloth.

Whilst describing the progression of uniform changes from 1829, I have used the Metropolitan Police as the example – however, the various county and town forces in the provinces, which were gradually being set up from 1840 onwards, tended to follow the new styles quite closely, although with some regional variations. Probably, in most cases, there would be a gap of one or two years for the design to become accepted and filter out to the other forces.

Very little of this early issue police uniform has come down to the present day, since in most cases it was either worn out before being changed, or storekeepers burnt the old issue when new styles came into fashion. I do not believe that there is a complete uniform from the original Metropolitan Police in existence now, although there are several well-made copies in museums. The provincial forces seem to have been a little luckier and one or two do have mid-Victorian uniforms in their museums –Merseyside County Museum in Liverpool and Portsmouth City Museum are two where these may be seen by appointment. For the amateur collector, however, it is always worth keeping one's eyes open since all sorts of things come up in sale rooms which may not be immediately recognised for their origins. There have also been one or two specialist police sales in recent years and it is sometimes possible to obtain quite early examples at these.

Salisbury City Police in 1895 wearing winter uniforms. Photograph courtesy of Mr. Charles Tompkins.

Salisbury City Police in 1905 wearing summer uniform with straw helmets. Even the flat caps of the two Inspectors are made from woven straw. Photograph courtesy of Mr. Charles Tompkins.

One of the biggest problems facing a collector of uniforms is how to preserve them and keep the moth away. The other problem, of course, is storage, since they can be heavy and bulky. My own feelings on the subject are that one or two examples are interesting to have from different periods to show the changes of styles. As an example I will list some of my own limited uniform collection which go some way to doing this.

The oldest uniform I have is an 1862 frock-coat for the Superintendent of the Wakefield Police – this was beautifully made with elaborate trimmings including small tassels at the back. I also have examples of the 'Number One' Metropolitan Police ceremonial uniform (pre-1949 style); a Thames River Police tunic from the early part of this century; a 1930s tunic for the Chief Constable of Edinburgh – very attractively trimmed in silver bullion; and finally, the 1960s ceremonial dress uniform for an Assistant Commisioner of the Metropolitan Police. I was fortunate to be able to purchase the latter with tunic, cocked hat and horse-cloak.

Finally, I must give one word of caution with regard to the collecting of police uniform. The Police Act of 1964 makes it an offence to be in possession of police uniform – this is usually interpreted to refer to modern police uniform - which could be falsely used in criminal activities.

Three old uniforms.
From left: *Superintendent of Wakefield – early 1860s.* (centre) *2. Chief Constable of Edinburgh – early 1930s. 3. Assistant Commissioner Metropolitan Police – full dress uniform – worn until the early 1960s.* Author's collection.

I would think it doubtful if a bona fide collector would ever be prosecuted for having items of modern uniform providing they were kept safely and not misused *and* that they had been bought lawfully and not under circumstances where they could have been thought to be stolen property. This can be demonstrated by using a police helmet as an example: a constable leaving the force may be required to hand in the main uniform, but is often allowed to keep his helmets as keepsakes – these could then be lawfully sold at a later date. However, many helmets are 'knocked off' during crowd demonstrations and if these were subsequently sold under suspicious circumstances the buyer could be charged with receiving stolen property.

With all collecting the watchwords should be 'caveat emptor' – let the buyer beware.

Collecting Items of Police Interest

Since their earliest days the police have been a constant source of interest, amusement, admiration and also general dislike by the criminal fraternity. It therefore comes as no surprise to find that in well over 150 years there have been many drawings, paintings, general illustrations and novelty items made in connection with the police. Although some of these are rarer than others, all are collectable and worth seeking out.

Since the items are so obviously varied, I cannot do more in this chapter than give a few personal examples which are within my own collection.

Postcards

These come from many periods but the number that I have are from the early 1900s and show the police in humorous situations. They were, I believe, fairly common at that time.

Some police related items which a collector may come across.
From left: *1. Wedgewood commemorative plate marking the 150th anniversary of the Metropolitan Police in 1979. 2. Four Edwardian humorous postcards. (centre) 3. Police Station cast iron badge for the Royal Irish Constabulary. This dates from 1904. 4. Early Victorian ceramic policeman. His head lifts off so the body was probably intended to hold salt. Unusually the uniform is painted dark green. (Worcester Police wore a green uniform in the 1880s.) 5. (bottom) Two keys from Belle Vue Prison Manchester. This prison was pulled down in the 1890s.* Author's collection.

Pottery

Caricatures of Victorian policemen were always popular as can be seen from the many *Punch* cartoons of the 1870s–1880s. I have one very interesting pottery example of a fat policeman carrying a truncheon and wearing a new style helmet which helps to date this to the period after the withdrawal of top-hats. His head lifts off to give access to the jar, so it was probably intended for kitchen use, perhaps for salt. It is interesting to note that his tunic and helmet are painted dark green, rather than dark blue.

Presentation pieces

By their very nature these are individual and their merit to a collector obviously depends on their quality, intrinsic appeal and past history. Many of these were sporting trophies and as such probably not of very much interest – retirement gifts however, particularly where they have an inscription, can provide a lot of valuable historical information.

Handbooks

All police forces – particularly at the time of their formation – issued guidance handbooks to the constables. These are often quite slim and contain basic rules of conduct with perhaps a simple map of the police area. Often in a hard cover, each had a triangular flap which folded over and had ribbons attached for fastening to keep it safe in the pocket. I have examples of these from Leicestershire, Oxford and from the Isle of Ely and it would seem likely that others were produced as standard items for other forces.

Police regulation booklets for Isle of Ely, Leicestershire and Oxford Constabularies. These all date from the 1860s. Author's collection.

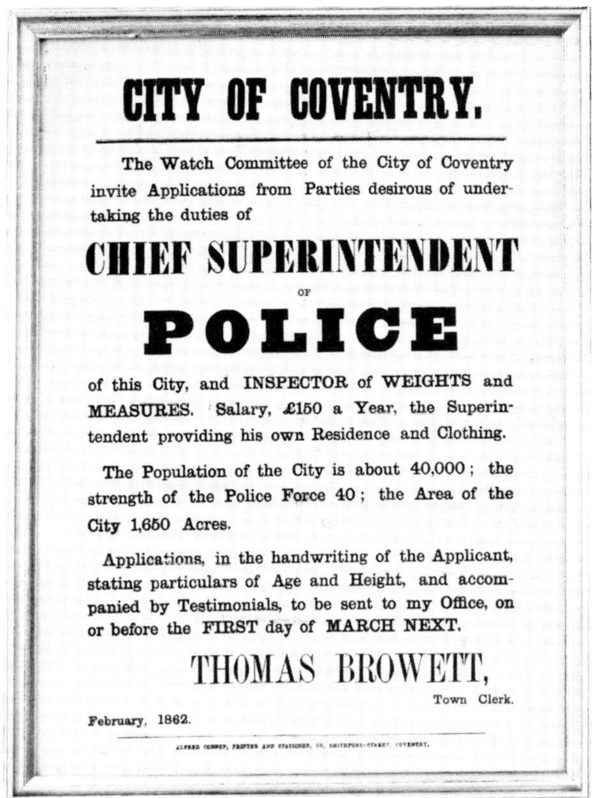

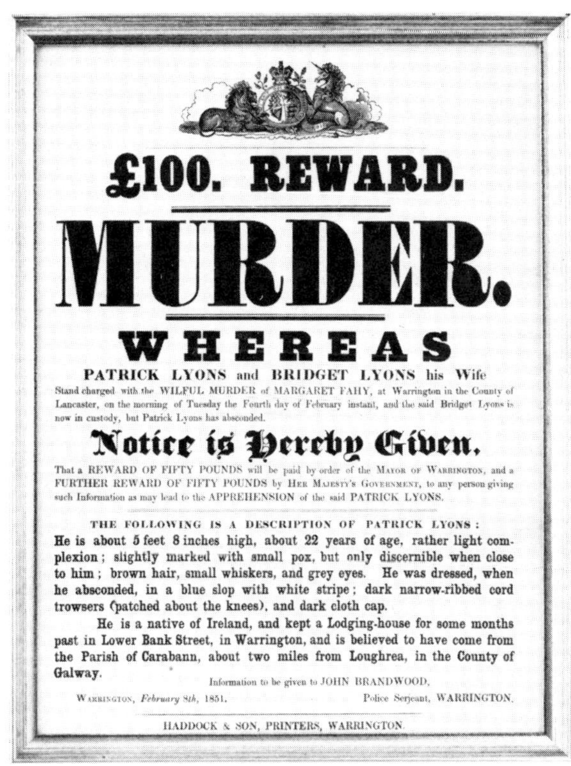

Interesting posters. Author's collection.

Early police almanacs can also be interesting, particularly with regard to advertisements for items of equipment such as handcuffs and painted truncheons.

The collecting of instruction books from later years and of general books with a police interest – such as biographies and reminiscences – is very much an individual hobby.

Keys

Providing that their authenticity is proved, prison and station keys, particularly of cell doors, can be quite attractive to the collector. I have two very fine brass examples from the Bell Vue Prison in Manchester which was pulled down in the 1890s.

Warrants, posters, handbills and discharge certificates

All these are very desirable, particularly the early examples which, in their own way, provide an historical record of the police in Victorian times.

Posters fall into two categories: those advertising for police constables or senior ranks which usually include salary details and conditions of work, and those used for publicising stolen items or wanted persons. The latter are naturally more common than the police recruitment posters.

When a constable leaves the force he is always given a discharge certificate which lists his personal details, his grading for conduct and, on

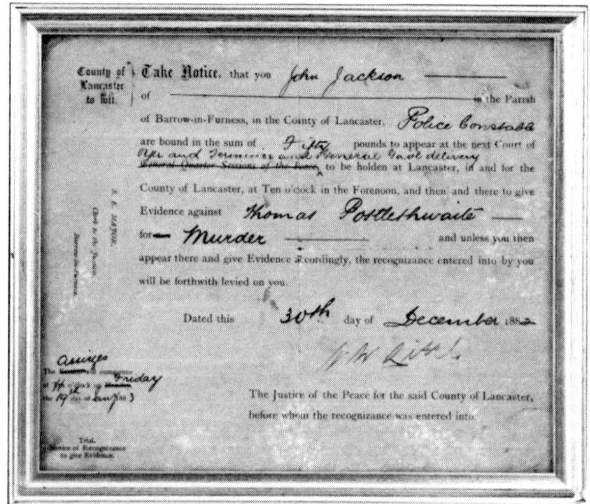 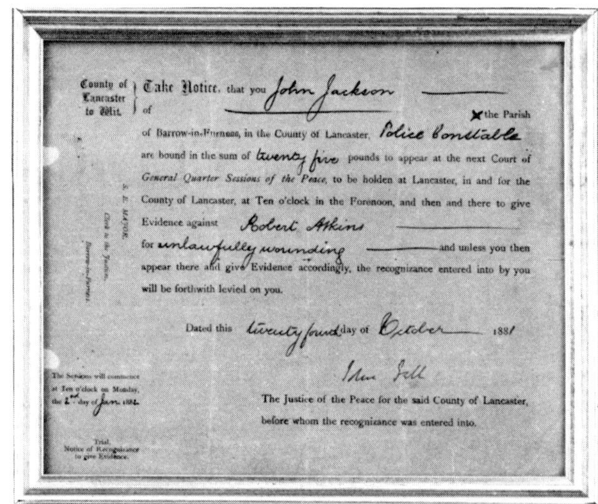

the reverse, measurement of height etc. to prevent misuse. Early examples of these discharge certificates were often on vellum and handwritten in copperplate – later ones are usually typewritten. They are always worth keeping as a record of officers serving in a particular police force at any given time.

Warrants issued by courts for the arrest of criminals are rare, since the warrant usually had to be returned to the court after the arrest was made. However, from time to time they can be found and, if made out for a serious crime such as murder, can be very rare indeed.

Two warrants for the attendance of a police constable in cases of unlawful wounding and murder dated respectively 1882 and 1883. Warrants such as these are rare and always worth collecting. Author's collection.

Photographs

Many of the available police photographs have gone into museum or force archives and, in order to build up as comprehensive a selection as possible, a collector should always consider giving small numbers that he may come across to the appropriate museums. However, the more serious collector who has the right facilities for storage should endeavour to build up his own collection, since pictorial sources are extremely valuable for reference when checking equipment and uniform.

The Colonial Period

Some years ago I was fortunate enough to purchase a large painted truncheon with the crown and cypher 'VR' and words 'Cape Police' within a cartouche. The thought occurred to me then as to whether any other of the old British territories had followed the English style of painted police truncheons? When circularising the British police forces and museums for the survey on truncheons and tipstaves, I therefore took the opportunity to make enquiry from a number of overseas countries. The results have been quite surprising and show conclusively that nearly all of what were the dominions and many of the larger colonies of the 19th century followed the British example, not only by having their truncheons decorated, but also with regard to rattles and in some cases, uniform and other equipment.

Further research will undoubtedly turn up larger collections than the ones traced so far and it will be interesting to account for them in the future. That these accoutrements of law – even to truncheons and tipstaves – should be transported from the mother country in such a way, shows the great liking of the British for stability and tradition. As the curator of one important Canadian museum put it, 'This is a most interesting field of investigation, with a number of social-political connotations'. However, my interest has been purely to track down these items and to make the public more aware of them in their respective countries so that they are less likely to neglect or destroy those in private hands.

The lists following this explanatory section will show by country those museums which hold equipment, together with their locations and other details. There are also a number of countries where admiralty oars and maces were originally used and, where known, I will list these in this first section.

Australia

The early penal settlements of Australia must be expected to have had English style constables, watchmen and prison warders, and in view of their original functions it is natural that their equipment was based on the English pattern of the time.

Truncheons have been reported in Tasmania, West Australia, New South Wales and Victoria and this must mean that there are reasonable numbers still to be found.

West Australia

A number of the truncheons held in the collection of the Western Australian Museum in Perth were either brought over from England by emigrating ex-policemen or were perhaps used by local constabularies, but without changing the designations on the paintwork. The museum has, for example, two Irish Constabulary truncheons and also one which I have identified as coming from Edinburgh. However, the ones which are directly attributable to Australia are the interesting ones. There is one issued to Mr. J. B. Ackland (Sen) who was a special constable in the Mitchem District Police in 1890. This was in Victoria. There are also two William IV (1830–1837) truncheons with the word 'Constable' painted on them and these were brought from England specifically for use in Western Australia. There is a further black painted truncheon which bears the inscription 'Convict Establishment – Western Australia'.

I was particularly interested to see that the museum has three tipstaves in its collection: these are some of the first which I have found outside England. Two of them are identical and are dated 1880. Their length is four-and-a-quarter inches and they were intended to be carried by police officers performing plain clothes duties. They are brass with a crown on the end and have, engraved along the barrel, 'West Australian Police Force Special Duty'. There is of course a parallel with the Metropolitan and Dublin Police Forces of the time which also issued engraved tipstaves to officers on plain clothes duty. However, by the 1880s, warrant cards had come into use in England.

There is a further tipstaff which is seven-and-a-quarter inches long. This has a brass barrel of one-and-three-quarter inches plus a crown on the end and, in addition, a wooden handle four inches long which has the initials 'L.R.' carved on the end. These could have represented the office or the officer.

There are a number of items of uniform in the collection, including two English-made blue covered helmets with silver mounts and a badge which has the letters 'U.R.' above 'Western Australia', all contained within a laurel wreath. Additionally, there is a cream summer helmet of similar shape.

The Art Gallery of Western Australia has one painted truncheon of 17½ inches which bears beneath the crown and cypher 'VR' the word 'Tasmania'. Tasmania replaced the original name 'Van Dieman's Land' in 1853.

Tasmania

The Queen Victoria Museum in Launceston, Tasmania, has seven truncheons with Tasmanian connections, plus three additional truncheons which may possibly have had local use, although one of them is painted 'East Riding Police' which means it comes from Yorkshire.

Three of the local truncheons are around 20 inches long and are painted dark blue with the carved initials 'V.D.L.' – these initials stood for Van

Dieman's Land. The dates given for these are between 1803 and 1853. There are a further three – 17½ to 18 inches long – which again have a dark blue background but this time have a painted crown, the cypher 'VR' and 'V.D.L.' in gold lettering underneath. This again stands for Van Dieman's Land and with the cypher 'VR' means that their date is between 1837 and 1853. The museum also has as a final example, a truncheon with a crown, 'VR' and 'Tasmania' painted gold and red on a black background. The length of this is 17¾ inches and the date is post-1853.

This museum also contains a number of handcuffs and leg irons, together with six rattles of the original English pattern. There are also a number of swords and cutlasses which were used by both the field police and by the warders at Port Arthur Penal Settlement. Two of the makers shown for these swords are 'Beddington & Co' and 'Woolley and Deakin'. There are also a number of guns and pistols, but as with English ones of the same period, they are basically of the military pattern.

The Tasmanian Museum and Art Gallery in Argyle Street, Hobart also has a number of truncheons with local connections, one of which was made by Parker, Holborn. Another has the initials 'C.B.' burnt into its side. They have a further Parker, Holborn truncheon with the crown, cypher 'VR' and 'Tasmania' which again dates it after 1853. Finally, there is one interesting item – a special voluntary constable's truncheon which has a crown and, painted in gold, the initials 'K.P.' and the number '85'. The maker's name impressed on the handle is 'Goules'. The other truncheons and life preservers in this collection are not attributable.

Two Police percussion cap carbines, a wooden watchman's rattle and a police sword. All used in Tasmania during Victorian times. Queen Victoria Museum, Launceston, Tasmania.

Victoria

The Glen Waverley Police Academy of the Victoria Police has two truncheons contained within a small collection of general early items. One of these is originally from Scotland but may, of course, have had local use, whilst the other one is an early Victorian police isssue. Other pieces in the collection include helmets, handcuffs, lanterns and a rattle.

I have been advised that there are a number of collectors of early police equipment throughout Australia and hope that, at some time in the future, it will be possible to make contact with them and find out the extent of their collections. For further information and reference it will also be interesting to learn of any other countries where the tradition of the English type of police equipment existed and I will, therefore, be very pleased to receive and collate any information regarding these.

New Zealand

I have not been able to find any painted truncheons which may have been used in New Zealand, but there are a number of old unpainted Victorian ones which were issued to the Missionary Police and to the armed constabulary.

The possibility must remain that some towns would have brought over the tradition of painted truncheons and tipstaves to give authority to their constables.

Other basic police equipment followed very closely the English pattern of the period; even today the New Zealand Police still wear helmets.

Tipstaff in ebony and silver for Ceylon (now Sri Lanka). The two place names spelt out by the separate silver letters are Madawachchi and Talaimannar. This was probably carried by a resident magistrate or district officer. Talaimannar is a town in the North East of Ceylon (now Sri Lanka) but I have been unable to find Madawachchi, which may well have changed its name since independence. Author's collection.

India

I have found no signs of painted truncheons being used in India and whilst this obviously does not rule out their existence, there are two factors which contribute to their absence. Firstly, relatively expensive painted truncheons would be unlikely to be given to indigenous constables – who more usually carried 'lathes' or long bamboo staves. Secondly, the hot and humid climate would soon flake the paint off.

Tipstaves, however, were most certainly used and only recently in London one appeared for sale. With an ivory handle and short brass tube and crown, its overall length was approximately 12 inches. It was engraved 'Jemadur Bullion Room' and, since this was a rank equivalent to sergeant, it was obviously the symbol of authority for a guard commander at a treasury. Most likely this would have been early in the 19th century when the Hon. East India Company was still the controlling power and had its own troops. There is also reference to a judge of one of the Indian courts actually carrying two tipstaves – each presumably for a different office he represented.

There is also in existence a silver admiralty oar for Calcutta. This is of Indian workmanship and has engraved on the blade the crown, cypher 'VR' and the foul anchor.

Sri Lanka

There is one admiralty oar which is still used in the High Court: 33¾ inches long and of silver, it was made in England in 1802 – although the royal arms are those usually used between 1816–1837. This oar was used originally for the Vice-Admiralty Court of Ceylon, as the country was formerly known.

I know of one other contemporary piece of police equipment for Ceylon, this is a silver tipstaff with the names of two Singhalene towns engraved on it. I suspect that it was probably carried by a visiting magistrate or resident commissioner.

Bermuda

One admiralty oar is recorded for this old colony. Originally intended to show the authority of the Vice-Admiralty Court, it was used as the mace for the Island Council and still functions as such.

Made of silver and 30 inches long, it bears the arms of William III, the foul anchor and the date 1701.

Jamaica

Only one silver admiralty oar is recorded for this important ex-colony. Now held in the Jamaica Archives on the island, it is 26½ inches long and is without markings. I am not sure of its date as it is not hallmarked, but it is possibly 17th century.

Canada

Enquiries in Canada have only revealed one truncheon – this is for Bytown which was later to become the City of Ottawa in Ontario Province. I am indebted to Mrs. V. Campbell, the Curator of the Bytown Historical Museum, for the following details.

The truncheon itself has been painted black in the traditional way and bears the queen's crown with the cypher 'VR', below which is the number '64'. It is believed that the truncheon dates from about 1840.

In 1835, the 'Bytown Association for Preservation of Public Peace' was founded using volunteer constables. This was followed in 1866 by a salaried police force with a chief constable and other constables. Prior to the full-time police, the volunteer constables were supported by the military forces who were stationed at Rideau Canal. The history of Bytown strictly speaking runs from 1826 to 1854 and that of Ottawa from 1855 to the present day.

Regulations were laid down that these original police constables were not to carry firearms, but only truncheons, or as they are called in Ottawa from the French, bâtons. Whilst so far only one painted truncheon has turned up in Canada, it would be most strange if the other towns there had not followed the traditions of the places from where so many of their new citizens had originated.

Probably the first admiralty oar to be presented to a court for many years was given in 1962. The inscription on the oar is 'Presented to the Exchequer Court of Canada, The Ontario Admiralty District by the Ontario Admiralty Bar 1962'. This was a replica of an original oar and it has the royal arms of Canada, the foul anchor and the provincial arms of Ontario.

USA

I have not been able to directly trace any painted truncheons held by American museums, but there must be a strong possibility that some do exist. The original colonies along the Eastern seaboard go back to the 1600s and it is unlikely that they would not have followed memories of home and given their local constables a stave of office. There are a number of American states who used the 'hundred' as a term for small community areas and this must have had its origins in the English hundred of ten tythings.

The City of New York, in its museum, still retains a large silver oar – (22½ inches long and with the royal arms 1714–1801) – which was granted in pre-Independence times to denote its having a court with admiralty jurisdiction. The oar is engraved 'Court of Vice-Admiralty New York'. Where a corporation had such a mace or oar in England, then usually the harbourmaster, water bailiff or, in the case of an Admiralty Court, its marshal, also carried a silver oar. Therefore, there is a strong possibility that these existed at the time.

There is another silver oar (23½ inches long, with royal arms, cypher 'GR' and engraved foul anchor) held by the Boston Museum of Fine Arts.

Even after Independence, the United States continued to follow many of the traditions of England. I found that a number of police forces used rattles during the 1800s – some as late as 1900. These rattles tended to be more ornate and in some cases were larger than their English counterparts – but, still most definitely, they were based on the rattles of the nightwatch in English towns and cities. Similarly, when whistles came into being in the

1880s in England, many American police forces adopted them, although not usually of the later English pattern.

Other police links with England are the felt helmets used in Boston, New York and other cities during the last quarter of the 19th century.

Whilst the American police may not have carried painted truncheons, many of those for the mid-1800s were ornate in their carving and not dissimilar to the larger versions of some English truncheons – which one should remember were not always painted, being often of polished mahogany, walnut or teak. The New York City Police in particular used these carved truncheons and it became a tradition with the patrolmen to make elaborate knots in the carrying cord.

After the turn of the century the American forces can be said to go their own way, since the development of the country was altogether more rapid and the policing problems of a different nature.

South Africa

The British influence in South Africa has traditionally been restricted to the coastal areas and, therefore, it is no surprise that, of the only two truncheons in museums, one is from Natal and the other from Cape Town.

The Cape Police truncheon is shown by the South Africa Police Museum as having been issued between 1882 and 1904 and these dates would match the style of the Cape Province truncheon which I have in my collection.

The other truncheon is for the City of Pietermaritzburg and shows the original town coat-of-arms, together with the dates 1838, 1848 and 1854. These apparently were all important events in the city's early history. The overall length of the truncheon is 16 inches.

After Cape Town was captured from the Dutch in the 16th century, a nightwatch was established and this continued from 1687 until the 1840s. They were known as the 'Rattle Watch' and were obviously based on their counterparts of the time in England. The surprising thing is that a watch should have been set up overseas so soon after the first organised force of bellmen in the City of London in 1663.

There is also an admiralty oar in existence for Cape Town – although this is apparently now in a private collection. Recorded details show that it has the royal arms for 1801–1816 and the admiralty oar. This was the authority for the Vice-Admiralty Court at Cape Town.

With the British being in South Africa for so many hundreds of years, there must undoubtedly be many other old truncheons and items of police equipment which are still in private households and small collections; it is to be hoped that these can eventually find their way into the safe keeping of museums.

South African Cape Police truncheon dating from the 1880s in the style of a Parker, Field truncheon there is the crown, a bold royal cypher and the words 'Cape Police' within a red cartouche. A further example of this truncheon is held in the South Africa Police Museum, Pretoria. Author's collection.

POLICE MATERIAL IN OVERSEAS COLLECTIONS

COLLECTION	HOURS OF OPEN	POLICE MATERIAL	ON DISPLAY	NOT ON DISPLAY
AUSTRALIA				
Glen Waverley Police Academy *Victoria*	By appointment	2 painted truncheons & other assorted early equipment incl. uniform, rattles & lanterns	On rota	Yes – to view contact Curator
Western Australian Museum Francis Street *Perth* Tel: 09-328 4411	Open daily (Not Christmas Day or Good Friday)	4 truncheons with W.A. association + 5 unknown. 2 tipstaves + uniform and 2 W.A. helmets	No	Yes – to view contact Curator
The Art Gallery of Western Australia 47 James Street *Perth* 6000 Tel: 328 7233	Not known	1 Tasmanian truncheon		
New South Wales Police Department G.P.O. Box 45 *Sydney*, N.S.W.	8.30am–4.30pm and by appointment	5 truncheons + rattles, whistles and uniform	Yes	
Tasmanian Museum & Art Gallery 5 Argyle Street *Hobart*, Tasmania Tel: 002-23 1422	Mon–Sun 10am–5pm	7 truncheons + 2 life preservers + handcuffs, leg irons and 1 rattle	Some	Yes – to view contact Curator
Queen Victoria Museum Wellington Street *Launceston* Tasmania 7250 Tel: 003-316777	Mon-Sat 10am–5pm Sun 2–5pm	7 truncheons for Tasmania + 3 unknown. Assorted material incl. rattles, leg irons, swords, guns & pistols	Some	Yes – to view contact Curator
CANADA				
Fort Steele Heritage Park Museum *Fort Steele* British Columbia Tel: 604-489 3351	Mon–Fri 8am–4pm	Uniform only for the N.W. Mounted Police and R.C.M.P.	No	Yes – to view contact Curator
Bytown Historical Museum P.O. Box 523 – Station B *Ottawa* Ontario Tel: 613–234 4570	Summer season only	1 truncheon for Bytown c. 1840, 1 N.W. Mounted police lantern	No	Yes – to view contact Curator

COLLECTION	HOURS OF OPEN	POLICE MATERIAL	ON DISPLAY	NOT ON DISPLAY
UNITED STATES Houston Police Museum 17000 Aldine-Westfield Road *Houston*, Texas 77034 Tel: 713-230 2300 Ext. 361	Mon–Fri 8am–4pm	American police equipment only from 1850	Yes	
Police Historical Society Museum Police Admin. Building 8th and Race Streets *Philadelphia* Pennsylvania 19106	Mon–Fri 9am–5pm	2 rattles (1860 & 1900), 3 whistles (1900–1925) + assorted material	Periodic-ally	
SOUTH AFRICA Africana Museum Public Library Market Square *Johannesburg* Transvaal Tel: 011-836 3787	Daily	1 truncheon for Pietermaritzburg (Natal), 1 Cape Watch rattle	Some	Yes – to view contact Curator
South Africa Police Museum Compol Building Pretoriuss Street *Pretoria* Tel: 021-214551 Ext. 401	Mon–Fri 8am–3.30pm	1 Cape police truncheon + handcuffs & rattles	Some	No

Previous Reference Books

This is the first book to deal with the whole field of Police Collecting – and strange as it may seem, only two have been published in the past on the major subject of truncheons. I have mentioned both of these in the text, as their general knowledge and illustrations have been the main source of identification for collectors over many years.

E. R. H. Dicken's book was published in 1952 and Erland Fenn Clark's *Truncheons – their Romance and Reality* was printed in 1935. Both of these have been out of print for many years and Fenn Clark's particularly now brings high prices at sales. His was probably the more important book as it is mainly illustrations and shows examples of many types – particularly helpful for identification purposes. Quite a number of the truncheons he shows are now in public collections and Bramshill Police College in particular are fortunate to have many of them.

Since the identification of truncheons is often a difficult task, the more illustrations which can be checked the better. With help from the Hutchinson Publishing Group – who took over the original publishers Herbert Jenkins – I have received their approval to reproduce the following pages from Fenn Clark's book. Taken from the original page plates, they are not to modern standards of quality, but nevertheless their detail is all there and they will provide a useful and additional source of reference.

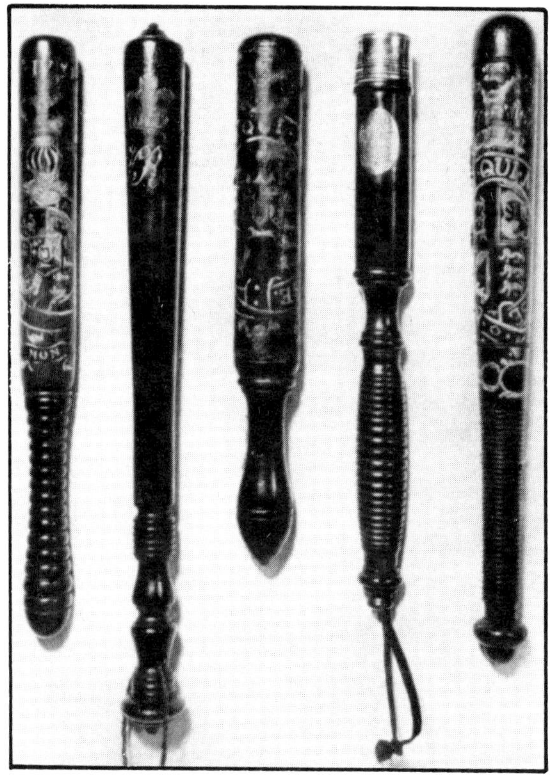

From left: *1. WIVR. Gold on blue background. 2. 'V.R.' Stamped S.O.R. (Sovereign Order Royal) 1837 on handle. 3. G.R. 4. Oak with silver top and ovals. Marked on front 'W. Turner, High Constable Division Warrington'. On back arms of Warrington. 5. 'V.R.'*

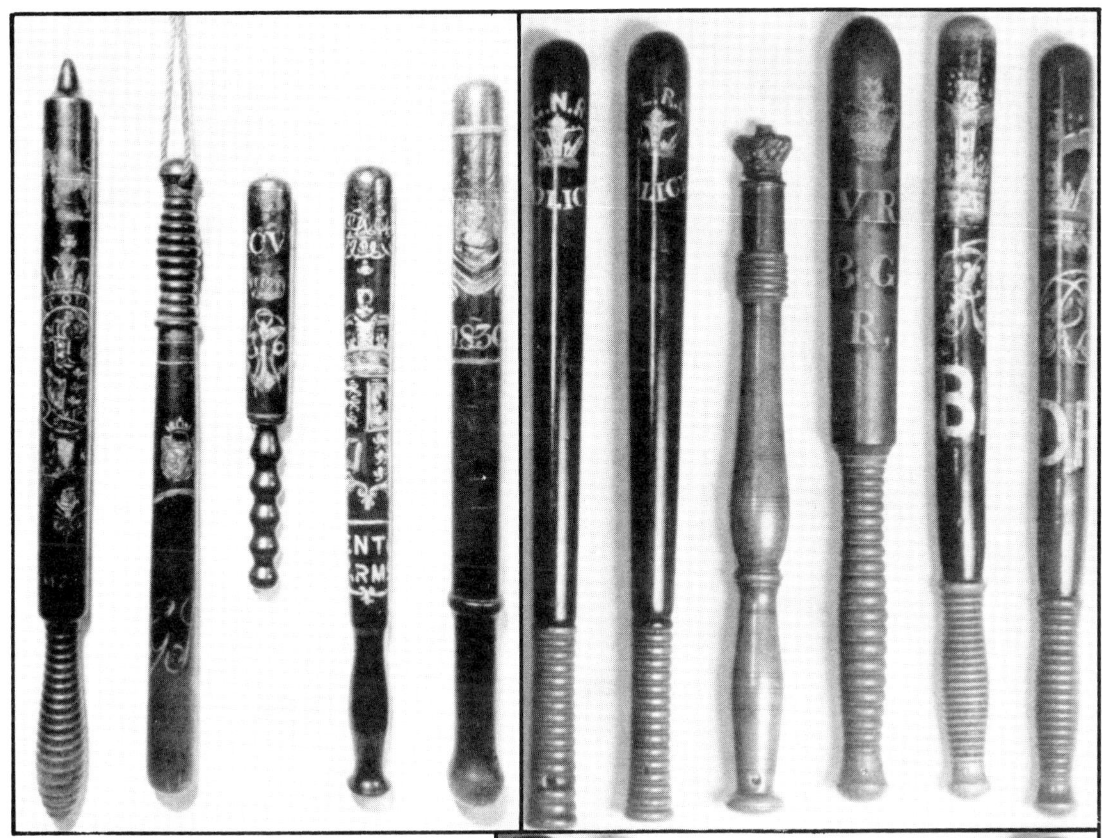

Top left

From left: *1. Inn truncheon, Portrait of innkeeper and details 'H.Ellis' Kings Head, Hampstead. 2. 'G.R.' Devonport Dockyard. Naval Crown. 3. 'R.C.V.Y. Gosport 1834' and fouled anchor (Royal Clarence Victualling Yard). 4. Inn truncheon marked 'Kent Arms'. 5. Inn truncheon. Portrait of the owner and 1830. 'Coach & Horses, Windsor'.*

Top right

From left: *1. 'G.N.R.' (Great Northern Railway. 2. 'E.L.R.C.' (East Lincolnshire Railway Company. 3. Bristol & Exeter Railway. 4. 'B.G.R.' – Birmingham & Gloucester Railway. 5. 'B.D.R.' – Birmingham & Derby Railway. 6. 'S.D.R.' – South Devon Railway.*

Right

From left: *1. 'L.B.R.' – London & Brighton Railway. 2. 'L.B.R.' – London & Birmingham Railway. 3. Eastern Union Railway. 4. 'N.E.R.' – North Eastern Railway. 5. 'G.W.R.' – Great Western Railway. 6. 'L.B.S.C.Ry' – London, Brighton & South Coast Railway.*

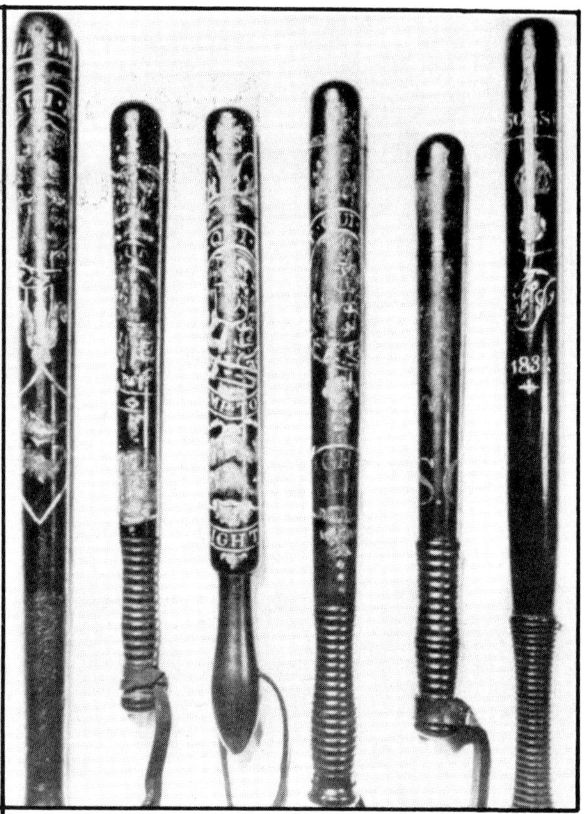

Top left

From left: *1. Carmarthenshire Constabulary 'V.R.'
2. 'V.R.' Sussex Police. 3. 'V.R.' Suffolk Police.
4. Surrey Constabulary SC1867. 5. Suffolk. 6. Sussex.*

Top right

From left: *1. Brighton. 2. Brighton. 3. Brighton –
Kemp Town. 4. Brighton Police. (All four of these
have the Brighton Arms of two dolphins.) 5. City of
Gloucester 'S.C.' 6. East Grinstead. Sussex. 'V.R.'
1832 (?)*

Left

From left: *1. 'G.IV.R'. Rusholme (near Manchester).
2. Havant – Hants. Possibly a railway truncheon.
3. Warwickshire Magistrates. Gilt crown above ivory
circle and with ivory set into base. 4. 'W1VR'
Edgbaston Parish, 1831. 5. 'W1VR'. Coventry.*

National Police Collections in Museums

When I first started the research for this book and enquired of different museums as to whether they had any police artefacts in their collections, I was surprised to find that many did indeed have quite extensive collections. Unfortunately, only a very few regarded them as more than local historical items and in the majority of cases there was very little information available.

I decided then that it would be a good idea to try to establish the exact numbers of truncheons and tipstaves held in the public collections around the country and, to this end, a detailed questionnaire was sent to every relevant museum and to all police forces. Almost without exception I received great help and support from both the museum curators and from those in charge of the police force collections. The result has been the first national survey of these historically valuable objects and one which I consider substantially accurate since only a few museums failed to return the form. Whilst I knew in advance that the total would not be great, I did certainly expect to find at least twice as many items as there are. The numbers break down as follows:

National museums

Truncheons	Tipstaves	Staves	Swords
3007	326	104	74

Police collections

Truncheons	Tipstaves	Staves	Swords
1305	54	22	17*

Colonial period collections in overseas museums

Truncheons	Tipstaves
32	2

The total therefore for all museums, both in the United Kingdom and abroad, together with police forces, is as follows:

Truncheons	Tipstaves	Staves	Swords
4344	382	126	91 (approx)

*Many of the large force museums have extensive amounts of equipment additional to truncheons and tipstaves and in many cases were unable to supply complete figures for items such as swords. The total of 17, therefore, should more realistically be at least 100.

When one considers that the period in question stretches for two hundred years from the 1750s when tipstaves and truncheons started to be used in more appreciable numbers, it will be seen that substantial quantities have undoubtedly been lost, or destroyed, over the years.

There are a number of private collectors in the country, many with only a few truncheons or tipstaves but some with probably many more; during the survey I received details of 47 truncheons and two tipstaves. My own collection, which is appreciably larger than that of any museum with the exception of the Police Staff College at Bramshill in Surrey, includes 360 truncheons, 90 tipstaves, 12 staves and 21 swords. (I only put truncheons into my main collection if they are in a well preserved condition – I have probably another 100 which I keep for reference only.) There are undoubtedly other large private collections, although I have not been able to track all of these down; it would be interesting to find out the numbers of truncheons and tipstaves which they hold in good condition. I have also heard of collections in the USA and in Japan, which means they are probably lost to this country permanently – a great pity.

With the totals given above for the public collections – and assuming that there are at least one-and-a-half times as many in private collections (a figure which could be on the high side) we are still only talking of total numbers of approximately –

Truncheons	*Tipstaves*	*Swords*
11,000	1000	300

These relatively small totals should act as an incentive to all collectors to search out, or locate, as many as possible in order to preserve them for the future and to prevent any further decrease in numbers.

There are a number of museum collections of truncheons, tipstaves and other antique police-related items which are worthy of note and one of the largest of these is undoubtedly the York Castle Museum which has over 224 truncheons. The nucleus of this collection goes back to the 1930s but has obviously been added to in recent years. The Horniman Museum, at Forest Hill in London, has a good selection which unfortunately has not been augmented since the late 1890s when Mr. Horniman, the founder, died. The Science Museum in London has a fine collection of railway truncheons and, of course, there are a number of other specialist museums which also have worthwhile collections. Probably the finest and most comprehensive collection of tipstaves is that held by the City of London Museum – amounting to 142. In addition, it has another 110 truncheons, many of them of very great interest. Blaise Castle Museum in Bristol specialises in brass Bristol truncheons and has 96 of these, together with a good general collection of 50 truncheons.

The largest overall collection in the country is that held at the Police Staff College as Bramshill. Due to the bequests of a number of famous collections – including those of Sir Arthur Dixon and the Rev. Acworth – the total is at least 500 truncheons and tipstaves. Many of those from the Dixon collection are particularly rare and in many ways it is a pity that such an important heritage should be held in a building in the depths of the countryside where, for security reasons, it is unlikely to be seen by many outside of the senior police officers who attend training courses.

The Lady Lever Gallery at Port Sunlight has 76 truncheons and tipstaves which were originally collected for their very fine quality and interest – therefore the serious collector should try to pay a visit. Other collections worthy of special mention are the Ashmolean at Oxford which has 67 truncheons, mainly associated with Oxford; the Newarke Houses Museum in Leicestershire with 161 truncheons and tipstaves; the Bridewell Museum at Norwich with 120 truncheons and the Birmingham City Museum and Art Gallery which has an interesting collection and also the Plymouth Museum for their collection of tipstaff/maces of local interest.

I would like to take this opportunity to thank all of the officials, both within the museums service and from the various police force headquarters, who have been so helpful in arranging details of their collections for the survey and also in providing additional help and information. Without wishing in any way to belittle the help given to me by the other museums, I would particularly like to acknowledge the Commandant and librarian at Bramshill Police College; Mrs. A. Herries, and the staff at the London Museum; the Greenwich Maritime Museum and the curator of the Worshipful Company of Goldsmiths. Readers interested is seeing some of the existing collections for themselves will find these listed in the following section, together with an indication of the numbers and type of exhibit.

Please note that museums are listed alphabetically under towns while the police collections are listed alphabetically under the name of the police force.

NATIONAL POLICE COLLECTIONS
IN PUBLIC MUSEUMS

MUSEUM	HOURS OF OPENING	POLICE MATERIAL	ON DISPLAY
Abergavenny Museum Castle Street *Abergavenny* Tel: 0873-4282	Winter: Mon–Sat Summer: daily	3 truncheons and assorted material	No – to view contact Curator
Ceredigion Museum Coliseum Terrace Road *Aberystwyth* Tel: 0970-617911 Ext. 252	Mon–Sat	2 truncheons	Yes
Abingdon Museum County Hall Market Place *Abingdon*, Berks Tel: 0235-23703	Daily	15 truncheons – beadles' staves including 1 gaoler's	Yes. Some – to view contact Librarian
Monklands District Council Collection c/o Airdrie Public Library Wellwynd, *Airdrie* Tel: Airdrie 63221	Not advised	4 truncheons, 11 sets handcuffs	Some – to view contact Librarian
Aldeburgh Moot Hall *Aldeburgh*, Suffolk	Summer: daily	1 Wm IV staff	Yes
Alnwick Castle Museum *Alnwick*, Northumberland Tel: 0665-602207	Not advised	1 truncheon – 1817	Not advised
Arbroath Abbey Abbot's House *Arbroath* Tel: 031-226 2570	Not advised	2 truncheons	Not advised
Armagh Co. Museum The Mall *East Armagh* Tel: 0861-523070	Mon–Sat	2 truncheons. Extensive collection of uniforms, helmets from Armagh City Watch & Royal Irish Constabulary	Some. Others to view contact Curator
Arundel Castle *Arundel*, West Sussex Tel: 0903-882173	April to Oct Not on Sat	3 truncheons, 4 long staves of office	No. Private appointments – contact Curator

MUSEUM	HOURS OF OPENING	POLICE MATERIAL	ON DISPLAY
Ashburton Museum 1 West Street *Ashburton*, Devon Tel: 0364-53278	4 days weekly	2 truncheons	Yes
Ashwell Village Museum *Swan St. Ashwell* Nr. Baldock, Herts	Not advised	4 truncheons & assorted material	Yes
Buckinghamshire County Museum Church Street *Aylesbury* Tel: 0296-82158 & 88849	Mon–Sat	29 truncheons, 1 tipstaff & assorted material	Yes
Old House Museum Off Church Lane *Bakewell* Derbyshire	Daily: Easter to Oct	Some police material	No. Yes – to view contact G. P. Challenger at Museum
Banbury Museum 8 Horsefair *Banbury* Tel: 0295-59855	Summer: Mon–Sat Winter: Mon, Wed & Sat	22 truncheons (including some illustrated in Fenn Clark's book) + assorted material	Some. Others at Woodstock
Museum of Welsh Antiquities Univ. Col. of N. Wales *Bangor* Tel: 2048-351151 Ext. 437	Tues–Sat	8 truncheons + rattles + some assorted material	Some. Others – to view contact Curator by letter
The Bowes Museum *Barnard Castle* Co. Durham Tel: 0833-37139	Summer: daily Winter: Sun pm only	2 truncheons + assorted material	Some. Others – to view contact Curator
Barnet Museum 31 Wood Street *Barnet*, Herts Tel: 01-449 0321 Ext. 4	Winter: Tues & Thurs pm Summer: same + all day Sat	6 truncheons, 4 staves of office	Yes
St. Anne's Chapel Civic Centre *Barnstaple* Tel: 0271-72511	Summer: weekdays (except Wed pm only)	2 truncheons, 10 staves, 2 tipstaves	Yes

MUSEUM	HOURS OF OPENING	POLICE MATERIAL	ON DISPLAY
The Furness Museum Ramsden Square *Barrow-in-Furness* Tel: 0229-20650	Thurs & Sat 10am–1pm All day other days. Closed Sun & Bank Hols	1 sword, 1 riot shield	Yes
Bagshaw Museum Wilton Park *Batley* Tel: 472514	Open daily Sun pm only	7 truncheons and assorted material	Some. Others – to view contact Curator
Beamish North of England Open Air Museum *Beamish Hall* Stanley, Co. Durham Tel: 0207-31811	Summer: daily Winter: Tues–Sun	27 truncheons (12 painted) & assorted material	No – to view contact Curator
Bedford Museum Castle Lane *Bedford* Tel: 0234-53323	All day Tues–Sat Sun pm only	12 truncheons, 6 tipstaves & assorted material	Yes
Bedale Hall Museum *Bedale* N. Yorks Tel: 0677-23131		3 truncheons	
Berwick-on-Tweed Museum 32 Marygate *Berwick* Tel: 0289-307320	Summer: daily Sat pm only	2 truncheons, leg irons	Yes
The Town Hall Marygate *Berwick-on-Tweed* Tel: 0289-307433	Variable	leg irons, branding iron	Yes
Bexley Museum Hall Place Bourne Road *Bexley* Tel: Crayford 526574	Mon, Thurs, Sat	2 truncheons, 1 stave of office	No – to view contact Museum
The Biggar Museum Gladstone Court *Biggar* Tel: 0899-21050	Easter to end Oct	6 truncheons	Most. Others – to view contact Museum
City Museum & Art Gallery Chamberlain Square *Birmingham* Tel: 021-235 4202	Mon–Sat Sun pm	54 truncheons, 5 tipstaves + pistols, swords & assorted material	Some. Others – to view contact Keeper of Local History
Bolton Museum & Art Gallery Le Mans Crescent *Bolton* Tel: 0204-22311	Daily – not Wed & Sun	1 truncheon	Some. Others – to view contact Curator
Bolton Local History Museum All Saints Street *Bolton*	Not advised	2 truncheons	Some. Others – contact Curator, Bolton Museum
Russell-Cotes Museum Bournemouth East Cliff *Bournemouth* Tel: 0202-21009		Some material associated with local force	
Bridport Museum & Art Gallery South Street, *Bridport* Tel: 0308-22116	Winter: am only Summer: all day Closed Sat, Thurs & Sun	1 truncheon	No – to view contact Curator
Brighton Museum Church Street *Brighton* Tel: 0273-603005	Tues–Fri	20 truncheons & assorted material	No – to view contact Curator
Blaise Castle Museum Henbury *Bristol* Tel: 0272-506789	Sat–Wed Some Bank Hols	96 Bristol truncheons, 50 general truncheons, & much associated material	Yes
Towneley Hall Art Gallery & Museum *Burnley*, Lancs Tel: 0282-24213	Daily except Sat	16 truncheons & assorted material	Periodically. Some – to view contact Curator
Bury Art Gallery and Museum Moss Street *Bury* Tel: 061-761 4021 Ext. 54	Daily except Sun	11 truncheons + assorted material including Sir Robert Peel's cradle!	Most. Some – to view contact Curator
Moyse's Hall Museum Cornhill *Bury St. Edmunds* Tel: 63233 Ext. 236	Daily	8 truncheons + assorted material including items from county goal	Yes

MUSEUM	HOURS OF OPENING	POLICE MATERIAL	ON DISPLAY
Surrey Heath Museum 271 London Road *Camberley* Tel: 0276-64483	Not advised	1 truncheon	Some. Others – to view contact Curator
The Welsh Folk Museum St. Fagans *Cardiff* Tel: 0222-569441	Daily Sun pm only	32 truncheons, 3 tipstaves, 9 handcuffs and assorted material including stocks, gibbet, irons	Some. Others – to view contact Curator
Carlisle Museum & Art Gallery Castle Street *Carlisle* Tel: 0228-34781	All day: Mon-Sat Sun in late May to August	16 truncheons & assorted material	No – contact Social History Assistant
Carmarthen Museum Abergwili *Carmarthen* Tel: 0267-231691	Mon-Sat	10 truncheons + assorted material	Yes
West Gate *Canterbury* Tel: 52747	Summer: Mon–Sat	Some truncheons + assorted material	Yes
Chelmsford & Essex Museum Oaklands Park Moulsham Street *Chelmsford* Tel: 0245-353066 or 260614	Daily Sun pm only	16 truncheons + assorted material	Possibly. If not contact Curator
Cheltenham Art Gallery & Museum 40 Clarence Street *Cheltenham* Tel: 0242-37431	Mon–Sat	16 truncheons, 4 tipstaves and assorted material	Some in rotation. Others – to view contact Dr. S. Blake
Chepstow Museum Gwy House Bridge Street *Chepstow* Tel: 029-125981	Summer: daily Sun pm only	2 truncheons	Yes
Grosvenor Museum 27 Grosvenor Street *Chester* Tel: 0244-21616	Daily Sun pm only	9 truncheons, 3 staves of office + assorted material	No – to view contact P. J. Broughton

MUSEUM	HOURS OF OPENING	POLICE MATERIAL	ON DISPLAY
Chichester District Museum 29 Little London *Chichester* Tel: 0243-784683	Tues–Sat	1 truncheon and assorted material	No – to view contact A. E. Bone
Yelde Hall Place Museum Market Place *Chippenham* Tel: Chippenham 651488	Mon–Sat April to Nov	Circulars from 1850s	No – to view contact Curator
Red House Museum Quay Road *Christchurch*, Dorset Tel: 0202-482860	Tues–Sat Sun pm only	5 truncheons, 3 tipstaves, 1 beadle's staff	Yes
Colchester & Essex 14 Ryegate Road *Colchester* Tel: 0206-577475	Weekdays	30 truncheons + assorted material	Possible displays. Otherwise to view contact Curator
Cotswold Countryside Collection Northleach, Glos Tel: 04516-715	April to Oct	Some assorted material	Some. Others – to view contact Curator
Herbert Art Gallery Jordan Well *Coventry* Tel: 0203-25555 Ext. 2934	Daily Sun pm only	5 truncheons + assorted material	No – to view contact Mr. D. Janes
Darlington Museum Tubwell Row *Darlington* Tel: 0325-463795	Daily	6 truncheons + assorted material	Yes
Dartford Borough Museum Market Street *Dartford*, Kent Tel: 0322-27266 Ext. 146	Daily	9 truncheons, 1 stave of office, 2 tipstaves + assorted material	No – to view contact Curator
Deal Town Hall Tel: 0304-361161 Ext. 262		5 truncheons, 7 tipstaves	No. Viewing by appointment only
Derbyshire Schools Resources Centre Kedlestone Road *Derby* Tel: 0332-371921	Mon–Fri	5 truncheons	Yes. Some – to view contact Peter Good

MUSEUM	HOURS OF OPENING	POLICE MATERIAL	ON DISPLAY
Devizes Museum 41 Long Street *Devizes* Tel: Devizes 2765	Tues-Sat	17 truncheons incl. 5 Union truncheons + assorted material	Yes
Doncaster Museum & Art Gallery Chequer Road *Doncaster* Tel: 0302-62095	Not advised	10 truncheons, 2 staves, 1 tipstaff	Some. Others – to view contact Curator
Dorset County Museum *Dorchester* Tel: 62735	Mon–Sat	11 truncheons	No – to view contact Mr. J. O. Roberts
Dover Museum Ladywell *Dover* Tel: 0304-201066	Daily except Wed & Sun	7 truncheons, 2 tipstaves	Yes
National Museum of Ireland Kildare Street *Dublin* 2 Tel: 01-765521	Daily except Mon	Uniforms of Royal Irish Constabulary	No – to view contact Curator
Dundee Museum & Art Gallery Albert Square *Dundee* Tel: 0382-27643	Mon–Sat	9 truncheons, 3 tipstaves and assorted material	Most. Rest to view contact Curatorial Assistant
Huntly House Museum 142 Canongate *Edinburgh* 8 Tel: 031-225 2424 Ext. 6689	Mon–Sat Sun during Festival only	6 truncheons + assorted material Fine collection of tipstaves	Yes
National Museum of Antiquities Queen Street *Edinburgh* Tel: 031-556 8921	Daily	6 truncheons + assorted material	Some. Others – to view contact Curator
The Almonry Museum Abbey Gate *Evesham*, Worcs. Tel: 0386-6944	Easter to Sept: daily except Mon	4 truncheons + assorted material including items from Evesham gaol	Some. Others – to view contact Curator
Rougemont House Museum Castle Street *Exeter* Tel: Exeter 56724	Tues–Sat	7 truncheons, 2 tipstaves	Yes

MUSEUM	HOURS OF OPENING	POLICE MATERIAL	ON DISPLAY
Farnham Museum 38 West Street *Farnham* Surrey Tel: 0252-715094	Tues–Sat	8 truncheons + assorted material	No – to view contact Keeper
Dunfermline Museum Viewfield *Fife* Tel: 0383-721814	Mon–Fri	9 truncheons + assorted material	Yes
Gainsborough Old Hall Parnell Street *Gainsborough* Tel: Gainsborough 2669	Not advised	3 truncheons	No
Gateshead Libraries Prince Consort Road *Gateshead* Tel: Gateshead 773478	Daily	1 truncheon	No – to view contact Librarian
Peoples Palace Museum Glasgow Green *Glasgow* Tel: 041-554 0223	Daily	18 truncheons, 3 tipstaves, 7 velvet covered ceremonial batons + assorted material	Yes (rotated). Some – to view contact Curator
Gloucester Folk Museum 99/103 Westgate Street *Gloucester* Tel: 0452-26467	Mon–Sat Closed Bank Hols	18 truncheons, 1 stave + assorted material	No – to view contact Curator
Godalming Museum Old Town Hall High Street *Godalming* Tel: 04868-4104 Ext. 545	Tues, Fri, Sat pm only	2 truncheons, 2 tipstaves	Not advised
Gravesend Museum High Street *Gravesend*	Daily except Wed & Sun	3 staves	Some. Others – contact Curator by letter
Thurrock Local History Museum Orsett Road *Grays*, Essex Tel: 0375-33325	Mon–Sat	2 staves of office + assorted material	Yes
Tolhouse Museum Tolhouse Street *Great Yarmouth* Tel: 0493-55746	Mon–Fri	4 truncheons + assorted material	Some. Others – to view contact Curator

MUSEUM	HOURS OF OPENING	POLICE MATERIAL	ON DISPLAY
Westholme Galleries Westholme Road *Grimsby* Tel: 0472-59161 Ext. 401	Mon–Sat Closed Bank Hols	7 truncheons	No – to view contact Curator
Guildford Museum Castle Arch *Guildford* Tel: 0483-503497	Mon–Sat	20 truncheons + assorted material	Some. Others – to view contact Curator
Bankfield Museum & Art Gallery Boothtown Road *Halifax* Tel: 0422-54823	Daily	19 truncheons, 24 police hangers + assorted material	No – to view contact Curator
Hartlebury Castle Nr. Kidderminster Tel: 0299-250416	Summer: daily except Sat	15 truncheons, 2 tipstaves + assorted material	Varies
Gray Art Gallery & Museum Clarence Road *Hartlepool* Tel: 0429-66522 Ext. 259	Daily	1 truncheon, 1 stave	Yes. Some – to view contact Museum Assistant
Hastings Museum & Art Gallery John's Place Cambridge Road *Hastings* Tel: 0424-435952	Daily	8 truncheons, 1 stave + assorted material	Yes, some at Old Town Hall Museum
Hatfield House *Hatfield*, Herts Tel: Hatfield 62823	Tues–Sun & Bank Hol Mon	2 truncheons	No – apply to Librarian
Hawick Museum & Art Gallery Wilton Lodge Park *Hawick*, Roxburghshire Tel: 0450-73457	Check with Museum	4 truncheons + assorted material	Yes
Castle Museum & Art Gallery The Castle *Haverfordwest* Tel: 0437-3708	Summer: Mon–Sat Winter: Tues–Sat	Some material but few details supplied	No – apply to Curator

MUSEUM	HOURS OF OPENING	POLICE MATERIAL	ON DISPLAY
Helston Folk Museum The Old Butter Market *Helston*, Cornwall Tel: 03265-61672	Mon–Sat Wed am only	6 truncheons, 1 tipstaff + assorted material	Yes
Hereford City Museum Broad Street *Hereford* Tel: 0432-268121 Ext. 207	Mon–Fri	Truncheons (quantity unknown) + assorted material	Occasion-ally
Herne Bay Museum Herne Bay Library High Street *Herne Bay*	Mon–Sat	5 truncheons, 1 beadle's staff + assorted material	Some. Others – to view contact Curator
Wycombe Chair Museum Castle Hill House Priory Avenue *High Wycombe* Tel: 0494-23879	Daily except Wed	1 truncheon + assorted material	Yes
Hitchin Museum & Art Gallery Paynes Park *Hitchin*, Herts Tel: 0462-34476	Mon–Sat Closed Bank Hols	8 truncheons	Some. Others – to view contact Curator
Allhallowes Museum High Street *Honiton*, Devon	Summer: Mon–Sat	3 truncheons + assorted material	Possibly
Horsham Museum 9 The Causeway *Horsham* Tel: 0403-54959	Tue–Fri pm All day Sat	5 truncheons + leg irons & manacles	Yes
Hove Museum of Art 19 New Church Road *Hove* Tel: 0273-779410	Not advised	4 truncheons	Yes
Tolson Memorial Museum Ravensknowle Park Wakefield Road *Huddersfied* Tel: 0482-30591	Daily Sun pm only	26 truncheons, 2 tipstaves + assorted material	Most. Others – to view contact Curator
Hythe Museum Oaklands Stave Street *Hythe*	Weekdays except Tues	5 truncheons + assorted material	Yes

MUSEUM	HOURS OF OPENING	POLICE MATERIAL	ON DISPLAY
Ilfracombe Museum Wilder Road *Ilfracombe* Tel: 0271-63541	Summer: daily Winter: am only	1 truncheon + some assorted material	Yes
Inverness Museum & Art Gallery Castle Wynd *Inverness* Tel: 0463-237114	Mon–Sat	2 truncheons + local uniforms	Some. Others – to view contact Mrs. E. Halley
Ipswich Museum High Street *Ipswich* Tel: 0473-213761	Mon–Sat	17 truncheons, 1 tipstaff, 2 beadles' staves + assorted material	Some. Others – to view contact Curator
Manx Museum & National Trust Kingswood Grove Douglas, *I.O.M.* Tel: 0624-5522	Mon–Sat	25 truncheons (all Isle of Man) + assorted material	Most. Others – to view contact Curator
Arreton Manor Arreton, *I.O.W.* Tel: 0983-528134		2 truncheons	
Carisbrooke Castle Museum Newport, *I.O.W.* Tel: 0983-523112	Daily Winter: Sun pm only	4 truncheons + assorted material	Yes
Jedburgh Castle Jail Castlegate *Jedburgh*	Not advised	1 truncheon + assorted material	Yes
The Museum Pier Road St. Helier *Jersey*, C.I.	Not advised	25 truncheons (incl. tipstaves)	Yes
Cliffe Castle Museum Spring Gardens Lane *Keighley* Tel: 0535-64184	Tues–Sat Not Good Fri	103 truncheons (painted), 23 truncheons (unpainted) + assorted material	Some. Others – to view contact Keeper
Abbot Hall Museum *Kendal* Tel: 0539-22464	All day Mon–Fri Sat & Sun pm only	1 truncheon + some assorted material	No – to view contact Director

MUSEUM	HOURS OF OPENING	POLICE MATERIAL	ON DISPLAY
Kendal Museum for Archaeology & Natural History Station Road *Kendal* Tel: 0539-21374	All day Mon–Fri Sat & Sun pm only	7 truncheons	Yes
The Lynn Museum Market Street *Kings Lynn* Tel: 0553-5001	Mon–Sat Closed Sun & Bank Hols	12 truncheons + assorted material	Some. Others – to view contact Curator
Lancaster City Museum Market Square *Lancaster* Tel: 0524-64637	Mon–Sat	8 truncheons, 2 staves + assorted material	Yes
Warwick Art Gallery & Museum Avenue Road *Leamington Spa* Tel: 0926-26559	Not advised	6 truncheons, 1 tipstaff (incl. items illustrated in Fenn Clark's book)	Occasion- ally
Abbey House Museum Kirkstall *Leeds* 5 Tel: 0532-755821		19 truncheons + assorted material	Occasion- ally
Newarke House's Museum The Newarke *Leicester* Tel: 0533-554100 Ext. 24	Daily except Fri Sun pm only	161 truncheons, 4 tipstaves, 6 staves + large collection of assorted material	Some. Others – to view contact Keeper
Museum of Local History Anne of Cleves House *Lewes* Tel: 07916-4610	Mon–Sat March to Oct	13 truncheons, 1 tipstaff, 18 rattles	Yes – varies. Sometimes – to view contact Curator at Barbican House, High Street, Lewes
Lincolnshire Life Museum Burton Road *Lincoln* Tel: 0522-28448	10am–5.30pm	28 truncheons	Some. Others – to view contact Keeper
Littlehampton Museum 12a River Road *Littlehampton* Tel: 5149	Winter: Thurs–Sat Summer: Tues–Sat	Some assorted material	Possibly. Some – to view contact Curator

MUSEUM	HOURS OF OPENING	POLICE MATERIAL	ON DISPLAY
Merseyside County Museum William Brown Street *Liverpool* Tel: 051-20700	Not advised	22 truncheons + large collection of uniforms & assorted material	Some. Others – to view contact Curator
Llandrindod Wells Museum Temple Gardens *Llandrindod Wells* Tel: 0597-4513	Summer: Mon–Sat Winter: Mon–Fri	Some assorted material	Some. Others – to view contact Curator
Ludlow Museum Butter Cross *Ludlow* Tel: Ludlow 3857	Not advised	2 truncheons + some assorted material	Some. Others – to view contact Curator
Luton Museum & Art Gallery Warwick Park *Luton* Tel: 0582-36941/2	Open daily except Tues Sun pm only Dec & Jan closed Sun	19 truncheons, 9 tipstaves + assorted material including old straw helmets	Some. Others – to view contact Curator

LONDON MUSEUMS

MUSEUM	HOURS OF OPENING	POLICE MATERIAL	ON DISPLAY
The Armouries Tower of London Tower Hill Tel: 01-709 0765	Daily	2 truncheons, 24 swords – police & prison service	No. Others – to senior students and for research only
Bruce Castle Museum Lordship Lane Tottenham Tel: 01-808 8772	Tues–Sat	2 truncheons + some assorted material	
Cuming Museum Walworth Road London SE17 Tel: 01-703 3324 Ext. 32	Mon–Sat	4 truncheons, 1 tipstaff + assorted material	No – to view contact Keeper
Goldsmith's Hall Foster Lane EC2 Tel: 01-493 8938	By appointment	12 tipstaves	No
Gunnersbury Park Museum Popes Lane London W3 Tel: 01-992 1612	Daily	7 truncheons + assorted material incl. beadle's bells & lanterns	Sometimes.
Horniman Museum London Road, Forest Hill Tel: 01-699 7328	Daily	97 truncheons, 3 tipstaves + large collection of assorted material	No – to view contact Curator
Kingston Heritage Centre Museum Fairfield West Kingston-on-Thames Tel: 01-5465386	Mon–Sat	12 truncheons, 2 tipstaves + assorted material	Sometimes. Also – to view contact Heritage Officer
Museum of London London Wall Tel: 01-600 3699	Tues–Sun	Approx. 110 truncheons, 142 tipstaves + rattles, swords, bludgeon	Some – Contact Museum
National Army Museum Royal Hospital Road Chelsea Tel: 01-730 0717	Daily Sun pm only	1 truncheon, 3 British police swords, 2 Indian police swords	Yes
National Maritime Museum Greenwich Tel: 01-858 4422	Daily	4 tipstaves including admiralty oars	No – Contact Keeper of Weapons
Plumstead & Greenwich Borough Museum 232 Plumstead High Street Tel: 01-854 1728	Daily except Wed & Sun	7 truncheons + assorted material	Some
Post Office Archives Postal HQ Building St. Martins Le Grand London EC1A Tel: 01-432 4521	Mon–Fri	2 truncheons, 2 tipstaves	No – to view contact Archives Search Room
Science Museum Exhibition Road S. Kensington Tel: 01-589 3456	Daily Sun pm only	34 truncheons, 6 tipstaves + assorted material	Some. Others – to view contact Curator
Victoria & Albert Museum S. Kensington Tel: 01-589 6371	Daily except Fri	3 tipstaves	No – contact Dept. of Metalwork

MUSEUM	HOURS OF OPENING	POLICE MATERIAL	ON DISPLAY
West Park Museum Prestbury Road *Macclesfield*	Summer: daily except Mon pm Winter: Sat & Sun pm only	6 truncheons + assorted material	Most. Others – to view write to Mrs. J. Goose, 162 London Road, Northwich
Maidstone Museum & Art Galleries St. Faiths Street *Maidstone* Tel: 0622-54497	Mon–Sat	3 identified truncheons + assorted material	No – to view contact Curator
Athelstan Museum Town Hall *Malmesbury*	Summer: Tues–Sat Winter: Wed–Sat pm	4 truncheons	Some. Others – to view contact Custodian
Manchester City Art Gallery Mosley Street *Manchester* Tel: 061-236 9422 Ext. 239	Not advised	1 tipstaff on display at Fletcher Moss Museum, Didsbury, Manchester	
The Harborough Museum Adam & Eve Street *Market Harborough* Tel: 0858-32468	Daily Sun pm only	3 truncheons	Some. Others – to view contact Keeper
Derbyshire Museum Services County Offices *Matlock* Tel: 0629-3411	Not advised	1 truncheon, leg irons and handcuffs	No – to view contact Museum's Officer
Monmouth Museum Priory Street *Monmouth* Tel: 0600-3519	Daily Sun pm only	2 swords + assorted material	Yes
Montacute House *Montacute* Somerset Tel: 0935-823289	Not advised	3 truncheons	Yes
Angus District Museums Panmure Place *Montrose* Tel: 0674-73232	Summer: daily Sun only July & Aug Winter: Mon–Fri pm only All day Sat	14 truncheons, 1 tipstaff + much assorted material	Some. Others – to view contact Curator
Newark D.C. Museum *Newark* Tel: 0636-702358	Weekdays Thurs pm only Closed Mon	11 truncheons, 1 tipstaff + assorted material	No – to view contact Curator

MUSEUM	HOURS OF OPENING	POLICE MATERIAL	ON DISPLAY
Newbury District Museum The Wharf *Newbury* Tel: 0635-30511	Winter: daily except Wed & Sun Summer: daily except Wed	6 truncheons, 1 tipstaff + assorted material	Some. Others – to view contact Curator
Borough Museum Brampton Park *Newcastle-under-Lyme* Tel: 0782-619705	Mon–Sat Sun (May to Sept)	2 truncheons + assorted material	Occasionally – to view contact Curator
Norfolk Rural Life Museum Beech House Gressenhall, Dereham *Norfolk* Tel: 0362-860563	Summer: Tues–Sat Sun pm only Winter: by appointment	3 truncheons + assorted material	No – to view contact Curator
Abington Museum Abington Park *Northampton* Tel: 0604-31454	Mon–Sat Summer only: Sun pm	13 truncheons, 6 tipstaves + assorted material	Some. Others – to view contact Keeper
Cotswold Countryside Collection *Northleach* Glos Tel: 04516-715	April to Oct	Some assorted material	Varies
Bridewell Museum Bridewell Alley *Norwich*, Norfolk Tel: 0603-611277 Ext. 299	Mon–Sat	120 truncheons, 8 tipstaves + assorted material	No – to view contact Keeper
Brewhouse Yard Museum Castle Boulevard *Nottingham* Tel: 0602-411881 Ext. 48	Daily	15 truncheons & assorted material incl. marked firearms	Some. Others – to view contact Curator
Oldham Library Art Gallery & Museum Greaves Street *Oldham* Tel: 061-6784657	Mon–Sat Tues pm only	13 truncheons + assorted material	Some. Others – to view contact Curator
Ashmolean Museum Beaumont Street *Oxford* Tel: 0865-512651	Tues–Sat Sun pm only -	67 truncheons, 4 staves of office + assorted material	Some. Others – to view contact Curator
Proctor's Office Wellington Square *Oxford* Tel: 0865–511359	Mon–Fri	18 ceremonial staves, 4 truncheons, 4 swords	No – to view contact University Marshal

MUSEUM	HOURS OF OPENING	POLICE MATERIAL	ON DISPLAY
Paisley Museum & Art Galleries High Street *Paisley* Tel: 041-889 3151	Mon–Sat	7 truncheons	Some. Others – to view contact Keeper
Perth Museum & Art Gallery George Street *Perth* Tel: 0738-32488	Mon–Sat	40 truncheons + assorted material	Some. Others – to view contact Keeper
City Museum and Art Gallery Priestgate *Peterborough* Tel: 0733-43329	Tues–Sat Winter: pm only	15 truncheons + assorted material incl. leg irons & handcuffs	No – to view contact Curator
Blair Castle Blair Atholl *Pitlochry*, Perth Tel: 079-681 355	Summer: daily April: Sun & Mon	4 truncheons	Yes
Plymouth City Museum & Art Gallery Drake Circus *Plymouth* Tel: 0752-668000 Ext. 4378	Mon–Sat	12 truncheons & 3 beadle's staves, 18 maces of office + assorted material	Yes (some at branch museums). Others – to view contact Asst. Keeper
Poole Museum The Guildhall Market Street *Poole*, Dorset Tel: Poole 675151	Daily Sun pm only	7 truncheons, 2 staves of office + assorted material	Some. Others – to view contact Curator
Portland Museum 217 Wakeham *Portland* Tel: Portland 821804	Summer: daily Winter: Tue–Sat	5 staves, 1 truncheon	Yes
Lady Lever Art Gallery *Port Sunlight* Village Wirral, Merseyside Tel: 051-645 3623	Daily Sun pm only	59 truncheons, 10 tipstaves, 7 beadle's staves	No – to view contact Curator
Portsmouth City Museum Museum Road *Old Portsmouth* Tel: 0705-827261	Daily	23 truncheons + extensive collection of old police uniforms & headdress	Occasionally.
Harris Museum & Art Gallery Market Square *Preston* Tel: 0772-58248	Mon–Sat	3 truncheons + assorted material	Yes
Reading Museum & Art Gallery Blagrave Street *Reading* Tel: 0734-55911 Ext. 2199	Mon–Sat	13 truncheons, 2 tipstaves + assorted material	Some. Others – to view contact Curator
Bassetlaw Museum Amcott House 40 Grove Street *Retford*, Notts Tel: 0777-706741	Not advised	3 truncheons + assorted material incl. 2 halberds used as staves of office	Some. Others – to view contact Curator
Guildhall Museum High Street *Rochester* Tel: 0634-48717	Daily	5 truncheons, 5 tipstaves + assorted material	Yes
Rossendale Museum Whitaker Park Rawenstall *Rossendale*, Lancs Tel: 0706-217777	Summer: daily Sun pm only	2 truncheons + assorted material	Yes
Bute Museum Stuart Street *Rothesay*, Scotland		1 sherriff's baton of office	
Rutland County Museum Catmose Street Oakham, *Rutland*	Not advised	1 truncheon + some assorted material	
City Museum Hatfield Road *St. Albans*, Herts Tel: 0727-56679	Mon–Sat	5 truncheons + assorted material	Yes
Norris Museum The Broadway *St. Ives* Huntingdon, Cambs Tel: 0480-65101	Summer: Tues–Sat Sun pm only Winter: Tues-Fri Sat pm only	9 truncheons, 2 staves of office + assorted material	No – to view contact Curator

MUSEUM	HOURS OF OPENING	POLICE MATERIAL	ON DISPLAY
Saffron Walden Museum Museum Street *Saffron Walden*, Essex Tel: 0799-22494	Daily Apr to Sept Sun pm only	3 truncheons, + tipstaff	No – to view contact Curator
Salford Museums & Art Galleries Peel Park Crescent *Salford*, Manchester Tel: 061-736 2649	Not advised	28 truncheons + assorted material	Some. Others – to view contact Keeper
Salisbury Museum 65 The Close *Salisbury*, Wilts Tel: 0722-332151	Mon–Sat July & Aug: Sun	35 truncheons + assorted material	Some. Others – to view contact Curator
Guildhall Museum *Sandwich*, Kent	Not advised	21 truncheons, 2 staves of office + assorted material	Some. Others – to view contact Curator, c/o Town Clerk
Scunthorpe Museum & Art Gallery Oswald Road *Scunthorpe* Tel: 0724-843533	Daily Sun pm only	11 truncheons + assorted material	Some. Others – to view contact Keeper
Shaftesbury Local History Museum Gold Hill *Shaftesbury*, Dorset Tel: Shaftesbury 2157	Summer: daily Sun pm only	1 truncheon + assorted material	Yes
Overbecks Museum *Sharpitor* Nr. Salcombe, Devon Tel: Salcombe 2893	Summer: daily	2 truncheons + assorted material incl. collection of handcuffs	Yes
Sheffield City Museum Weston Park *Sheffield* Tel: 0742-27226	Daily	18 truncheons + assorted material	No – to view contact Keeper
Sherborne Museum Abbey Gate House *Sherborne*, Dorset Tel: Sherborne 812252	Not advised	1 truncheon	Yes
All Saints Church *Shillington* Beds.		35 truncheons all connected with the 'Swing Riots' in 1830	No – to view contact Rev. R. P. Lanham
Staffordshire County Museum *Shugborough*, Stafford Tel: 0889-881388	Summer: Tues–Fri Sat & Sun pm only Winter: Tues–Fri 1st & 3rd Suns in month pm	25 truncheons + much assorted material incl. police uniforms	Some. Others – to view contact Museum Officer
Sidmouth Museum Church Street *Sidmouth*, Devon	Daily Sun pm only	6 truncheons	Some. Others – to view contact Curator
Tudor House Museum Bugle Street *Southampton* Tel: 0703-24216	Not advised	3 truncheons	Eventually – to view contact Curator
Southend-on-Sea Central Museum Victoria Avenue *Southend-on-Sea* Essex Tel: 0702-330214	Tues–Sat Mon pm only Not Bank Hols	4 truncheons + assorted material	Most.
South Molton Museum Town Hall The Square *South Molton*, Devon Tel: 07695-2501	Mon, Tues, Thurs, Fri Wed & Sat am only	35 truncheons, 8 staves of office + assorted material	Some. Others – to view contact Curator
Botanic Gardens Museum Churchtown *Southport*, Lancs Tel: 0704-27547	Tues–Sat Sun pm only Open Bank Hol Mon	2 truncheons + assorted material	Some. Others – to view contact Curator
South Queensferry Museum Burgh Chambers High Street *S. Queensferry*, Lothian Tel: 031-225 2424 Ext. 6689	May to Mid-Sept Thurs & Fri pm only	2 truncheons	Yes
South Shields Museum Ocean Road *S. Shields*, Tyne & Wear Tel: S/Shields 568740	Daily Sun pm only	3 truncheons	Yes
Stevenage Museum St. George's Way *Stevenage*, Herts Tel: 0438-354292	Mon–Sat	1 truncheon + assorted material	No – to view contact Curator
Vernon Park Museum Turncroft Lane *Stockport*, Cheshire Tel: 061-480 3668	Mon–Sat pm only	10 truncheons + assorted material	Some. Others – to view contact Curator

MUSEUM	HOURS OF OPENING	POLICE MATERIAL	ON DISPLAY
City Museum & Art Gallery Broad St. Hanley *Stoke-on-Trent* Tel: 0782-29611	Mon–Sat	5 truncheons + assorted material	Some. Others – to view contact Curator
Museum of East Anglian Life Crowe Street *Stowmarket* Suffolk Tel: 0449-612229	Summer: daily	5 truncheons + assorted material	No – to view contact Curator
New Place Museum Chapel Street *Stratford-on-Avon* Warwicks Tel: 0789-292325	Summer: daily Sun pm only Winter: Mon–Sat	5 truncheons + assorted material	No – to view contact Director of Shakespeare Trust
Stroud District (Cowle) Museum Lansdown *Stroud*, Glos Tel: 04536-3394	Mon–Sat	10 truncheons + assorted material	Some. Others – to view contact Curator
Sunderland Museum Borough Road *Sunderland* Tyne & Wear Tel: 0783-41235	Daily Sun pm only	7 truncheons + assorted material	Some. Others – to view contact Curator
Thamesdown Museum & Art Gallery 1–4 Euclid Street *Swindon*, Wilts Tel: 0793-26161 Ext. 3118	Daily Sun pm only	9 truncheons (8 railway truncheons)	Some in G.W.R. Museum – to view contact Mr. Dickinson
Somerset County Museum Taunton Castle *Taunton* Tel: 0823-55507	Mon–Fri 10am–5pm	27 truncheons, 1 staff of office, 6 tipstaves and assorted material	Some. Others – to view contact Curator, Rural Life Museum, Glastonbury. Tel: 0458-32903
Tenby Museum Castle Hill *Tenby*, Dyfed Tel: 0834-2809	Daily	2 truncheons, 6 tipstaves + assorted material	Some. Others – to view contact Curator
The Museum 64 Barton Street *Tewksbury*, Glos	Not advised	Some truncheons but details not advised	Yes

MUSEUM	HOURS OF OPENING	POLICE MATERIAL	ON DISPLAY
Tiverton Museum St. Andrew Street *Tiverton*, Devon Tel: 0884-256295	Mon–Sat	5 truncheons and assorted material	Yes
The Waterways Museum Stoke Bruerne, *Towcester*, Northants Tel: 0604-862229	Summer: daily Winter: Tues–Sun	2 truncheons (not painted) + assorted material	Yes
Trowbridge Museum Civic Hall *Trowbridge*, Wilts Tel: 02214-65072	Tues and Sat am only	17 truncheons	
County Museum & Art Gallery River Street *Truro*, Cornwall Tel: Truro 2205	Mon–Sat Closed Bank Hols	19 truncheons + assorted material	Yes
Tunbridge Wells Museum Civic Centre Mount Pleasant *Tunbridge Wells* Tel: 0892-26121 Ext. 171	Mon–Sat Closed Bank Hols	11 truncheons + assorted material	Some. Others – to view contact Curator
Wakefield Art Gallery & Museum Wentworth Terrace *Wakefield*, Yorks Tel: 0924-370211 Ext. 8031	Mon–Sat	19 truncheons + assorted material	Sometimes. Others – to view contact Keeper
Dewey Museum c/o Warminster Library Three Horse Shoes Mall *Warminster*, Wilts Tel: 0985-216022	Mon pm only Tues, Thurs, Fri & Sat all day	3 truncheons	Some. Others – to view contact Curator
Warrington Museum & Art Gallery Bold Street *Warrington*, Cheshire Tel: 0925-30550	Mon–Sat	5 truncheons + assorted material	No – to view contact Curator
Warwickshire Museum St. John's House St. John's *Warwick* Tel: 0926-493431 Ext. 2021	Tues–Sat Sun in summer pm only	8 truncheons + assorted material incl. 16 police hangers & assorted material	Some. Others – to view contact Curator

MUSEUM	HOURS OF OPENING	POLICE MATERIAL	ON DISPLAY
Wells Museum 8 Cathedral Green *Wells*, Somerset Tel: 0749-73477	Not advised	3 truncheons	No – to view contact Curator
Woodspring Museum Burlington Street *Weston-Super-Mare* Avon Tel: 0934-21028	Mon–Sat	6 truncheons + assorted material incl. paintings of 2 policemen c. 1850	Sometimes. Others – to view contact Curator
Wigan Museum Service 9–10 Bridgeman Terrace *Wigan*, Gr. Manchester Tel: Wigan 36141	Not advised	4 truncheons + assorted material	Some. Others – to view contact Curator
Priest's House Museum High Street *Wimborne*, Dorset	Summer: daily	12 truncheons and assorted material	Yes
Court Hall Museum High Street *Winchelsea*, E. Sussex	Summer: daily Sun pm only	2 truncheons	Yes
Winchester City Museum 75 Hyde Street *Winchester*, Hants Tel: 0962-68166 Ext. 269	Mon–Fri	4 truncheons	Some. Others – to view contact Keeper
Hampshire County Museum Service Chilcomb Lane Barend, *Winchester*, Hants Tel: 0962-66242	8 museums with various openings – check for details	48 truncheons + assorted material	Some. Museums throughout Hampshire. For details contact Mr. C. Goldthorpe
Simms Collection Old Town Hall Museum *Winchcombe*, Glos Tel: 0242-602614	Summer: Mon–Sat Sun by arrangement	90 truncheons + extensive collection of over 400 police uniforms (many foreign)	Some
The Borough Collection The Stationmaster's House Thames Street *Windsor*	Daily	4 truncheons	Some. Others – to view contact Curator
Windsor Castle		1 staff of office (Constable of Windsor Castle, 1833–42)	Not known

MUSEUM	HOURS OF OPENING	POLICE MATERIAL	ON DISPLAY
Wisbech & Fenland Museum Museum Square *Wisbech*, Cambs Tel: 0945-583817	Tues–Sat	4 truncheons – 1 tipstaff marked 'Jonathan Wild 1720' + assorted material	Some. Others – to view contact Curator
Worthing Museum & Art Gallery Chapel Road *Worthing*, Sussex Tel: 0903-39999 Ext. 121	Mon–Sat	13 truncheons + assorted material	Some. Others – to view contact Curator
Oxfordshire County Museum Fletcher's House *Woodstock*, Oxford Tel: 0993-811456	Not advised	10 truncheons, 2 beadle's staves + extensive collection of assorted material	No – to view contact Keeper
Yeovil Museum Hendford Manor Hall *Yeovil*, Somerset Tel: 0935-75171	Daily except Thurs & Sun	8 truncheons + assorted material	Yes
York Castle Museum *York* Tel: 0904-53611	Daily	224 truncheons and tipstaves. Representative collection of police badges	Some. Others – to view contact Curator
National Railway Museum Leeman Road *York* Tel: 0904–21261	Daily Sun pm only	14 truncheons, 2 tipstaves + assorted material	Some. Others – to view contact Manager

NATIONAL POLICE COLLECTIONS IN POLICE MUSEUMS

POLICE FORCE	OPEN TO PUBLIC	POLICE MATERIAL	ON DISPLAY
Bedfordshire Police Headquarters Woburn Road *Kempston*, Beds Tel: 0234-855222	By appointment	12 truncheons + assorted material incl. helmets, swords, uniforms	Yes

POLICE FORCE	OPEN TO PUBLIC	POLICE MATERIAL	ON DISPLAY
Police Staff College Bramshill House *Bramshill* Nr. Basingstoke Hants	By appointment	Probably the largest collection in the country. Approximately 500 truncheons and tipstaves – many of them very rare	Yes – by appointment only, contact Librarian
Cheshire Constabulary Museum Force Training Centre Nantwich Road *Crewe*, Cheshire Tel: Crewe 211098	By appointment	Not supplied	On rotation
City of London Police 26 Old Jewry *London* EC2R 8DJ	By appointment	33 truncheons + 9 tipstaves. Also extensive collection of items connected with City of London	Yes
Garda Museum Police Headquarters *Dublin* Tel: 01-771156	By appointment	1 truncheon – c. 1840 + much assorted material from the 3 forces between 1822 and the present	Yes – view by appointment
Derbyshire Constabulary Butterley Hall *Ripley* Tel: 0773-43551 Ext. 316	By appointment	12 truncheons + assorted material including uniform, handcuffs & swords	Yes
Durham Constabulary Police Headquarters Aykley Heads *Durham*	By appointment	11 truncheons	Yes
Essex Police Force Museum Police Headquarters P.O. Box 2, Springfield *Chelmsford*, Essex Tel: 0245-267267	Not to general public	2 truncheons, 1 tipstaff + assorted material	
Gloucestershire Constabulary Police Headquarters Holland House Lansdown Road *Cheltenham*, Glos Tel: 0242-521321 Ext. 267	Organised party visits only	12 truncheons	Yes
Grampian Police Museum Police Headquarters Queen Street *Aberdeen* Tel: 0224-639111	By appointment	16 truncheons, 1 ceremonial baton + assorted material	Some. Others – view by appointment
Gwent Police Headquarters Croesyceiliog *Cwmbran*, Gwent Tel: 06333-2011	Mon–Fri 9am–5pm Check first	10 truncheons + assorted material	Yes

View of reconstructed Victorian Police Station at the Bradford Police Museum Very authentically carried out. Note the original height indicator for prisoner's details. West Yorkshire Metropolitan Police.

POLICE FORCE	OPEN TO PUBLIC	POLICE MATERIAL	ON DISPLAY
Herts Police County Headquarters Stanborough Lane *Welwyn Garden City* Herts Tel: 31177	No	6 truncheons + assorted material	Some. Others not available for inspection
Kent County Constabulary Police Headquarters Sutton Road *Maidstone*, Kent Tel: 0622-65432	By appointment only	75 truncheons, 4 nightsticks, 6 tipstaves + extensive collection of police material	Some. Others – by appointment
Lancashire Police Museum Police Training School Hutton Hall *Hutton* Tel: 0772-614444	Not open to public	9 truncheons + assorted material	Yes
Leicestershire Constabulary 420 London Road *Leicester* Tel: 0533-700911	Not advised	35 truncheons + assorted material	Not on display for public
Lincolnshire Police P.O. Box 999 *Lincoln* Tel: 0522-32222	Not open to public	3 truncheons + assorted material	Yes – by appointment
Greater Manchester Police Museum Newton Street *Manchester* Tel: 061-855 3290	Mon–Fri By appointment	25 truncheons, 1 tipstaff + much assorted material incl. uniform, handcuffs, swords, & lanterns	Some. Others – by appointment
Merseyside Police Headquarters Canning Place *Liverpool* Tel: 051-709 6010	Not open to public	10 truncheons + assorted material	No
Metropolitan Police Historical Museum c/o Room 104 New Scotland Yard *London* SW1 Tel: 01-230 4398	Not open to public	Approx. 150 truncheons, 25 tipstaves + large collection dealing with Met. Police. New Museum from 1986	No
Northamptonshire Police Headquarters Wootton Hall *Northampton* Tel: 0604-63111	By appointment	81 truncheons + assorted material incl. 17 swords	Some. Others – by appointment
Northumbria Police Headquarters *Ponteland* Newcastle-on-Tyne Tel: 0661-72555	Annual Force Open Day only	24 truncheons + assorted material incl. some uniforms	No
North Wales Police Headquarters *Colwyn Bay* N. Wales Tel: 0492-517171	Not open to public	1 truncheon + some assorted material incl. Chief Constable's uniform	No
Nottinghamshire Constabulary Sherwood Lodge Arnold *Nottingham* Tel: 0602-269700	By appointment	2 truncheons	Some. Others – by appointment
Ripon Prison & Police Museum St. Marygate *Ripon* Tel: 0765-3706	Summer: Tues-Sat	9 truncheons, 1 ceremonial staff. A unique collection of prison and police equipment in their original settings	Yes
Scottish Police College Tulliallan Castle *Kincardine*, Fife Tel: 0259-30333	Mon–Fri by appointment	92 truncheons	Some. Others – by appointment
Central Scotland Police *Stirling* Tel: 0786-3161	By appointment	8 truncheons, 1 tipstaff	Yes
South Wales Police Museum Police Headquarters *Bridgend* Mid-Glamorgan Tel: 0656-55555	By appointment	Approx. 30 truncheons + extensive collection of police-related items	Yes

POLICE FORCE	OPEN TO PUBLIC	POLICE MATERIAL	ON DISPLAY
South Yorkshire Police Headquarters Snig Hill *Sheffield*, Yorks Tel: 0742-78522	By appointment	10 truncheons	Yes
Suffolk Constabulary Force Headquarters Martlesham Heath *Ipswich* Tel: 0473-624848	By arrangement	22 truncheons + assorted material incl. lamps	Yes – by appointment
The Police Station Old Nelson Street *Lowestoft*, Suffolk	Not known	A small collection of items	Not known
Sussex Police Headquarters Malling House *Lewes*, E. Sussex Tel: 5432	By appointment	19 truncheons + assorted material incl. useful photographic record of badges and police officers	Yes – by appointment
Strathclyde Police Museum 173 Pitt Street *Glasgow* Tel: 041-204 2626	Mon–Fri by appointment	28 truncheons, 10 tipstaves + assorted material incl. swords, handcuffs, uniform	Yes
Divisional Headquarters Strathclyde Police 10 St. Marnock Street *Kilmarnock*, Ayrshire Tel: 0563-21188 Ext. 308	Mon–Fri by appointment	4 truncheons, 1 staff of office + assorted material	Yes
Tayside Police Museum Police Headquarters *Dundee* Tel: 0382-23200	By appointment	9 truncheons + 1 Perth High Constable's stave, 1 tipstaff + assorted material	Some. Others – to view contact Curator
Tayside Police Museum (Eastern Division) Divisional Headquarters West High Street *Forfar*, Angus Tel: 0307-62551 Ext. 64	By appointment	12 truncheons + assorted material incl. many records for area	Yes
Thames Valley Police Force Training Centre *Theale* Near Reading, Berks Tel: 0734-302601	By appointment	9 truncheons + inspector's silver headed night stick, + assorted material	Yes
Royal Ulster Constabulary Museum Constabulary Hdqrs 'Brooklyn' Knock Road *Belfast* Tel: 0232-650222 Ext. 2474	Not open to public	5 truncheons + large collection of assorted material dealing with Ireland and dating back to 1787	No
West Mercia Constabulary Hindlip Hall *Worcester* Tel: 0905-27188	Not advised	Extensive collection of all police material	
West Midlands Police Training Centre Pershore Road *Birmingham* Tel: 021-472 3201	Fri morning or by appointment	Many items – particularly with reference to Birmingham City Police	
West Yorkshire Metropolitan Police The Tyrle *Bradford*, Yorks Tel: 0274-723422 Ext. 7719	By arrangement. (This is the Force Museum and deals only with the original Bradford City Police Force)	32 truncheons and tipstaves & large assortment of original equipment in facsimile Victorian police station	Yes – by arrangement
West Yorkshire Metropolitan Police 10/12 Laburnum Road *Wakefield*, Yorks Tel: 0924-375222 Ext. 22218	By appointment	13 truncheons, 3 tipstaves and assorted material, uniform and swords	
Wiltshire Constabulary London Road *Devizes*, Wilts Tel: 0380-2341	Not open to public	19 truncheons, 2 tipstaves and assorted material	Not advised
Prison Services Museum Officers Training School *Leyhill* Wotton-under-Edge Glos	Not advised	12 presentation truncheons	